WITHDRAWN

Management and Language

Books are to be returned on or
the last date below.

Management and Language

The Manager as a Practical Author

David Holman and Richard Thorpe

SAGE Publications

London • Thousand Oaks • New Delhi

SAGE Publications Ltd
6 Bonhill Street
London EC2A 4PU

SAGE Publications Inc.
2455 Teller Road
Thousand Oaks, California 91320

SAGE Publications India Pvt Ltd
32, M-Block Market
Greater Kailash – I
New Delhi 110 048

British Library Cataloguing in Publication data
A catalogue record for this book is available from the British Library

ISBN 0 7619 6907 1
ISBN (pbk)0 7619 6908 X

Library of Congress Control Number available

Typeset by Photoprint, Torquay, Devon
Printed and bound in Great Britain by Athenaeum Press, Gateshead

I would like to thank my parents,
Annette and Bob Holman,
for all their support throughout my life.
David.

Contents

About the editors

David J. Holman is a Research Fellow at the Centre for Organisation and Innovation, which is part of the Institute of Work Psychology, University of Sheffield. After graduating in psychology at Manchester Polytechnic, he worked as Psychological Technician supporting people with learning disabilities at home and at work. He then went back to academia and completed a Diploma in Personnel Management at Manchester Polytechnic. It was during this period that he met Richard Thorpe, who was to become his supervisor on his PhD that examined the experience of skill development in undergraduates on management courses.

On completing his PhD, David joined the Institute of Work Psychology where his research focuses on the affects of job design on employee wellbeing, learning and innovation. He has maintained an interest in management education and development and has continued to work with Richard Thorpe in this area. David is the co-editor of *The New Workplace: A Guide to the Human Impact of Modern Technology and Working Practices* and has published in journals such as *Human Relations*, the *Journal of Occupational and Organisational Psychology*, the *Journal of Occupational Health Psychology*, *Management Learning* and the *British Journal of Management*.

Richard Thorpe is Professor in Management and Director of the Graduate School of Business at Manchester Metropolitan University. After spending the early part of his career in industry culminating in the management of a manufacturing company in the Highlands of Scotland, he joined Strathclyde University. There, as a Research Fellow, he undertook a national study of payment systems in Britain. This research led to collaboration in three publications – *Incentive Schemes in Britain, 1978–1980* (Department of Employment, 1982), *Payment Systems and Productivity* (Macmillan, 1986) and *Strategic Reward Management* (Financial Times International, 2000).

In 1980, he joined Glasgow University where he continued to widen his research experience making contributions to the Scottish Business School's Doctoral Programme. In 1983 he was accepted for the International Teachers Programme in Sweden and embarked on a PhD in small firm growth and development, the experience of which led to a collaboration with his supervisor (Mark Easterby-Smith) on a research text book, *Management Research: An Introduction*, 2nd edition (Sage, 2002).

On leaving Scotland, he settled at Manchester Metropolitan University where the focus of his work and research took a new turn, focusing on the Management of Change and the Learning and Development of Managers. It was a PhD research project supervised by Richard and conducted by David that was the genesis of the collaboration on this book.

Contributors

David M. Boje, Professor, Department of Management, New Mexico State University, USA.

Francois Cooren, Associate Professor, Department of Communication, State University of New York, Albany, USA.

Joep Cornelisson, Assistant Professor, University of Amsterdam, Netherlands.

Ann L. Cunliffe, Assistant Professor, Department of Public Administration, California State University, USA.

Stanley Deetz, Professor, Department of Communication, University of Colorado, USA.

Gail T. Fairhurst, Professor, Department of Communication, University of Cincinnati, USA.

Jeffrey D. Ford, Associate Professor, Max M. Fisher College of Business, Ohio State University, USA.

Laurie W. Ford, PhD, Critical Path Consultants, Ohio, USA.

Jeff Gold, Senior Lecturer, Leeds Business School, University of Leeds, UK.

Joy L. Hart, Associate Professor, Department of Communication, University of Louisville, USA.

David J. Holman, Research Fellow, Institute of Work Psychology, University of Sheffield, UK.

Dorothy Lander, Assistant Professor, Department of Adult Education, St Francis Xavier University, Canada.

Mike Pedler, Revans Professorial Fellow, Revans Institute for Action Learning and Research, University of Salford, UK.

Craig Prichard, Senior Lecturer, Department of Management, Massey University, New Zealand.

John Shotter, Professor, Department of Communication, University of New Hampshire.

Richard Thorpe, Professor, Graduate Business School, Manchester Metropolitan University, UK.

Charles A. Willard, Professor, Department of Communication, University of Louisville, USA.

Shirley Willihnganz, Associate Professor and Chair, Department of Communication, University of Louisville, USA.

Figures and tables

Introduction
Management and language:
the manager as a practical author

David J. Holman and Richard Thorpe

Almost anyone connected to the practice and study of management will, at some point, have heard managers ask questions such as:

'How should I act in this situation?'
'What can I do in this context?'
'What is the best way to proceed?'
'What can I use to help me inform my action?'

In response, one might offer a range of suggestions, e.g., consider this, notice that, think of that, or even make a number of prescriptions, e.g., do this, do that. Whether instructive or prescriptive, the comments made in the ensuing discussion would probably be informed by one's personal experience and knowledge of management practice.

Another significant factor informing a person's response to questions such as those above would be his or her beliefs about how managers should approach their practice, i.e., a perceived ideal of managerial action. For example, one person might suggest that a manager should proceed like a scientist, by being as rational and objective as possible, by constructing and testing hypotheses and by applying general principles and theories. A person advocating such a view could be seen as having a scientific/technical understanding of managerial action, and an image of the manager as a practical scientist (Alvesson and Willmott, 1996; Holman, 2000a; Reed, 1989). Another person might quote Mintzberg, who stated that 'brief observation of any manager will quickly lay to rest the notion that managers practise a science' (1999: 302), and argue that this 'scientific' ideal is practically impossible to achieve and not particularly useful even if it was. Rather, they might suggest that a manager can proceed by reflecting closely on the social and political processes of organisational life and on one's personal knowledge of the situation, and use the insights gained from this to transform the situation rather than simply test a hypothesis on it. This person might be seen as having a 'practice' perspective of management and an image of the manager as a 'reflective practitioner' (Reed, 1989; Schön, 1983).[1]

The 'scientific/technical' and the 'practice' perspective of management, and their associated images of the manager (respectively, the manager as practical scientist and the manager as reflective practitioner), have been highly influential in the study and practice of management. However, within the practice perspective there has been a growing interest in how language is used in organisational practice – sometimes referred to as the 'linguistic turn' (Jablin and Putnam, 2001; Westwood and Linstead, 2001). Thus, another person in a discussion on how a manager might proceed, might agree with the advocate of the practice perspective, but argue that the manager needs to play closer attention to the way that language is used to shape the organisational landscape in ambiguous and uncertain conditions. She or he might argue that closer attention to language use is important, as it is the primary means through which managerial action occurs and with which organisations are created, maintained and changed. This person, while also coming from a practice perspective of management, might suggest an alternative image of the manager, and one that conjures up more linguistic connotations, namely, the manager as a 'practical author' (Shotter, 1993).[2]

The aim of this book, then, is to examine what it might mean to be a practical author and to show how it applies to different facets of managerial life. However, to show why we believe this idea to be valuable and timely, we first provide a more detailed account of how it relates to the two other dominant images of management, the manager as a practical scientist and the manager as a reflective practitioner. We then go on to examine the linguistic turn in management and organisational studies. Finally, we show how Shotter's idea of the manager as a practical author resonates with many of the concerns and themes in this linguistic turn.

The manager as a practical scientist

Perhaps the most dominant image of management has been the manager as a scientist or practical scientist (Kolb, 1984) and a scientific/technical perspective of management has underpinned this image. From a scientific/technical perspective, managerial activity is characterised as a rational, technical and morally neutral process of planning, controlling and decision-making aimed at securing the organisations ends through the efficient use of administrative, human and productive resources (Reed, 1989). These activities are thought to be most effective, and the aims of management most likely to be achieved, when based on 'hard' information and grounded in the rigorous application of scientifically validated knowledge and techniques. Furthermore, the 'best' managers are seen to act according to a hypothetico-deductive scientific model of action, i.e., that action should involve constructing and testing hypotheses and applying general principles and theories to problems (Schön, 1983).

The image of the manager as scientist has 'exerted a powerful influence on the development of management thought' (Reed, 1989: 74). Indeed, through the influence of writers such as Frederick Taylor, management thought was largely founded on the belief that managerial activity should be akin to scientific activity. It is perhaps of no surprise then that management education, particularly during its postwar expansion, sought to teach management as a scientifically based practice and teach only those ideas and techniques that had been scientifically validated. There are also numerous examples of managers using the image and aura of science when trying to justify, legitimate and account for actions made (Pavlica, 1996; Watson, 1994).

The idea that managers (or the 'best' managers) act in a scientific manner and the ideal of management as a scientific practice has been subject to a sustained, and some would say fatal, critique. One 'nail in the coffin' has come from studies of management activity that have pointed to the fact that managerial work is characterised by brevity, fragmentation, a fast pace, a high degree of informal interpersonal contact and much ritual activity (Hales, 1986; Kotter, 1982; Stewart, 1967; Mintzberg, 1973). Such studies have also highlighted the social and political nature of managerial work. Moreover, they have demonstrated that managers often have to make sense of and take action in ambiguous and contradictory conditions in which both the means and ends of action are highly uncertain. These descriptions of managerial activity seem far removed from the image of the manager as scientist and this alternative view of managerial activity, i.e., as a pragmatic, social and political activity, can be labelled a 'practice perspective'. It is worth noting that 'critical' perspectives of management also share this view of management action, although they are more explicit about understanding management within its wider social, historical and economic context and with examining the ends of management practice.

The manager as a reflective practitioner

It could be argued that even if managers do not act according to the ideal of management as a scientific activity, this does not necessarily mean that the ideal is a poor one and that it should not be adhered to. The proponents of this view might suggest that the problem does not lie in the theory but in its execution. Yet, even the ideal of management as a scientific activity has come under attack. One of the most notable of these critiques comes from Schön (1983) in his book *The Reflective Practitioner*. In this highly influential work,

Schön argues strongly against the ideal of professional and managerial activity as a scientific and technical activity. Schön suggests that such a model, based on what he calls a technical rationality, is inappropriate for many professional activities. For Schön, a 'technical rationality holds that practitioners are instrumental problem solvers who select technical means best suited to particular purposes. Rigorous professional practitioners solve well-formed instrumental problems by applying theory and technique derived from systematic, preferably scientific knowledge' (1983: 3–4). Schön demonstrates that one of the main difficulties of a technical rationality is its assumption that, when a person is confronted by a problem, the problem is already fairly well defined. Yet, many of the situations and problems that managers have to contend with are not well defined but uncertain, messy and ambiguous. In these situations the problem is not just problem solving but also problem setting. In other words, the issue is not just 'What techniques do I use?' but also 'What is the problem with which I am faced?' A further assumption of a technical rationality is that the knowledge or means with which to solve a problem can be applied to it in a relatively easy manner. However, even when a problem has been defined and 'set', the outcome may still escape the categories of applied science as the problem may be multi-faceted, unique and riven with value conflicts. Simply applying scientific knowledge and technique to a problem may therefore prove problematic.

Schön is also critical of the notion that technical problem solving requires an objective stance, that it involves acting in a way that is akin to hypothesis-driven testing and experimentation, and that it is primarily concerned with the implementation and testing of technical decisions. Thus, according to a technical rationality, a manager can be viewed as someone who manipulates a situation from the outside, like a scientist observing experiments in a laboratory. Yet serious doubts can be raised about whether a person could ever 'step outside' of their worldview, as such a belief misses the fact that the manager is embedded within his or her situation and that it is their experientially derived knowledge from within a context (i.e., their social, political and cultural knowledge) that is essential for successful action. Schön therefore stresses the importance of attending to the social and political context in which problem setting, problem solving and knowledge application occurs – something that a technical rationality tends to ignore or downplay. A further consequence of a technical rationality is that the social and political abilities required in these processes can sometimes be viewed as less important. Indeed, personalities and politics are often blamed for the failure of managerial activities, instead of recognising that it was possibly failure to address the interests of different individuals and groups that helped to undermine the potential 'success' of managerial activity.

Schön argues that activity could be approached differently. He labels this different approach 'reflection-in-action' and those who practise it, 'reflective practitioners'. Reflection-in-action is considered to be particularly appropriate for guiding action in unique and uncertain situations and to have a number of important characteristics. One characteristic is a focus on problem setting, i.e., the need to frame a situation and 'impose' an order on it. In this process the reflective practitioner is not dependent upon established theory but employs an array of personal knowledge, theoretical knowledge, heuristics and techniques. Furthermore, the person attempts to actively transform or create a new situation – action goes beyond testing existing knowledge. Moreover, in reflection-in-action, problem setting and transformation are intertwined and, as such, knowing and doing and means and ends are not held to be separate and distinct entities.[3] Schön also suggests that engaging in reflection-in-action is like having a reflective conversation with the situation. By making this comparison, he draws attention to the inherently social nature of practice and many of his examples show how reflection-in-action occurs through discussion. Another important characteristic of reflection-in-action is that it recognises that practice is embedded in a context of meanings. This highlights the need to attend to the contextually specific nature of one's own and others' understandings. It also highlights the limits of one's personal understanding and, in particular, that others with different commitments may not share the 'compellingness' of one's personal knowledge.

With regard to the study and practice of management, Schön's work provided a powerful and cogent argument that professional activity could be modelled on principles different to those emanating from a scientific/technical perspective. In addition, Schön provided a powerful metaphor, the reflective practitioner, which could act as guiding ideal. Indeed, the idea of the reflective practitioner has been widely adopted in many spheres and in the field of management it resonated especially well with the practice and critical perspectives of management. This resonance occurred because they each emphasise how practitioners deal with messy and ambiguous problems, because they each highlight the social and political nature of practice and because they all share a subjectivist epistemology. Studies of management emanating from a practice perspective also highlighted that managers engaged in little reflective activity, something for which managers were often criticised. Schön's notion of the reflective practitioner could therefore be held up to managers as an exemplary model of professional activity and, importantly, as a model that was in tune with the difficulties faced by managers in their everyday lives.

The linguistic turn in the study of management and organisation

Since Schön's work on the reflective practitioner, ideas about the nature of management have progressed. From within the practice perspective of management, greater attention has been given to the nature, role and function of language in organisational life (Jablin and Putnam, 2001; Westwood and

Linstead, 2001). For example, studies have looked at how linguistic resources, such as stories, metaphors and discourses, are used to construct notions of management, leadership and self-identity (Calás and Smircich, 1991; Townley, 1993; Watson, 1994). Other studies have attempted to understand how language-based constructs (e.g., scripts, schema, cognitive maps, frames) are used to make sense of the organisation and how they guide action (Fairhurst and Sarr, 1996; Gioia et al., 1989; Huff, 1990). There has also been an emphasis on how social practices (e.g., negotiation, storytelling, rituals, teamwork, persuasion, arguments) and symbols (e.g., totems, myths, sagas) are structured and unfold over time (Boje, 1991; Gersick, 1989; Holman, 2000b). Yet another area of interest has centred on how these different linguistic resources and social practices are employed by organisational members to create, maintain and alter 'the organisation' (Bastien et al., 1995; Boden, 1994; Donnellon et al., 1986; Fairhurst, 1993; Ford and Ford, 1994; McPhee, 1989; Weick, 1995). An assumption in these studies is that language use is central to the generation of the organising process. Indeed, for some, language is the *very thing* with which organisations are constituted (Taylor and Van Every, 2000) and organisations are likened metaphorically to texts (Putnam et al., 1996; Tompkins et al., 1989).

The linguistic turn in organisation and management studies has been prompted, in part, by the increasing influence of social constructionist ideas about reality, knowledge, language and communication; ideas that differ from those underlying the traditionally dominant scientific/technical approaches. Thus, scientific/technical approaches to management and organisational theory have assumed that reality is objective and that valid knowledge reflects this reality (Burrell and Morgan, 1979). Flowing from this is the idea that language is predominantly a system of representation, i.e., depicting reality, objects, rules, norms, etc. In organisational studies, this has meant that there has tended to be a focus on the conditions needed for effective communication (often conceptualised as information exchange) within organisations and the interpersonal skills/abilities needed for effective communication (Deetz, 2001). Furthermore, language and communication has generally been viewed as one explanatory factor among many. On the other hand, the linguistic turn has placed language use at the centre of organisational and managerial life. Language use is considered to be one of *the* key phenomena to be studied. This change was prompted, in large part, by the view that social reality is socially constructed and that social interaction is an essential part of this process (Berger and Luckmann, 1966). Language is not, therefore, just a system of representation used to exchange information. Rather, language is predominantly performative, productive and formative. In other words, language does things, it makes things happen and it gives form to reality (Austin, 1962; Garfinkel, 1967).

For organisational and management studies, this means that language use is seen to be the means through and with which organising and managing occur. Psychology too has not been unaffected by the linguistic turn and the increasing interest in social constructionism (Billig, 1987; Edwards and Potter, 1992; Gergen, 1985; Smith et al., 1995). For example, in approaches variously labelled as discursive, relational and dialogical psychology, primacy is given to social relationships. In particular, there is a focus on the conversational or dialogical practices that people use to coordinate everyday activities and how these everyday performances emerge from the uncertain, ambiguous and vague conditions that often exist in the social world. There is an emphasis, then, on the linguistic processes that create, make and shape the social world and ourselves. A further feature of these approaches is an assumption that it is only from within these ways of relating to each other that people can make sense of their surroundings and come to know the world around them. The way in which we 'come to know' and what we know is based within these wider relational activities (Hosking et al., 1995). Another feature, and one emphasised by Shotter, is that because normally we must respond to others in a way that takes their actions and intentions seriously, and because we must coordinate our activities in socially acceptable and legitimate ways, the problem of 'how to act' is not just a technical issue but also a moral one.

The manager as a practical author

When we read Shotter's chapter on 'The Manager as a Practical Author' (1993), we were struck by how it resonated with the linguistic turn in management studies, just as Schön's reflective practitioner resonated with the practice perspective.[4] This resonance occurs because Shotter's notion of the manager as a practical author highlights and dramatises practical language use in organisations, the performative role of language and the centrality of language to the process of organising. However, we also thought that what made the idea of the practical author so appealing was that it went further than simply reiterating the importance of language to managerial practice. What we found so illuminating was the wider theoretical position in which it was placed, namely, a relational/dialogical approach to psychology. We felt that much could be gained in the study and practice of management by considering some of its implications. In particular, we were drawn to the idea that 'good' managers recognised the formative power of language and that they could jointly author some shared sense of organisational space within which they and others could be situated (Cunliffe, 2001). We also liked the fact that Shotter drew attention to the types of conversational activities that would be needed in authorship – and these were quite different from those prescribed in most management textbooks. They include:

1 To articulate a clear formulation of what for others might be chaotic and vague, and to give them a shared or sharable significance.
2 To create a landscape of enabling constraints relevant for a range of next possible actions.

3 To set out a network of moral positions or commitments (understood as the rights and duties of players in that landscape).
4 To be able to argue persuasively and authoritatively for this landscape among those who must work in it.
5 To do the above in joint action with others.

The structure of the book

Although Shotter's original chapter on the practical author was highly instructive, it was also relatively short. We therefore wanted to expand on his original ideas, to consider what other activities or abilities might be useful for practical authorship and to examine how it might be applied to aspects of managerial practice. This book is an attempt to meet those aims and is laid out in the following four parts.

Part 1 introduces and extends the idea of the practical author. In it, John Shotter and Ann Cunliffe situate the practical author within a wider theoretical framework, define practical authorship, focus on how managers create intelligible formulations through everyday linguistic practices (see also chapters 6 and 8), highlight the linguistic and poetic resources available to help managers in authorship (see also chapters 2, 3, 5, 6, 7, 8), and argue for the need for ethical forms of discourse (see also chapters 2, 3, 6 and 7).

Parts 2 to 4 offer a variety of perspectives that one might consider in relation to the broad framework set out in Part 1. In particular, there is a focus on the linguistic resources that can be used in authorship and on how authorship might come into play when engaging in certain managerial techniques.[5] Using the metaphor of 'authorship' we have grouped the remaining chapters into three further parts, namely, 'Developing and Understanding the Story', 'Developing the Author's Position', and 'Rewriting the Script, Rescripting the Author'. It should be noted that we do not seek to provide an exhaustive account of how managers use language, nor do we seek to provide a definitive version of what a practical author might be and the 'skills' needed. We also do not aim to offer a singular perspective on the practical author. Rather, our intention is to be inclusive and to expand on the concept of practical authorship from a variety of theoretical perspectives.

Part 2 focuses on the types of resources that can enable managers to gain a better understanding of the work context and themselves. In chapter 2, David Boje argues that, although storytelling is important in creating organisational realities, managers also need to be aware of how the storytelling process can be problematic, both practically and ethically. He defines four major types of storytelling that are used by managers, draws attention to the ways in which they are problematic, and goes on to suggest an alternative type of storytelling process that is more sensitive to the concerns of the different communities within an organisation. Storytelling is one resource that managers can employ and important aspects of any story are the characters in it and the identities of those characters. Chapter 3, by David Holman, Jeff Gold and Richard Thorpe, proposes a relational approach to identity. In particular, the chapter explores how identity is important in shaping action, how a relational understanding of identity might improve one's understanding of how organisational practices unfold and explores the links between a relational understanding of identity and practical authorship. Until this point, much of the focus has been on words, but not all stories are told in words. Cartoons, pictures and diagrams are all means with which a story can be told or enhanced. In chapter 4, Richard Thorpe and Joep Cornelisson address these issues and look at some of the ways in which visual media can be employed to aid the process of practical authorship.

While Part 2 concentrates on how practical authors can use language and visual media to gain a better understanding of themselves and the work context, Part 3 looks at some of the ways in which language can be used more prospectively to create and restore flows of action. In chapter 5, Francois Cooren and Gail Fairhurst start by drawing attention to the importance of narrative in understanding organisational action. They then combine this with actor-network theory (Latour, 1996) to demonstrate how leaders can accommodate the multiple perspectives of those in an organisation and *translate* them into new inclusive landscapes of action. In other words, they provide a detailed insight into one way in which a practical author's position can be created, developed and used to shape the flow of action within organisations.

Shotter (1993) also suggests that practical authors need to argue persuasively for the landscapes of action that they propose. Chapter 6, by Shirley Willihnganz, Joy Hart and Charles Willard, therefore concentrates on the different ways that arguments can be made in an organisation. Based on O'Keefe's (1988) theory of Message Design Logistics, they suggest that being a practical author requires the rhetorical and argumentative skills that are unique to a Rhetorical Message Design Logic. In this logic, argument is seen as a cooperative, negotiated and creative dialogue that can generate new responses to situations and reframe situations to allow room for action rather than impasse. Another important feature of the argumentative process is that it creates a shared space where incompatible agendas are acknowledged and, possibly, reconciled. Thus, as in the chapters by Boje and Cooren and Fairhurst, the need to recognise and accommodate alternative perspectives is highlighted as an important factor in moving organisational action forward and as central to organisational ethics.

The need to engage constructively with different perspectives means that an ability to negotiate between them is paramount. In chapter 7, Stanley Deetz draws attention to how identity, social orders (e.g., organisational practices), knowledge and policies are negotiated products. He argues that managers are sometimes 'guilty' of trying to stabilise the meanings of these facets or acting as if meanings were fixed. This, he argues, is counterproductive, as it prevents individuals and organisations from creating new potentialities. Rather, managers should be actively involved in complicating and opening up the meanings associated with identities, social orders, etc., so that new potentialities can be negotiated and jointly authored in collaboration with others.

The first two chapters of Part 4 look at the ways in which practical authors can engage in organisational change, i.e., re-writing the script of the organisation. Thus, in chapter 8, Jeffrey Ford and Laurie Ford argue that change is an unfolding of many conversations over time. They show that in order to move action forward, managers need to engage in 'committed conversations' in which each participant commits to engaging in certain acts in the future. They then define and illustrate four different types of committed conversations and compare committed conversations to uncommitted conversations. Chapter 9, by Mike Pedler, is also concerned with organisational change. He starts by comparing action learning and practical authorship and uses a practical example to show how action learning can be used to coauthor change. The last chapter of Part 4, by Dorothy Lander and Craig Prichard, is written as a conversation. In this conversation they aim to upset the grammar of the practical author – to re-script the author – by taking a critical examination of some of the assumptions that Shotter and Cunliffe make in their writings about the practical author.

Notes

1 The two perspectives of management described here are derived from those offered by Reed (1989) and Alvesson and Willmott (1996). The 'scientific/technical' perspective is derived from Reed's 'technical' and Alvesson and Willmott's 'technocratic' perspectives of management. The 'practice' perspective is similar to Reed's 'political' and Alvesson and Willmott's 'progressive' perspectives. It must be noted, however, that Reed also uses the practice perspective to denote an understanding of management that subsumes technical, political and critical perspectives. That is not the intention here. The term practice is preferred to political and progressive as it emphasises that this perspective is rooted in empirical studies of managerial practice. The term practice is also preferred as political is thought to be too narrow an understanding of the social practices involved in management. The critical perspective is derived from the 'critical' perspectives of Reed and Alvesson and Willmott.
2 As we locate the practical author within a practice perspective, we see it as complementing the notion of the reflective practitioner and not as some competing alternative.
3 Schön describes a range of practices through which problem setting and transformation might be achieved, although we will not detail these practices here.
4 We are not suggesting that the practical author is a better approach to practice than the reflective practitioner. Rather, we view the practical author as another 'instructive account' and one that complements that of the reflective practitioner.
5 We do not seek to provide an exhaustive account of practical authorship, our intention is to illustrate how authorship can be applied to aspects of managerial practice.

References

Alvesson, M. and Willmott, H. (1996) *Making Sense of Management: A Critical Introduction*. London and Thousand Oaks, CA: Sage.

Austin, J. (1962) *How to Do Things with Words*. London: Oxford.

Bastien, D.T., McPhee, R.D. and Bolton, K.A. (1995) 'A study and extended theory of structuration of climate', *Communication Monographs*, 62: 87–109.

Berger, P. and Luckmann, T. (1966) *The Social Construction of Reality*. New York: Doubleday and Co.

Billig, M. (1987) *Arguing and Thinking: A Rhetorical Approach to Social Psychology*. Cambridge: Cambridge University Press.

Boden, D. (1994) *The Business of Talk: Organisations in Action*. Cambridge: Polity Press.

Boje, D.M. (1991) 'The story telling organization: a study of story performance in an office-supply firm', *Administrative Science Quarterly*, 36: 106–26.

Burrell, G. and Morgan, G. (1979) *Sociological Paradigms and Organisational Analysis*. London: Heinemann.

Calás, M.B. and Smircich, L. (1991) 'Voicing seduction to silence leadership', *Organisation Studies*, 12: 567–602.

Cunliffe, A.L. (2001) 'Managers as practical authors: reconstructing our understanding of management practice', *Journal of Management Studies*, 38: 351–71.

Deetz, S. (2001) 'Conceptual foundations', in F.M. Jablin and L.L. Putnam (eds), *The New Handbook of Organizational Communication: Advances in Theory, Research and Methods*. Thousand Oaks, CA: Sage.

Donnellon, A., Gray, B. and Bougon, M.G. (1986) 'Communicating, meaning and organized action', *Administrative Science Quarterly*, 31: 43–55.

Edwards, D. and Potter, J. (1992) *Discursive Psychology*. London, Sage.

Fairhurst, G. (1993) 'The leader–member exchange patterns of women leaders in industry: a discourse analysis', *Communication Monographs*, 60: 321–51.

Fairhurst, G.T. and Sarr, R.A. (1996) *The Art of Framing. Managing the Language of Leadership*. San Francisco, CA: Jossey-Bass.

Ford, J.D. and Ford, L.W. (1994) 'The role of conversations in producing intentional change in organizations', *Academy of Management Review*, 20: 541–70.

Garfinkel, H. (1967) *Studies in Ethnomethodology*. Englewood Cliffs: Prentice Hall.

Gergen, K.J. (1985) 'The social constructionist movement in modern psychology', *American Psychologist*, 40: 266–75.

Gersick, C. (1989) 'Marking time: predictable transitions in work groups', *Academy of Management Journal*, 32: 274–309.

Gioia, D.A., Donnellon, A. and Sims, H.P. Jr (1989) 'Communication and cognition in appraisal: a tale of two paradigms', *Organization Studies*, 10: 503–30.

Hales, C. (1986) 'What do managers do? A critical review of the literature', *Journal of Management Studies*, 23: 88–115.

Holman, D. (2000a) 'Contemporary models of management education in the UK', *Management Learning*, 31 (2): 197–217.

Holman, D. (2000b) 'A dialogical approach to skill and skilled activity', *Human Relations*, 53: 957–80.

Huff, A. (1990) *Mapping Strategic Thought*. New York: John Wiley.

Hosking, D.-M., Dachler, P.H. and Gergen, K.J. (1995) *Management and Organization: Relational Alternatives to Individualism*. Avebury: Aldershot.

Jablin, F.M. and Putnam, L.L. (2001) (eds) *The New Handbook of Organizational Communication: Advances in Theory, Research and Methods*. Thousand Oaks, CA: Sage.

Kolb, D. (1984) *Experiential Learning*. Englewood Cliffs, NJ: Prentice Hall.

Kotter, J.P. (1982) *The General Managers*. New York: Free Press.

Latour, B. (1996) 'On interobjectivity', *Mind, Culture, and Activity*, 3: 228–45.

McPhee, R. (1989) 'Organizational communication. A structurational exemplar', in B. Dervin, L. Grossberg, B. O'Keefe and E. Wartella (eds), *Rethinking Communication: Vol. 2, Paradigm Exemplars*. Newbury Park, CA: Sage, pp. 199–212.

Mintzberg, H. (1973) *The Nature of Managerial Work*. New York: Harper and Row.

Mintzberg, H. (1999) 'Debate', *Harvard Business Review*, November/December: 129.

O'Keefe, B.J. (1988) 'The logic of message design: individual differences in reasoning about communication', *Communication Monographs*, 55: 80–103.

Pavlica, K. (1996) 'Management Identity – Czech Republic and Britain', unpublished PhD thesis, Manchester Metropolitan University.

Putnam, L.L., Phillips, N. and Chapman, P. (1996) 'Metaphors of communication and organization', in S.R. Clegg, C. Hardy and W.R. Nord (eds), *Handbook of Organizational Studies*. Thousand Oaks, CA: Sage, pp. 375–408.

Reed, M. (1989) *The Sociology of Management*. Hemel Hempstead: Harvester Wheatsheaf.

Schön, D. (1983) *The Reflective Practitioner: How Professionals Think in Action*. London: Maurice Temple Smith.

Shotter, J. (1993) *Conversational Realities: Constructing Life through Language*. London: Sage.

Smith, A., Harré, R. and Van Lagenhoven, L. (eds) (1995) *Rethinking Psychology*. London: Sage.

Stewart, R. (1967) *Managers and their Jobs*. Maidenhead: McGraw-Hill.

Taylor, J.R. and Van Every, E.J. (2000) *The Emergent Organisation: Communication as Site and Surface*. Hillsdale, NJ: Lawrence Erlbaum.

Tompkins, E.V.B., Tompkins, P.K. and Cheney, G. (1989) 'Organizations, texts, arguments, premises: critical textualism and the study of organizational communication', *Journal of Management Systems*, 1: 35–8.

Townley, B. (1993) 'Foucault, power/knowledge and its relevance for human resource management', *Academy of Management Review*, 18 (3): 518–45.

Watson, T.J. (1994) *In Search of Management: Culture, Chaos and Control in Managerial Work*. London: Routledge.

Weick, K.E. (1995) *Sensemaking in Organizations*. Thousand Oaks, CA: Sage.

Westwood, R. and Linstead, S. (2001) *The Language of Organization*. London: Sage.

PART ONE

Setting the scene

Managers as practical authors: everyday conversations for action

John Shotter and Ann L. Cunliffe

What is most difficult here is to put this indefiniteness, correctly and unfalsified, into words. (Wittgenstein, 1953: 227)

Though he was trained both to develop such models [of his country's economy] and to evaluate the models others developed, he [Fernando Flores] seldom found time to do this work. Instead, he was constantly talking: he explained this and that, to that and this person, put person A in touch with person B, held press conferences, and so forth . . . Because he was sensitive to [this] anomaly [i.e., to the fact that his work was not producing any particular products but that he was working nonetheless], it led him to take a course on the theory of speech acts, and in that course he found the key to the anomaly . . . He saw that work no longer made sense as the craftsmanship of writing this or that sentence or the skilled craftsmanship of banging this of that widget into shape but that currently work was becoming a matter of coordinating human activity – opening up conversations about one thing or another to produce a binding promise to perform an act . . . Work never appears in isolation but always in a context created by conversation. (Spinosa et al., 1997: 45–6)

> *Lisa* [a project manager]: So the understanding of what's real and what's . . . um . . . it isn't OK to do, is not well understood . . . I have no control over the information and it really gets uncomfortable when you think the construction company has a whole lot of subcontractors they pull in, so you're left with a lot of fuzziness . . . and the whole project has that from start to finish . . . I was saying to someone yesterday that a lot of what I do at work is I have conversations with people and sometimes I feel I should be having more output, and they said to me, 'well . . . you tend to be in jobs with a high degree of ambiguity and in those circumstances, talking things out with people and discussing them, that probably is your job. It's to help figure out where are you in those circumstances and what needs to get done.' So a lot of what I have been doing in my job is calling together meetings which say we need to grapple with these issues, we need to confront this stuff, or . . . I need to question these things.

> *Rob* [a program manager]: We've set a goal that 95 per cent of the issues I hear about shouldn't go further than me – only 5 per cent should go to the next level of managers. Knowing which 5 per cent to escalate and

when to escalate them consumes a fair amount of time because there are no rules. The rule that I use is that if I start to feel in the pit of my stomach, or if I can't sleep at night – it's time!

Expressing in words the view 'from within'

A radical change is occurring in our attitudes to human inquiry. We are moving away from analysing our surroundings objectively as external observers of static forms of reality and moving away from studying the activity of others while standing at a distance from them. Indeed, in the past, we have attempted to make sense of others' activity in terms of the realm of *behaviour* (explained as a naturally causal sequence of events) and the realm of *action* (in which we explain the reasons why individuals act the way they do). We have also tried to understand those around us in a one-way fashion, by fitting our observations of their activities into static theoretical schemas. Now, we are beginning to conduct our inquiries in terms of the special practical understanding that emerges from the interplay between our own responsive expressions toward others and their equally responsive expressions towards us. We shall call this a *relationally responsive* understanding to contrast it with the *representational-referential* understanding more familiar to us in our traditional intellectual dealings. Through this reorientation we are beginning to recognise the special, first-time quality of unique events. We are beginning to appreciate the importance of our living, embodied involvements and our own unique spontaneous responses in generating new ideas. As Merleau-Ponty puts it, such bodily responses generate 'a spontaneity which teaches me what I could not know in any other way except through it' (1964: 93). Managers themselves recognise this living relationship within their everyday practice, as Rob's quote above shows. He talks of his spontaneous bodily responses in the sense of an 'instructive spontaneity' that teaches him something that he cannot learn in any other way. Such responses constitute a sensitive instrument for him, indicating, perhaps vaguely at first, something of the nature of his involvements with others and, what may emerge from this, are new, practical ways of relating to orienting ourselves to one's surroundings.

In this third relationally responsive realm, activity is understood to possess some features that are quite different from those of the other two realms discussed above. First, what is so special about these jointly structured activities is that they are always incomplete. Indeed the central defining feature of relationally responsive activity is its openness to being specified or determined yet further by those involved in it. No wonder Wittgenstein (1953) remarks, as we indicate above, that the task of putting the unique indefiniteness of activity, correctly and unfalsified, into words, is not an easy one. Yet managers, such as Lisa and Rob, find themselves struggling with these issues of uniqueness, ambiguity, and 'fuzziness' on a day-to-day basis.

Secondly, relationally responsive dialogical activity is not simply to do with two self-contained people having a two-way conversation. Rather, what matters when a listener perceives and understands the meaning of another's voiced utterance is that

> he simultaneously takes an active, responsive attitude toward it. He either agrees or disagrees with it (completely or partially), augments it, applies it, prepares for its execution, and so on . . . [Likewise, a speaker] does not expect passive understanding that, so to speak, only duplicates his or her own idea in someone else's mind (as in Saussure's model of linguistic communication . . .). Rather, the speaker talks with an expectation of a response, agreement, sympathy, objection, execution, and so forth . . . (Bakhtin, 1986: 68–9)

Furthermore, it is the particular ways in which our utterances are responsive to the circumstances of their use that gives them their specific meanings:

> What is important for the speaker about a linguistic form is not that it is a stable and always self-equivalent signal, but that it is an always changeable and adaptable sign . . . [T]he task of understanding does not basically amount to recognising the form used, but rather to understanding its meaning in a particular utterance, i.e., it amounts to understanding [responding to] its novelty and not to recognising its identity. (Voloshinov, 1986: 68)

In other words, practical meaning occurs between us spontaneously in the living responses a second person gives to the expressions (utterances) of a first. It is the particular way in which we voice our utterances, shape and intone them in responsive accord with our circumstances that gives our utterances their unique, once-occurrent meanings. Also, it is in the way that listeners act in response to our utterances that we judge whether they have understood them or not. Put simply, meanings are created in the spontaneously coordinated interplay of people's responsive relations to each other.

We can talk of participants within such dialogically structured activities as being *practical authors*, who create between them a unique sense of their shared circumstances that enables them to act in ways intelligible to each other. Just as authors create a text with a felt unity in collaboration with their readers, so conversational participants create meaning in a practice with its own shared 'structure of feeling' (Williams, 1977). And as we go on together, certain styles or ways of speaking, certain 'language-games', may become intertwined into our shared practices (Wittgenstein, 1953). Such ways of speaking may serve to express and specify intricate ways in which our practices may be refined, elaborated, or otherwise be made more fitting to our circumstances. It is in this more developed way that we speak here of people as practical authors. Thus, practical authors speak in such a way that other participants can creatively respond in their own unique way but in ways that still makes sense to all those involved.

This concern with authoring connects with this book's overall aim. For, as David Holman and Richard Thorpe point out in the introduction, its aim is to explore and develop the image of the manager as a practical author, first outlined in the book *Conversational Realities* (Shotter, 1993a). That chapter was originally written in 1990. Much has happened since then, both in philosophical circles and in the sphere of organisational studies. In particular, management and organisational studies have taken a linguistic turn and much new literature of direct relevance to the approach taken here has appeared. Organisational analysts have explored the notions of dramatisation, dialogue and rhetoric in organisational life from many perspectives (for example, Alvesson and Karreman, 2000; Czarniawska, 1997; Deetz, 1994; Hatch, 1997; Höpfl, 1995; Law, 1994; Pye, 1995; Tulin, 1997; Watson, 1994).

What we would like to do in this chapter is to deepen and extend the connections between the idea of the manager as a practical author and recent work in philosophy. We seek to do this in two main ways. First, we would now like to bring certain aspects of the work of Wittgenstein, Merleau-Ponty, Bakhtin, Voloshinov, and Heidegger to bear on the issues of concern. Secondly, while the original chapter drew on the work of Morgan (1986), Schön (1983) and Winograd and Flores (1986), and upon *their* reflections on managerial and organisational problems, it contained no data at all from actual managers themselves! We are now in a much better position to remedy that weakness. In an exploration of the idea of managers as practical authors, Ann Cunliffe has accumulated a certain amount of conversational material in which managers discuss issues, events and problems occurring to them in their everyday experiences of managing (Cunliffe, 2001). We would like to bring some of the words of these managers to bear on some of the points we shall try to make. In doing so, we offer a number of excerpts drawn from audio and video taped conversations with managers, which formed part of research designed to explore the notion of managers as practical authors. These conversational excerpts are intended to portray how poetic language may orient our responses and ways of relating.[1] In particular, we are concerned with studying words-in-their-speaking and with the moment-by-moment unfolding of relationally responsive events occurring in 'the interactive moment' (Shotter, 1993a: 3). Furthermore, rather than wanting to talk 'about' such events, we want to explore the functions of this talk. We offer an embedded interpretation of the possibilities for meaning construction from within the talk itself, and a reflective commentary. Indeed, these exemplary utterances add to the 'practical-descriptive' aim of the original chapter: as 'instructive accounts', they are useful in drawing attention to how we create meaning and action in our relations with others. They also offer resources for refining our relational practice.[2]

What is practical authorship?

Rob: Other program managers, who have the same job description, have
   different measures and different things they key in on . . . the project

manager manages the people who are doing the design . . . they are managing the task, and the term I've used is 'managing the interactions' – which is what I do. That's different from managing the actions. The project managers are managing the actions – this person needs to get this task done by this date so this person can do their work . . . I manage the interactions which says that the marketing person needs to know what the project is going to look like so they can develop some sales brochures.

Managers such as Rob recognise both implicitly and explicitly the need to 'manage interactions'. Indeed, many management education and training programmes focus on communicating effectively. However, we suggest that practical authorship is not just about managing communication, but also creating meaning in a relationally responsive way. It is a different way of being and relating – a different understanding of how language constitutes our social realities and sense of self – that we wish to explore in the remainder of this chapter.

The original chapter took a remark of Winograd and Flores (1986) as its point of departure. Rather than urging managers to study theories established for them by outsiders, by scientific experts, they characterised the responsibilities of managers 'as participation in "conversations for possibilities" that open new *backgrounds* for conversations for action' (1986: 151, our emphasis) and new ways of relating to one's surroundings. We shall make a somewhat similar claim to theirs: that it is not yet more or different theories that we need in management studies, but a better understanding of how conversation intertwines with an organisation's other activities, and of how such intertwining can lead to the creation of yet further kinds of conversationally structured realities.[3] Indeed, the implication of our comments is that management studies will fare much better as a *humane* rather than theoretical study, one which draws upon the special knowledge we have 'from within' ourselves as conversationally competent human beings rather than on our knowledge of propositions, rules or principles.[4]

We are now in a position to move on to our exploration of the image of the manager as a practical author. We must begin the aim of trying to reveal the beginnings of a new way of doing things, in our everyday activities, by reminding ourselves of the momentary nature of our access to such organisational landscapes, that their nature is not continuously accessible to external public scrutiny, and that their 'shapes' become known to us only from within our particular, momentary, living involvements in them. As we have already suggested, such moments of involvement are unique. They are situated within the background flow of people's ongoing, everyday, talk-entwined, spontaneously responsive activities. It is from within this background that the following four issues will be explored: who are 'good' author managers; how managers create intelligible formulations through everyday linguistic practices; the linguistic and poetic resources available to help managers; and, the need for ethical forms of discourse.

Who are 'good' author managers?

> The basic practical-moral problem in life is not what *to do* but what [kind of person] *to be*. (Shotter, 1993a: 118, *emphasis in original*)

Often in the human sciences it is said that there is nothing so practical as a good theory. Does this mean that good managers should, before going out to participate in the life of their organisations, prepare themselves like academics by spending time devising and discussing theories? This is where a focus solely on the idea of the manager as a scientist can mislead us. We suggest good management is *not* to do with finding and applying a true or false theory, or acting out specific roles or functions (Kotter, 1982; Mintzberg, 1973; Stewart, 1967). In attending to the many possible external frameworks or 'systems' when trying to make sense of events, we can easily ignore the many other special preparatory activities relevant to the development of new practices. Rather, we would suggest that practical author managers need to create *intelligible formulations* of what has become, for other organisational members, either a chaotic welter of impressions, or a static, fossilised view (a single order of connectedness). By doing so, in the course of their everyday conversations they, along with other organisational participants, author the shape of their organisation's operational space or social landscape. In this sense, a manager might be seen as someone able to restore a flow of action, giving shape and direction to the actions of other participants in the organisation when they are either disoriented or stuck. Thus, rather than 'doing science', they are involved in 'making history' (Spinosa et al., 1997). For, although they must often operate (in Marx's well known phrase) 'under conditions not of their own choosing', good managers, when faced with such un-chosen conditions, can create a shared landscape of possibilities for action by producing appropriate responsive utterances when conversing with those around them.

Good author managers can go further. Just as good novelists or playwrights can move others to experience a felt and actively lived sense of an (as yet) non-existent reality, so, as Rob suggests above, good managers move those they manage toward such a shared sensing through acting jointly with them. More than just 'giving us a picture' – which lies dead on the page – the good author manager can bring us to experience a *living reality*, a dynamic landscape, which spontaneously offers us a set of 'action guiding advisories', a 'shaped and vectored sense' of where we are now and where we might go next. Indeed, from within such a felt and actively lived reality, what is 'in front' and 'behind', what is 'in reach' and 'out of reach', and so on, becomes directly apparent to us. It is as if each event occurs, so to speak, with 'strings attached', so that those who are involved in it create a sense of 'what leads to what' or 'what can go with what'. Managers can be seen, then, as creating in concert with those around them, new possibilities within which both they and others can live and work. It is in this sense that, more than just an individual reader or repairer of situations, a good manager can also be seen as a coauthor of them.

Managers also author a sense of their own identities and the identities of those around them, i.e., the different parts all involved must play in relation to each other upon that landscape. In this way, managers are more like artists and novelists than scientists or engineers. As Heidegger notes with respect to his inquiry into the general meaning of Being, although we do not know what Being means, 'this vague average understanding of Being is still a Fact' (1962: 25). It exists in us in terms of felt or sensed deviations or variations from all the currently existing, public or official attempts to define its character. Just like Heidegger himself, we say to ourselves: 'There is something there I still do not quite grasp.' We gain this vague average understanding *from within* our engaged involvements with the others around us. Indeed, good managers actively pursue such required *in situ* involvements to gain an understanding of Being in their own local settings – a sense of being-in-relation-to-others.

> *Rob*: We've actually done a fair amount of discussing around that and what successful managers tend to do and at least here in our environment we tend to be fairly participative. We want people on the project teams to self-manage as much as possible, we want people to take ownership for the deliverables and really feel a part of setting the plan and executing the plan, and so for that reason, the job of manager tends to be more of a leader and integrator. To provide leadership in saying, 'this is where we're heading, this is what's important, this is what we need to do together', to provide leadership to get different people to put their part in place and make it fit and then integrate that over time to make sure all the pieces continue to fit and if this person didn't meet this objective, that this person over-achieved and as a whole we continue to meet the objective.

How should we *be* in relation to the others around us? Our stance here is that authorship is a way of being-in-relation-to-others/self/surrounding and that managers must contest and negotiate who they *are* in responsive dialogue. Clearly, Rob wants to be a leader without followers, i.e., he wants people on the project teams to be self-managing as much as possible. He doesn't want to be a coercive, threatening leader – yet wants to provide direction and integration so 'all the pieces fit'. Managing is therefore not separate from who we are, or based on a detached knowledge of the world, but is intimately linked with what we feel, say and how we relate with others. Furthermore, while managers may recognise themselves as being in conversational relations with others, they are also acting from, and working on, their own sense of themselves as they talk. What they do is entwined within embodied, responsive dialogues and therefore part of who they are and want to be. We cannot separate talk and action from self, nor self from others, as highlighted by Rob's comments above and Mike's below about credibility and faith. Rob and Mike are each extremely knowledgeable about their own inner 'workings', about how they must orchestrate the unfolding movement of their own management activities, what precisely and concretely must be related to what, and in what order.

One further aspect of practical authorship is to do with entering into the realities of others around one and making meaning *with them*, jointly:

> *Mike*: I think the essential management skills – as I use the term, the management of people – reside on this continuum that has things about communication, your ability to communicate your ideas, to empathise with other people . . . you make meaning with them jointly . . . you present ideas that are powerful – but you can't do that unless people have faith in you.

In summary, authorship is a dialogical practice in which features of experience and surroundings are articulated and brought into prominence. To do this, besides talking to or at others, good author managers must talk *with* others; they must be sensitive and subtle listeners, as well as sensitive and subtle talkers. And within the relational interplay between their own outgoing talk (and other actions) and the incoming responses from others to what they do, they must be able to sense those aspects of other's responses which are not just the mere reflection of their own responses back to them. In other words, they must be able to hear the possibility of something new in the nuances and tones of those around them. Furthermore, what makes managers good authors, is that they are able to draw on a variety of linguistic resources to help those around them who might experience themselves as occupying indeterminate, ill-defined realms of activity, make intelligible sense of their surroundings. In so doing, they help create new possibilities for action and new ways of being and relating. From this perspective, good managers do not enact a series of activities, roles or core competencies, but recognise managing as a way of being and relating with others in terms set by, so to speak, the possibilities made available to them by their organisation's momentary landscape.

It is this momentary nature of experience – that everything we do in the sphere of language use is never a mere repetition of something already done, but requires us to be responsive as we negotiate with others the emerging meaning of our actions – that makes the notion of creative authorship especially appropriate. More than merely finding an already existing category into which to fit an action, the task is to create or craft a unique response to a unique circumstance. But the good manager must do more than this. As we shall see, good managers coauthor intelligible formulations of the situation at hand, develop a shared common sense, use talk poetically to make noticeable the unique details of the surroundings, and author an ethical discourse.

How do managers make intelligible formulations? New beginnings and dramatisations

How do managers create intelligible formulations, a scenic sense of an organisation's social landscape and possibilities for action, through responsive dialogue? The good manager is able to start with the vague sense of possibility, i.e., a sense of something not previously noticed in the background to everyone's daily circumstances, and work *from within* that vague under-standing toward a much more explicit, linguistically expressible, account. But more than that, the account offered must provide participants with a sense of the organisation both as it is now and of the moves they might make next. (This is related to what Weick [1979, 1995] talks of as the enactment of sensible organisational environments.)

Talk in terms of objective theories is not oriented towards influencing events *from within* one's living involvement in them in this way; it actively excludes the provision of such a directed sense. Indeed, such theoretical talk can often seem to *exclude* action: 'OK, I get the picture, but . . . so what?' A sense of being disempowered by one's own analyses is still possible even with the most complex and sophisticated forms of theory.[5] Good managers must do more than provide a picture. Through their use of words, like a good novelist, they must create between and around themselves and their asso-ciates a dynamic dialogical landscape within which all involved can find an orientation, places in which to take a stand and places to which to move.

If managers are to do this, they must be sensitive to their environment and see their surroundings in a special way. Thus they must not only see the given (i.e., unchosen) conditions, which all in the organisation must face; they must also see them afresh as a poet might see them, as if for another first time. They must see them as offering, permitting or affording *new possibil-ities unnoticed by others*. They must then be able, linguistically, to stop others in their tracks, to disrupt routine ways of seeing things, to draw attention to the presence of something previously unnoticed in their shared circumstances, and give it a distinct initial formulation so that others can contribute toward 'its' further specification. They must also be able to give a sharable linguistic formulation, to already shared feelings, arising out of shared circumstances.

In order to do all this, practical authors must do more than merely touch on possibilities and then move on, they must also, as in an artistic presenta-tion or performance, *dramatise* it. What is done in a dramatisation is to foreground and to make sensibly graspable the shape and character of 'a something' which, nonetheless, still remains invisible. One must portray or display in one's performance its *presence* as a unitary whole (just as the mime artist Marcel Marceau displays the existence of an invisible wall in his hand movements as he struggles to find an opening in it). If one is original enough (in one's words), then one can express the fleeting, flickering presence of new possibilities merely glimpsed in such a way that others can glimpse them too and dwell on them long enough to make them items of public discussion. Due to the vagueness of things, this is, perhaps, best done through the use of *metaphors* and other poetic devices, on which we shall elaborate below.

By dramatising and creating intelligible formulations, organisational participants author an organisational common sense[6] (i.e., a figurative understanding that incorporates shared responsive understandings rather than literal descriptions). This process involves the attempt to change an unarticulated 'imaginary' organisational landscape into an 'imagined' one

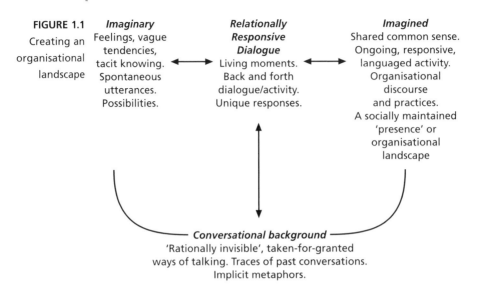

FIGURE 1.1 Creating an organisational landscape

(Shotter, 1993a) (see Figure 1.1). This transition, from a fleeting sense to a grasp of a presence that is open to exploration, is central to our stance here. The imaginary is something tacit: feelings, tendencies, anticipations, projected possibilities, i.e., entities that are still emergent in the internal relations of our experience but which nonetheless play a real part in structuring our activities. When such relations are made rationally visible by being articulated, they become the imagined or imaginable. And, when talking with various images in mind, which resonate with the contoured movement of our experience, we become more sensitive to possible connections and relations between aspects of our surroundings.

Managers, perhaps both consciously and unconsciously, help to construct an organisation's common sense by responding to aspects available to all in the conversational background, and by creating shared ways of talking about features of its organisation. This common sense, and the discourse it sustains, unlike the generalised talk of outside theory-driven experts, is unique to organisational members; it emerges from within the relationally responsive activities occurring between people. A conversation with the president (Vince) and various managers (Dave and Jeff) of a small manufacturing organisation offers an example of how language may constitute intelligible formulations and 'features' for organising activity:

> *Vince*: I live in this world of uncertainty, I'm not naive any longer. Maybe, Ann, one of the problems is the way you operate as a manager – I come in in the morning now and I'm a sceptic. I say, 'Okay, first tell me about all the casualties, I want to set priorities. What are the things that might take us out of business today?' I'm not being wise, I'm being a realist . . . right now we're wrestling with keeping two boilers up and running . . . Yeah, we gotta game plan and we try to set a course of direction, but then I live with the reality of the situation. I can go back Monday and the

boiler is gone – so how do we address this problem? You really have to be nimble of foot here, you've got to be able to react, you don't know what's going to be thrown at you. You try to prepare yourself for the unexpected, and with a number of eyes looking ahead with me, maybe we'll see a few of the potholes that are approaching us . . . if you look at the plant, the plant itself is like a rickety old car with band aids and rubber bands!

Dave: You plan to use this machine and have to use that, and some weeks this breaks and then that breaks – so it's very difficult . . . You plan something then 'Boom!' something happens . . . that's one of the dark tunnels.

Jeff: For half of every decision that's made, there's some sort of unantici- pated personnel backlash!

Vince is perhaps trying to deal with the chaotic welter of impressions by constructing contoured poetic images: 'casualties' and 'wrestling', metaphors of the battlefield. These linguistic practices may help him construct oppor- tunities for shared responsive understandings (with both the researcher he is talking to as well as with organisational members) as he articulates features (the imaginary) and brings them into the realm of talk (the imagined). In using the root metaphor of a battlefield and other instructive forms of talk to draw the attention of other organisational members, Vince may be coauthor- ing a common organisational discourse and themes around which further organising activity can take place (e.g., his response 'Okay, first tell me about the casualties'). Such imagery can be very powerful in shaping meaning by evoking responses and perhaps similar ways of talking. Indeed, this met- aphor was shared in conversations with other managers in his organisation, as can be seen in the excerpts from Dave and Jeff. Each is perhaps taking all the complex strands of experience, the language used in responsive inter- action, and weaving them into a coherent text. It is in this way that managers can create and shape features of their organisation's landscape by dramatis- ing a not-yet-visible dynamic whole, which then may take on a 'presence' by becoming a taken-for-granted part of shared organisational discourse. This shared discourse, in turn, provides the background conversation in which further possibilities for action are constructed.

There is, however, a danger that these vague but rich images may become 'literalised' (Rorty, 1989) into precise but sparsely detailed models and theories. While persuasive in seminar and conference halls, such models and theories can be totally unresponsive and unrelated to involved partici- pants and their surroundings. Rather than disrupting routine ways of paying attention to and responding to our surroundings, such talk assumes them to still be in place and open to 'objective' theoretical manipulation. In contrast, talk that articulates the imagined within the imaginary, works within the living moment. It is a living part of the everyday conversational background which functions practically and persuasively by influencing and being influ- enced by our actions and talk – thus enhancing our responsive relations to our surroundings (see Figure 1.1).

We suggest that it is through responsive dialogue and linguistic practices that a shared organisational discourse or architecture emerges – a sense of organisational reality, into which we then act (see also chapter 10). Metaphors and poetic forms of talk are used extensively in our everyday conversations (Lakoff and Johnson, 1980; Watson, 1995: 812) and are key resources, potent in creating vivid images, immediate reactions and embodied responses, which can lead to shared significances and intelligible formulations. Organisational features are often spoken of in metaphorical ways (see excerpts above), yet may take on a 'presence' by becoming a taken-for-granted part of the shared organisational discourse on which possibilities for action are constructed: reality takes on the characteristics of images created in language. In this way, the good practical author manager renders the invisible visible by engaging with and dramatising his or her sense of the surroundings. The good practical author also creates an 'imagined' from the many imaginaries by jointly authoring acceptable features and possibilities for action, in fluid responsive ways, from the welter of impressions organisational members experience.

Social poetics: noticing previously unnoticed details in one's surroundings

While the use of systematic theory may seem to help in enabling one to prepare one's reactions ahead of time, it precludes all the possibilities of authorship we are discussing here. In fact, if we are to understand authorship, what we need, as we have argued above, is to move away from thinking of language as to do with representations. We need an account of language use which emphasises what we might call its *constitutive* or *formative* powers: the ability of people in otherwise vague, or only partially specified, incomplete situations to lend to such situations a more determinate linguistic formulation. However, from an academic and even personal perspective, situations of this relationally responsive kind, in which novel realities gradually come into existence for a first time, are very unfamiliar to us. We lack an appropriate vocabulary in terms of which to characterise them. As academics, we are much more used to talking in representational terms 'about' objective entities we suppose to be already in existence somewhere and whose hidden order awaits our discovery. It is as if with all our scholarly training, we arrive on the scene much too late and then look in the wrong direction. The once-occurrent, first-time, originary events of importance escape our notice. They are too fleeting; they are already over. What we can see with all the special framing devices we invent for ourselves, are only the finished products, a finalised and static picture of reality 'over there', a 'dead' actuality existing independently of our involvement in it.

To overcome this tendency, we need a new way of relating ourselves to our circumstances. For Vico (1990: 34) this meant adjusting oneself to the 'contours' of the context, and the kind of knowing we need in dealing with those passing moments we call an event's circumstances is *practical wisdom*. Practical wisdom is a special third kind of contextualised knowing, *sui generis*, that we have already mentioned above, i.e., knowing of a *relationally responsive* kind – which takes into account (and is only accountable within) the social situation within which it is known. Thus, says Vico, the difference between the imprudent individual and the wise person is this:

> The learned but imprudent individual, travelling in a straight line from general truths to particular ones, bulls his way through the tortuous paths of life. But the sage who, through all the obliquities and uncertainties of human actions and events, keeps his eye steadily focused on eternal truth, manages to follow a roundabout way whenever he cannot travel in a straight line, and makes decisions, in the field of action, which, in the course of time, prove to be as profitable as the nature of things permits. (1990: 35)

Imprudent individuals must use force because they act in accordance with how, according to their theories, they think circumstances *ought* to be, rather than acting in accordance with how they actually are.

How can managers shape their talk to fit the contours of a circumstance? What kind of talk is required to make their invisible contours visible to people for a very first time, and to orient them toward fresh, unnoticed possibilities? What linguistic resources can we use in this process? Vico, Wittgenstein, Bakhtin and Heidegger all claim that the kind of talk required is poetic talk and, as we will see in the conversational excerpts that follow, managers tend to talk in poetic and imaginative ways as they make sense of, act in and negotiate their way through organisational life. We suggest that in these ways of talking, managers use particular social poetic methods to create possibilities for meaning and action.

Before we turn to these poetic forms of talk, we would like to draw attention to what it is that makes them have a completely different role to theoretical forms. First, they are aimed at 'arresting' our routine forms of thought and perception, thus orienting us toward previously unnoticed aspects of our surroundings. Often, it does this by bringing two very ordinary words or phrases, not usually juxtaposed, into strange new combinations. While the words used may themselves be quite vague, their unusual juxtaposition directs us to attend to specific aspects of what is before us in new ways. In doing so, they can also provoke us into the construction of a poetic image, a 'dynamic landscape', a felt 'presence' (Steiner, 1989), to provide us with a previously lacking orientation. Such talk can then work further to put the imaged scene on freeze-frame and then instruct us in searching over the frozen presence for ways in which to relate ourselves responsively to aspects that might not otherwise have occurred to us. So, although such talk may in itself seem vague, it can be quite precise in its use. Its precision comes from the public witnessing of new, previously unnoticed, nuanced details in our circumstances.

More than merely giving us some information about our circumstances, a poetic image helps us *form* or *constitute*, for the very first time, a way of orienting toward or relating ourselves to our surroundings and the circumstances of our lives. It leads to a kind of understanding which 'consists in "seeing connections" ' (Wittgenstein, 1953: no. 122). And we can make use of such images – to look *through* them, to think *with* them, so to speak – in seeing and making connections between aspects of our surrounding circumstances that might not otherwise have occurred to us. As Merleau-Ponty remarks: 'To think is not to possess the objects of thought; it is to use them to mark a realm to think about which we therefore are not yet thinking about' (1964: 160).

These resources have been explained in depth elsewhere (Shotter and Katz, 1996). What we are interested in here is how they may be used by managers (unselfconsciously or otherwise) to constitute organisational realities and identities. As managers and researchers we are using the 'responsive instructions' in such poetic images to make sense; to guide us in organising and assembling bits and pieces of information available to us. Their function is to relate us to our surroundings in more refined, nuanced, elaborated and, ultimately, more creative ways. We are usually unaware of our talk working, spontaneously, in this creative fashion.

In organisations, because managers must work with the others around them and make meanings with them jointly, we shall call the kind of poetic methods at work a *social* poetics (Cunliffe, 1999; Katz and Shotter, 1996a, 1996b; Shotter and Katz, 1996). Social poetics embraces the notion of the living experience of authorship and sense-making by exploring how meaning may be created between people, both in the moment of speech and after the moment in reflection upon it. We will therefore focus on interactive moments in which opportunities occur for constructing shared significances, and draw attention to the type of dialogue in which such moments of connection and meaning may be created. Wittgenstein's later work (1953) offers a number of resources for grasping these practical and taken-for-granted aspects of our talk. They may be summarised as follows:

1 *Noticing in practice*: 'giving prominence to distinctions which our ordinary forms of language easily make us overlook' (no. 132): 'stop' 'look', 'listen to this', 'look at that' (breaking routine ways of responding by pointing out features of the flow from within the flow) (no. 144);
2 *New connections and relations*: 'a *picture* held us captive' (no. 115): the use of new metaphors to reveal new possible connections and relations between events hidden by the dead metaphors in routine forms of talk;
3 *To continue to gather examples*: 'don't think, but look!' . . . 'and the result of this examination is: we see a complicated network of similarities overlapping and criss-crossing' (no. 66);
4 *Making comparisons*: to bring some order to our experiences by making comparisons using (sometimes invented) '*objects of comparison* which are meant to throw light on the facts of our language by way not only of similarities but dissimilarities' (no. 130);

5 *Establishing 'an order in our knowledge of the use of language*: an order with a particular end in view [so that we can all participate in discussions toward that end]; one out of many possible orders, not *the* order' (no. 132);

6 *Seeing not something* behind *or* underlying *appearances*: but seeing 'something that lies open to view and that becomes surveyable by a rearrangement' (no. 92).

Indeed, the aim of all these moves is to achieve a 'perspicuous representation' a way of surveying a sequence of experiences (as if they were moments of fixation in one's visual scanning over a landscape) with the aim of producing 'just that understanding which consists in "seeing connections" ' (no. 122). They lead, not to theory, but to the kind of understanding which enables us to be more 'at home' within our own cultural creations, to know our 'way about' (no. 123) within them, and thus to avoid becoming 'as it were, entangled in our own rules' (no. 125), i.e., to avoid being at cross-purposes with each other. Wittgenstein calls these 'reminders' (no. 89) because they direct attention to 'what we have always known' (no. 109), about our relations to our circumstances and about how we intertwine our activities with those of others to make sense of our surroundings and create living relationships.

We have seen some examples of how such methods may exert their effects and contribute toward the idea of managers as practical authors. Business schools do not explicitly teach the linguistic skills we think of as associated with good practical authorship. Yet, the managers we depict here are not wholly unaware of their skills in this sphere. Indeed, they seem to possess a reflexive self-awareness of how they construct the very features they think of themselves as talking about, and how their linguistic practices influence this process of construction. In the example below, Rob is quite clear of the relation between his talk and its function. It is not and cannot be to *impose* a plan externally. He must help to create a network of *participatory* relationships within which all involved call on each other to play their parts:

> *Rob*: Ideally, the strategy would be set, I would be charted to deliver a piece of that strategy, and then I would tactically implement that. The reality is that we never nail down the strategy part to a level where it's purely tactical for the programme team. It's always still fairly strategic, fairly open and undefined . . . Problems are at a much higher level of abstraction; nothing is designed, nothing is given, everything is what you decide it is. If you ask somebody, 'What is this product going to do?' – 'Well I don't know, you tell me.' 'When is it going to be finished?' 'Well I don't know – you tell me.' 'How much is it going to cost?' 'Well I don't know – you tell me.'

Rob's comments highlight the importance of creating meaning by being responsive to others both in terms of what he says and how he speaks. He talks about the difficulty of creating a precise strategy. He speaks rhythmically, using alliteration, repetitive words in tempo, e.g., 'nothing is designed, nothing is given . . .', and uses dialogue within dialogue in an iterative way, e.g., 'Well, I don't know – you tell me . . . well, I don't know . . .'. To me (ALC), as a conversational participant, this seemed not only to emphasise his point about the openness of the process but also gave me a sense of the unrelenting, back and forth nature of these problems. His verbal perform-ance, his practical use of words, their very rhythms in their voicing, like being another's dance partner, helped to create a more holistic sense of experience for me as conversational participant. In such instances, managers evoke images in which meaning seems to be authored by images and by how the words are spoken.

Social accountability and ethical discourse

> *Mike*: I think it's also possible to act out of values . . . particularly I think when people sense themselves making a decision that has a moral component to it. It's probably one of the times we do get intentionally reflective. You know, if someone comes in and says, 'Gee the numbers look really bad this quarter, but I think I've found a way . . . I'm not sure it's exactly right, but I think I've found a way we can maybe rework the numbers and it won't look as bad as it really is.' Most of us, I think, with any kind of sense of moral element to management would be very reflective about that and say, 'Well, what are you talking about!' 'Well, I could do this and this' and you would say, 'Well, is this right?'

Conventional views of management as a science and managers as technocrats making economically rational decisions often deny the moral aspects of managing because the ends and means are taken for granted (Alvesson and Willmott, 1996; Jackall, 1988; Mumby, 1988). Managers are often perceived as morally neutral technicians (Roberts, 1996) and manage-ment itself as a value-free practice in which moral judgements are validated against objective, technically rational, system-oriented criteria of efficiency and effectiveness. An alternative argument suggests managers are not value-neutral but often act in self-interested and political ways (Jermier et al., 1994). If we accept this position (although already, Mike's comments above should caution us against an easy acceptance of it), then how do/might managers act in an ethical and morally responsible way? And how can managers do this from within an already morally textured yet continually contested social landscape?

A dialogic perspective offers possibilities because it draws attention to how we relate with each other ethically: 'We must go forward to the selves hidden in each moment of opportunity and realise that the irreducible conflicts between our many legitimate selves are not different from the conflict with diverse others . . . ethics rests not in agreement to principles, but in avoidance of the suppression of alternative conceptions and possibilities' (Deetz, 1995: 223).

But more than this, at a deeper level, practical authorship brings issues of social accountability and morality to the fore by emphasising the nature of our being-in-relation-to-others. If I need you in order to be me, if my sense of personal worth depends upon your response to my expressions, then, strange though it may seem, ethical values are prior to, not a consequence of, our knowledge of the others around us. To appreciate this, consider for a moment occasions when, simply, we meet the eyes of another, when we are struck just for a moment by the presence of another before us. If we dwell for a while on the character of such moments, we find within them a sense of being obligated to another which we *must* play out according to the local (moral) requirements. We become aware of such obligations if, for instance, we stare too long at someone, or look away from them too quickly – either response seems to express disrespect and can occasion anger. Similarly, if in the course of our involvement with another, they sense us as failing to respond to their expressions appropriately, they feel justified in complaining: 'Hello,' they say, 'anyone at home?' Goffman (1967) explores in detail what he calls our 'involvement obligations' and the many different forms of 'alienative misinvolvement' that we can experience in our relations with others. We need not list them here. Suffice it to say that only if we honour our 'involvement obligations' in our conversations with those around us can we each gain a sense of each other's unique 'inner worlds', i.e., where we each are coming from and/or going to.

Palshaugen notes that although many problems arising in an organisation consist of 'trifling things', they often remain unresolved

> because they are considered 'insignificant' by those whose responsibility it is to do something about them. (1998: 60)

But,

> when these problems are brought into a common arena, a public sphere inside the company, then their significance changes and increases . . . A hand wheel on a machine which is difficult to turn, too narrow a stairway next to a machine, a failure in the planning route, the lack of a spare part, a problem with raw deliveries – all these are examples of trifles that form a problem both for efficient production *and* for the working environment. (1998: 61, *emphasis in original*)

The significance of these trivial problems changes and increases as they become publicly visible because, in fact, they are not just technical, mechanical problems: each time workers who have taken the trouble to articulate a problematic detail they have noticed in carrying out their daily task are ignored, not only is a small, possible improvement in efficiency lost, but their dignity as caring workers has been slighted – their identity as someone of moral worth within the company is diminished.

Indeed, in Palshaugen's account of the effects of direct, two-way verbal contact replacing or supplementing customary written contacts, he gives us an example of a seemingly trivial problem which has often been ignored. He quotes union workers' comments on the drawbacks of *written* contacts, e.g., 'Letters simplify.' While a departmental head articulates the issue in more detail as follows: 'Personal contact means that both the problem and those who are responsible for its solution, in every section, become visible in a way that both deepens our understanding of the problem and our obligation to do something about it. Far more than impersonal notes' (1998: 64). In other words, both the unions and the departmental head spontaneously note that something of importance is lost in one-way, monologic forms of communication that is restored in two-way dialogic forms. The departmental head gives more detail. He or she suggests that it is not just a detail of possible technical importance that is being ignored, but also an *obligation* and if management can ignore their obligations, can't the workforce also ignore theirs? Thus, to have a visible place within a company's public sphere requires more than just a matter of giving everyone the opportunity to participate in the development of the company's production capacity. Just as crucial, it is a matter of everyone being able to see the nature of each other's *moral* involvements (i.e., their rights and duties) and to come to a much more detailed grasp of what, justifiably, is expected of them and what they can expect of others. Human values do not disappear from a company just because its dominant, organisational discourse only allows expression of technical matters, but what does disappear are the arenas within which human values can be publicly discussed and resolved.

To have a voice in establishing one's own conditions of work, and to be listened to seriously (in the sense of others visibly responding to what one has to say) is a part of what it is to feel oneself fully a person, and not subject to a reduced status in one's workplace (Braverman, 1974; Sennett and Cobb, 1972; Shotter, 1984, 1993b). Indeed, to insist on judging everything that occurs within a person's work life solely in terms of production values and to reduce human relations to mechanical ones – even in a factory, where it may seem justifiable – is to discount the complexity of people's moral and ethical relations to each other. It is to act as if we already knew their unimportance, when in fact, the opposite is the case – as those with any sensitivity to their surrounding circumstances appreciate.

In creating a common sense, participants should recognise a morally textured landscape of opportunities for joint action, and act in a socially shared responsive way. This entails moral *interdependence*, a moral requirement to make available communicative opportunities (socio-ontological resources) to each other (Shotter, 1993a: 163). This means recognising our place in creating ethical discourse, respecting the rights of those around us to speak, and understanding how our use of words orients responses and ways of relating. In other words, a 'knowing how, knowing how to live, knowing how to listen' (Lyotard, 1984). A crucial aspect of ethical discourse is reflexive dialogical practice (Cunliffe, 2002) – engaging in dialogue to explore how our own actions and conversational practices may create and be sustained by particular ways of relating and by implicit or explicit power relationships. In doing so, we can work towards more linguistically expressible and reflexive accounts, from within experience itself, so that we may act as critical practitioners and influence events from inside.

Conclusion: implications for knowledge and practice

We began this chapter by emphasising the importance of our living, spontaneously responsive relations to our surroundings. This leads to a recognition of the embedding of our everyday activities in a third, background realm of dialogically constituted, intricately structured, joint activity. This third realm is quite different from the other two realms of action and behaviour that have occupied our attention in human affairs in the past. Situating management in this third realm of activity led us to claim that the essential core ability to do with being a good manager is *not* that of finding and applying true theories. Managers should not be looked upon as experts in theoretical talk, as experts in devising models to be used in calculating rational solutions to problems by their manipulation. While persuasive in certain contexts, the unresponsiveness of such talk to its context can make it of little use to involved practitioners. They can try to impose externally the effects of such talk. But, as Vico (1990) puts it, that is to try to 'bull [one's] way through the tortuous paths of life'. We argued that we need forms of talk that work from within the living moment to enhance people's responsive relations to their surroundings.

Good managers must be good conversationalists, both responsive listeners and responsive speakers; what marks off the manager from those they must manage is their attention not to this or that specific job within the organisation, but to making a comprehensive set of connections and relations between them all. As Rob says in one of our quotes, while others 'manage the actions', the good manager must 'manage the interactions'. And they must do this by helping to promote among all concerned a shared common sense (a shared *sensus communis*), a shared spontaneous responsiveness to events within the organisation, no matter whereabouts within it such events may occur. In particular, being a good manager is to do with a whole complex set of issues centring on the provision of *intelligible formulations* of what, for the others in the organisation, appears to be a chaotic welter of unconnected impressions.

Thus, our view of managers as practical authors has implications not only for how we think about meaning and meanings, of the relation of knowledge and knowing to management, but also for how we think about their relation to thinking and to the development of new ways of doing things, i.e., to our practices. Indeed, what we have been suggesting in this chapter is *not* a new theory that people might put into practice, but a set of new, dialogically structured, mostly linguistic practices, that people might put into their already existing practices. Simply by uttering certain crucial words at certain crucial moments in the routine flow of current practice we can move those involved to notice aspects of experience previously unnoticed. It is the equivalent of saying: 'Hey, stop! Wait a moment! Lets look more closely at what's happening here. Look at it *this* way!' – We can then go on from such new but fleeting beginnings to fashion new ways of acting, which do not solve the problems of the old ways, but leave them behind. Like the 'anomaly' to which Fernando Flores became 'sensitive' (in our opening epigraph quote), the good manager must be continually sensitive to those events in which routine ways of making sense no longer work. But rather than implementing a few very basic principles and insisting that everyone derive their actions from these, the good manager (like a good Wittgensteinian philosopher) must continually produce a 'synoptic view' of a whole, interrelated melee of particular, concrete events and conditions. From all the small details, he or she must fashion a dynamic, scenic sense of the circumstances they all share, toward which everyone concerned can orient, and within which they can know their way about. It is through their invention, and with the 'authorial' help of others, that the participants of an organisation can conversationally fashion for themselves a shared, dynamic, relational landscape for action. In so doing, organisational participants can develop themselves into a 'mutually enabling community', in which, instead of obstacles to each others projects, we can come to see each other as resources, as resourceful conversational partners.

Notes

1　These research conversations should be seen from the perspective of an embodied dialogical practice in which a manager and researcher coconstruct momentary connections about how each makes sense of the manager's lived experience. We are not claiming the conversations are representative of an actual reality but rather offer a way of exploring possibilities of how the discursive practices of participants may help coconstruct meaning and how these practices may spill over into organisational lives. In other words, the manager and researcher are both practical authors in the process of ordering impressions.

2　We also feel it is necessary to point out that the original chapter took an essentially social constructionist approach toward management problems – that is, such problems are much more to do with *making* (poiesis = Gr. making) and creating something quite new than with finding or discovering something already in existence. It is worth emphasising that it espoused a social constructionism of a quite specific kind, one which embodied a strong leaning toward the primary or originary importance of our spontaneous, pre- or non-cognitive, bodily responsiveness – an emphasis explicit in the work of Vico mentioned in the original chapter, but crucial also in the work of Bakhtin and Wittgenstein explored in other chapters of the book (Shotter, 1993a). There, it was called 'rhetorical-responsive' social constructionism. Here, to emphasise our central focus on relational understandings, we would like to call it a *relationally responsive* version of social constructionism, one that is crucially concerned with 'once-occurrent events of Being' (Bakhtin, 1993) which are occurring for yet 'another first time' (Garfinkel, 1967: 9). We mention this here because many other postmodernist and poststructuralist versions of social constructionism still focus on patterns or repetitions, on structures of rules or conventions, on frames, systems or structures and also take something of a cognitive, Cartesian, *referential-representational* stance toward the events they study.

3   Spinosa, Flores and Dreyfus say in the opening sentences of their book – a book which in many ways is very close to our concerns in this chapter: 'This book does not present a *theory* of entrepreneurship, democratic action, and solidarity production. Nor is it a manual that will tell you how to succeed in these domains. Rather, we hope that this book will help you develop a skill that is essential for being an entrepreneur, a virtuous citizen, and a solidarity cultivator – that is, for regularly and as matter of course seeing yourself and the world anew. Your ability to appreciate and engage in the ontological skill of disclosing new ways of being will, we hope, be expanded when you re-examine your old experiences from the perspective of this book's descriptions and analyses' (1997: 1).

4   Elsewhere, Shotter (1993b) has characterised this as a third kind of knowing, distinct from 'knowing that' and 'knowing how' (Ryle, 1949). Unlike the two other forms of knowing, which can give rise to bodies of knowledge within an individual, it is a form of knowledge that one only has *from within* a social situation, and which depends on the judgements of others as to whether one is properly in possession of it or not.

5   As Morgan notes, a complex and sophisticated understanding of our lives, as determined by the logic of unfolding oppositions, for instance, may still lead us to experience our lives as 'shaped by forces over which we have little control. [Thus] a manager may feel that he or she has no option but to follow the rules of the market and general environment in shaping corporate policy. [Or] a worker may feel that job opportunities and career prospects are predetermined by his or her education or social background. [Where] in each case, the logic of "the system" or "the environment" is seen as being in the driving seat' (1986: 266).

6   'Common sense [*sensus communis*] is judgement without reflection, shared by an entire class . . .' (Vico, 1968, para. 142). It gives rise to a whole integrated set of spontaneous responses to events shared by all participants in a social group.

References

Alvesson, M. and Karreman, D. (2000) 'Varieties of discourse: on the study of organizations through discourse analysis', *Human Relations*, 53 (9): 1125–49.

Alvesson, M. and Willmott, H. (1996) *Making Sense of Management: A Critical Introduction*. London and Thousand Oaks, CA: Sage.

Bakhtin, M.M. (1986) *Speech Genres and Other Late Essays*, translated by Vern W. McGee. Austin, TX: University of Texas Press.

Bakhtin, M.M. (1993) *Toward a Philosophy of the Act*, with translation and notes by Vadim Lianpov, edited by M. Holquist. Austin, TX: University of Texas Press.

Braverman, H. (1974) *Labour and Monopoly Capitalism: The Degradation of Work in the Twentieth Century*. New York: Monthly Review Press.

Cooper, R. (1983) 'The Other: A Model of Human Structuring', in G. Morgan (ed.), *Beyond Method. Strategies for Social Research*. London: Sage.

Cunliffe, A.L. (1999) 'Everyday conversations: a social poetics of managing', paper presented at the Critical Management Studies Conference, July 1999.

Cunliffe, A.L. (2001) 'Managers as practical authors: reconstructing our understanding of management practice', *Journal of Management Studies*, 38: 351–72.

Cunliffe, A.L. (2002) 'Reflexive dialogical practice in management learning', *Management Learning*, 33: 35–61.

Czarniawska, B. (1997) *Narrating the Organization: Dramas of Institutional Identity*. Chicago: University of Chicago Press.

Deetz, S. (1994) 'The micro-politics of identity formation in the workplace: the case of a knowledge intensive firm', *Human Studies*, 17 (1): 1–22.

Deetz, S. (1995) 'Character, corporate responsibility and the dialogic in the postmodern context: a commentary on Mangham', *Organization*, 2 (2): 217–25.

Garfinkel, H. (1967) *Studies in Ethnomethodology*. Englewood Cliffs: Prentice Hall.

Goffman, E. (1967) *Interaction Ritual*. Harmondsworth: Penguin.

Hatch, M.J. (1997) 'Irony and the social construction of contradiction in the humor of a management team', *Organization Science*, 8 (3): 275–88.

Heidegger, M. (1962) *Being and Time*. Oxford: Blackwell.

Hertz, H.H. (1956) *The Principles of Mechanics*. New York: Dover (orig. German pub. 1894).

Höpfl, H. (1995) 'Organizational rhetoric and the threat of ambivalence', *Studies in Cultures, Organizations and Societies*, 1: 175–87.

Jackall, R. (1988) *Moral Mazes: The World of Corporate Managers*. New York: Oxford University Press

Jermier, J., Knights, D. and Nord, W. (eds) (1994) *Resistance and Power in Organizations: Agency, Subjectivity and the Labour Process*. London: Routledge.

Katz, A.M. and Shotter, J. (1996a) 'Resonances from within the practice: social poetics in a mentorship program', *Concepts and Transformations*, 1 (2/3): 239–47.

Katz, A.M. and Shotter, J. (1996b) 'Hearing the patient's voice: toward a "social poetics" in diagnostic interviews', *Social Science and Medicine*, 43 (6): 919–31.

Kotter, J.P. (1982) *The General Managers*. New York: Free Press.

Lakoff, G. and Johnson, M. (1980) *Metaphors We Live By*. Chicago: University of Chicago Press.

Law, J. (1994) *Organizing Modernity*. Oxford: Blackwell.

Linstead, S. (1994) 'Objectivity, reflexivity, and fiction: humanity, inhumanity, and the science of the social', *Human Relations*, 46 (1): 1321–45.

Lyotard, J.F. (1984) *The Postmodern Condition: A Report on Knowledge*, translated by G. Bennington and B. Massumi. Minneapolis: University of Minnesota Press.

MacIntyre, A. (1981) *After Virtue*. London: Duckworth.

Merleau-Ponty, M. (1964) *Signs*, translated by Richard M. McCleary. Evanston, IL: Northwestern University Press.

Mintzberg, H. (1973) *The Nature of Managerial Work*. New York: Harper and Row.

Morgan, G. (1986) *Images of Organization*. Thousand Oaks, CA: Sage.

Mumby, D.K. (1988) *Communication and Power in Organizations: Discourse, Ideology and Domination*. Norwood, NJ: Ablex.

Palshaugen, O. (1998) *The End of Organization Theory? Language as a Tool in Action Research and Organizational Development*. Amsterdam: John Benjamins.

Pye, A. (1995) 'Strategy through dialogue and doing: a game of "Morningtown Crescent"?', *Management Learning*, 26 (4): 445–62.

Roberts J. (1996) 'Management education and the limits of technical rationality: the conditions and consequences of management practice', in R. French and C. Grey (eds), *Rethinking Management Education*. London: Sage. pp. 54–75.

Rorty, R. (1989) *Contingency, Irony and Solidarity*. Cambridge: Cambridge University Press.

Ryle, G. (1949) *The Concept of Mind*. London: Methuen.

Schön, D. (1983) *The Reflective Practitioner: How Professionals Think in Action*. London: Maurice Temple Smith.

Sennett, R. and Cobb, J. (1972) *The Hidden Injuries of Class*. Cambridge: Cambridge University Press.

Shotter, J. (1984) *Social Accountability and Selfhood*. Oxford: Blackwell.

Shotter, J. (1993a) *Conversational Realities: Constructing Life through Language.* London: Sage.

Shotter, J. (1993b) *Cultural Politics of Everyday Life: Social Constructionism, Rhetoric, and Knowing of the Third Kind.* Buckingham: Open University Press.

Shotter, J. and Katz, A.M. (1996) 'Articulating a practice from within the practice itself: establishing formative dialogues by the use of a "social poetics" ', *Concepts and Transformations*, 1 (2/3): 213–37.

Spinosa, C., Flores, F. and Dreyfus, H.L. (1997) *Disclosing New Worlds: Entrepreneurship, Democratic Action, and the Cultivation of Solidarity.* Cambridge, MA: MIT Press.

Steiner, G. (1989) *Real Presences.* Chicago, IL: University of Chicago Press.

Stewart, R. (1967) *Managers and their Jobs.* Maidenhead: McGraw-Hill.

Tulin, M. F. (1997), 'Talking organization: possibilities for conversational analysis in organizational behavior research', *Journal of Management Inquiry*, 6 (2): 101–19.

Vico, G. (1968) *The New Science of Giambattista Vico*, translated and edited by T.G. Bergin and M.H. Fisch. Ithaca, NY: Cornell University Press.

Vico, G. (1990) *On the Study Methods of our Time*, translated by Elio Gianturco. New York: Bobbs-Merrill.

Voloshinov, V.N. (1986) *Marxism and the Philosophy of Language*, translated by L. Matejka and I.R. Titunik. Cambridge, MA: Harvard University Press (first pub. 1929).

Watson, T.J. (1994) *In Search of Management. Culture, Chaos and Control in Managerial Work.* London: Routledge.

Watson, T.J. (1995) 'Rhetoric, discourse and argument in organizational sense making: a reflexive tale', *Organization Studies*, 16 (5): 805–21.

Weick, K.E. (1979) *The Social Psychology of Organizations.* Reading, MA: Addison-Wesley.

Weick, K.E. (1995) *Sensemaking in Organizations.* Thousand Oaks, CA: Sage.

Williams, R. (1977) *Marxism and Literature.* Oxford: Oxford University Press.

Winograd, T. and Flores, F. (1986) *Understanding Computers and Cognition: A New Foundation for Design.* New York: Addison-Wesley.

Wittgenstein, L. (1953) *Philosophical Investigations.* Oxford: Blackwell.

PART TWO

Developing and understanding the story

Using narrative and telling stories

David M. Boje

We know that managers are storytellers and use stories to accomplish their everyday work. But, what stories are they telling, how do managers control which stories get told and how can they tell a better story in a pluralistic world? In this chapter, I want to make three practical author points:

1 Managers are taught and socialised to participate in organising processes that control stories, storytellers, and the construction of storytelling in complex organisations.
2 Managers learn to listen to and evaluate stories told through administrative processes that make the experiences of employees and customers difficult to hear.
3 Managers have to deal with the ethical consequences of these two points.

Let us begin with a story.

As we sat at our tables in La Provinceal restaurant in the Paris resort hotel, every half-hour the waiters and waitresses did a choreographed dance routine. They formed a chorus line, waving flags, kicking their feet in unison, lip-syncing their lines, as they maintained the biggest smiles I have seen any food workers display. Our friends from France assured us 'this does not exist in France'. We remarked, 'It is the Las Vegasisation and Disneyfication of Paris, this is fake Paris.' When our French friends ordered dishes in French, the waitress replied that she only spoke a few words of French, such as 'Bonjour and Merci'. 'Is Angelique your real name?' I asked. 'It is really Angela' she replied. As we watched the waiters and waitresses perform, it struck us that they were performing stories that were not their own. They were apparently trained in just enough French to take on the role of a French employee but their training (as at Disney) rendered them little more than 'smiling robots' in a simulation of a Parisian restaurant. As customers we participated in the spectacle, applauding their narrative performances, sometimes failing to notice differences between their ritual tellings and what we had each experienced in the 'real' Paris. In what ways did the managers of this 'simulated' restaurant control Angela's story and her presentation of self? In what ways do managerial processes control storytelling?

The role of stories in organisations and the importance of storytelling for managers

Managers tell and hear stories everyday and they play an important role in the process of managing and organising. Stories are used to exchange information, to instruct others how to act, to articulate the future (what are vision statements, if not the synopsis of a story of a quest to some utopian future?), as an oral cultural memory and as ways to rewrite history in order to legitimate moves made in the present. Organisational members also use stories to collectively make sense of the organisation. Indeed, it takes a community of tellers to construct and control the stories of an organisation and the meaning given to a story is fashioned by creating and interpreting stories in relation to other stories. People in organisations are therefore embedded in a web of stories; and while some navigate the web, others get caught in it and lose their ability to narrate a personal account. It is this point that is central to this chapter.

Problems with storytelling: recapturing the narration of personal experience

Prior work has argued that organisational storytelling processes can overwhelm and marginalise the capacity for experiencing the self and community. It is thought that the individual feels unable to recount their life story; their experiences become marginal to various 'modern' storytelling processes which Lyotard (1984) has called the grand narrative (e.g., scientific and bureaucratic narratives). For example, workers and customers may live out the story as told by the CEO to the *Wall Street Journal* and are unable to articulate an unmediated narrative of their personal experience. Other writers have suggested that, faced with a chaotic 'postmodern' world of fragmentation (Bauman, 1993, 1995) and complexity (Kauffman, 1993; Stacey, 1996), the individual can no longer narrate a sense of cohesive personal identity. In more radical postmodern versions, we live lives without coherence or meaning, slipping down a slope that simulates both time and place but is no longer grounded.

But, not everyone wishes to live the 'robotic' narratives of modernity or the fragmented narratives of postmodernity and this highlights my concern about whether individuals feel able to narrate their personal experience at all. In particular, I seek to create a space for a form of dialogue that might return the individual to the centre stage of narration and storytelling. To do so it is first necessary to explore the 'stages' in which storytelling is performed, and how storytellers are controlled and constructed, in what I call the 'storytelling organisation'.

Defining the 'storytelling organisation'

The 'storytelling organisation' is defined as the collective storytelling system in which the performance of stories is a key part of members' sense-making. Storytelling organisations exist to tell or 'narrate' their collective stories,[1] to live out their collective stories and to be in constant struggle over getting the stories, plots and characterisations of insiders and outsiders straight, and 'to supplement individual memories with institutional memory' (Boje, 1991a: 106). At one extreme, the storytelling organisation can oppress by subordinating everyone and collapsing everything (including personal narratives) to one grand narrative. For example, in a narrative analysis, Walt Disney enterprises was theorised as a storytelling organisation in which an interplay of official stories triumphed over or accommodated more marginal ones.[2] At the other extreme, the storytelling organisation can be a pluralistic and liberatory construction of a multiplicity of stories, storytellers and story performance events.

In this chapter, I extend prior work in this area by exploring the differences among five ideal type storytelling organisations. Initially I will focus on four ideal types of storytelling organisation, the bureaucratic, the quest, the chaotic and the postmodern (see Figure 2.1).[3] However, as noted, I also hope to show that it may be possible to create a type of storytelling organisation that returns the individual to the centre stage of narration. Thus, after describing the first four types, I will place the manager of the storytelling processes in what I term the 'inter-story storytelling organisation'. The hybrid inter-story storytelling organisation is seen to be important as the employee's and the customer's life story is more than any reconstructed version that a single type of storytelling organisation can re-author, retell and control. It is also important to point out that, rather than seeing any one type of storytelling organisation as being supplanted and replaced by another, I theorise them in interaction, in layers and strands, as intertextual and multilayered processes.

Figure 2.1 has two dimensions that I use to categorise the ideal types of storytelling organisations. The first is monophonic–polyphonic. A monophonic narrative has one voice that narrates for everyone else. In organisation studies, this narrator is typically the voice of the CEO, the spokesperson for bureaucratic and quest storytelling organisations. In polyphonic narrative processes, there is a plurality of narrators. The narratives themselves can lack cohesion and consensus, and can be suspended in complexity and fragmentation. Bureaucratic and quest narratives tend to be monophonic, while chaos and postmodern tend to be polyphonic.

The second dimension is scientific–aesthetic knowledge. For Lyotard (1984) the scientific narrative is one of progress and economic growth

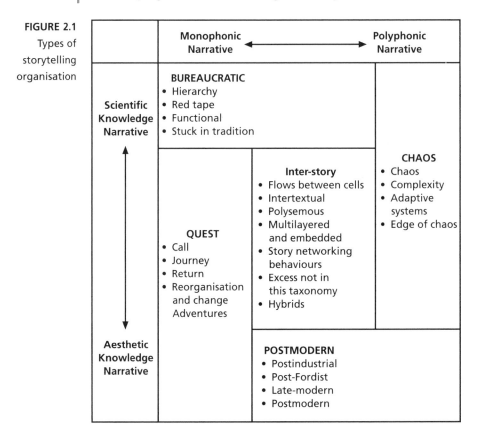

FIGURE 2.1
Types of storytelling organisation

Figure 2.1 content:

	Monophonic Narrative ⟷		Polyphonic Narrative
Scientific Knowledge Narrative	**BUREAUCRATIC** • Hierarchy • Red tape • Functional • Stuck in tradition		
	QUEST • Call • Journey • Return • Reorganisation and change Adventures	**Inter-story** • Flows between cells • Intertextual • Polysemous • Multilayered and embedded • Story networking behaviours • Excess not in this taxonomy • Hybrids	**CHAOS** • Chaos • Complexity • Adaptive systems • Edge of chaos
Aesthetic Knowledge Narrative		**POSTMODERN** • Postindustrial • Post-Fordist • Late-modern • Postmodern	

realised through technical knowledge. Both bureaucratic and chaos storytelling organising processes appeal to the legitimacy of scientific knowledge, be it Taylor's scientific management or Fayol's science of administration, reengineered information systems, Total Quality Management (TQM) or examples of fractals and complexity curves. These 'scientific knowledge narratives' compete with other kinds of knowledge narratives that I choose to call 'aesthetic'. An 'aesthetic knowledge narrative' does not make appeals to technical rationality as the basis for its legitimation. In the quest storytelling organising processes, legitimacy is the function of what Joseph Campbell calls mythic journeys told in ritualised formulas, as well as self-reflective accounts that defy formulas. In postmodern narratives, formulas for how to tell and listen to stories are meaningless because they lack any 'horizon of consensus' or agreement on any one-language game or ways of speaking (Lyotard, 1984: 24–5). If the legitimacy of scientific knowledge narratives is functionality, usefulness and performativity played out in games of technology, then the legitimacy of aesthetic knowledge is derived from the 'life-of-the-spirit'.

Ethics also comes in to play throughout Figure 2.1. Ethical questions raised include, for example: 'Whose story is being told by the organisation?',

'Who gets to tell a story to whom?' and 'What narrative framework is being given authority?' (Bauman, 1993; Hallstein and O'Brien, 1999; Newton, 1995).

I now turn to describe the ideal types of storytelling organisation, show how they are problematic and examine the manager's role in them.

The bureaucratic storytelling organisation   In the bureaucratic storytelling organisation, stories are linear, quantified, rationalised and attempt to make the control of people and processes more predictable. Indeed, linear story lines are seen to correlate with the linear processes of the bureaucratic organisation. For example, the manager participates in bureaucratic processes that render story lines predictable; life is always getting better through successive reforms in administrative process, be they TQM, reengineering or knowledge organisation transformations. Furthermore, managerial acts such as appraisals can play a role in creating linear, rationalised and over-controlled storytelling processes that reduce 'individual stories' to entries in personnel databases. However, if one peels back the narratives of rationality, there is a swarm of 'vulnerability, futility, and impotence' (Frank, 1995: 97). This means that the coherent sequences of events told in the official and proper bureaucratic narrative are always more linear, rationalised and controlled than accounts given by customers or employees and do not adequately reflect their lived experience. Another consequence of this is that the bureaucratic storytelling organisation turns other types of story (e.g., the chaotic or quest) into linear accounts of the self. The narrative process thus becomes ritualised and we are seduced into abandoning our experiences of complex organisations. As such, the bureaucratic storytelling organisation can overwhelm personal experience narratives and the ethical challenge for bureaucratic storytelling organisations is to hear the personal experience narrative.

The quest storytelling organisation   The quest narrative focuses upon the voice of the hero who has a compelling story to tell. There are three essential segments in a quest narrative: the call, journey and return. Thus, after the call to adventure and after some false starts and recruiting companions, the hero departs on the journey. The journey begins with some act of initiation that normally involves a series of trials and overwhelming events. These usually mould the actors in the quest into a mighty team. Along the journey the hero can be tempted and even atone for transgressions. The hero of the quest meets difficulty and even chaos head on and seeks to master its secrets. At the end of the journey, the hero is transformed, returning not only with the 'loot', but also with values that have been transformed. In the return, the hero has mastered the pain and suffering of the quest.

In film and literature we encounter at least two types of quest journeys. In one, the hero slugs his way through a never-ending list of more and more powerful opponents. At the last match, he nevertheless triumphs against overwhelming odds and great risk. The other motif is more spiritual.

Through the agony of trial and even defeat, the hero makes atonement for past failures or misdeeds. Both hero-types return and convince others who did not go on the journey that they have the magic sword or the magic wisdom.

Quest storytelling organisations often construct the romantic tale of the heroic CEO and this affords the CEO the most distinctive voice. For example, most Harvard business case studies are variations of a quest narrative, with the triumphant CEO, returning from the reorganisation or acquisition adventure with the 'booty'. Disarray itself can be part of the organisational call that prompts the journey into the unknown and promises that the struggle to transform the disarray will produce a gain. Other recent writings about CEOs stresses their 'spiritual journey', as a discovery of great wisdom and enlightenment, not to mention higher existential meaning. Strategy narratives, including SWOT analysis, also adopt a heroic and romantic emplotment (Barry and Elmes, 1997).

But, can the heroic journey, the quest for the magic elixir that will transform corporate excess and inefficiency, be an oppressive narrative? The quest storytelling processes, I believe, can mask the stories of other voices. The quest narrative is prone to ignore the rifts, confusions and gaps in the essential fabric of an organisation and this tends to marginalise others who participate in the journey or the experience of those who await the hero's return. Its outcome or resolution may be no more than a band-aid rather than the transformation that is really needed. The CEO journey and the tale of the transformed organisation may mask and overwhelm the more mundane, chaotic and even tragic kinds of consciousness that are the experience of everyday participants in quests within complex and fragmented organisations. Indeed, bureaucratic and quest storytelling organisations cannot practically fill the narrative holes with which we are confronted when we 'read' or tell chaotic and postmodern narratives.

The chaos storytelling organisation   The defining characteristic of a chaos narrative is that 'events are told as the storyteller experiences life: without sequences or discernible causality' (Frank, 1995: 97). The chaos narrative is thus fragmented, with a syntactic structure of 'then this happened and then that happened and then another event occurred'. Chaos stories are lived, not told in acts of cohesion. Indeed, the chaos story is in one way an 'anti-narrative', without a coherent sequence of events connected to each other in time and space, and relatively unmediated by acts of retrospective sense-making (Frank, 1995). A caveat is necessary here. When I refer to chaos, I do not mean here the chaos of chaos theorists, i.e., the emergence of discernible, yet non-linear patterns that can revert to linear pathways or even to randomness and noise at any moment. Rather, I focus on chaos as it is narratively experienced by employees and customers – as a wound, as the narrative wreckage of existence or as senseless suffering (Kauffman, 1993) – and before they attend an 'edge of chaos' postmodern consulting seminar (Bergquist, 1993) or read the latest Santa Fe Institute reports.

The chaos storytelling organisation, then, provides a space to tell stories without plots and causal sequence, where no one is in control.[4] The general plot of a chaos story organisation is that 'life never gets better, especially when one tumbles into the abyss'. In this way, the chaos storytelling organisation is at the opposite end of the continuum to the bureaucratic storytelling organisation, which presupposes order, coherence and control. The plot also differs from those found in the quest storytelling organisation, in which chaos is confronted and the abyss is not fallen into. The chaos storytelling organisation thus opens the can of worms that bureaucratic and quest storytelling organisations seek to cover.

However, within organisations, the chaos stories that are told as part of the chaos storytelling organisation often draw on chaos theory and shroud organisational practice in the form of abstractions such as theories of fractal chaos, complexity and strange attractors. Indeed, when I explained the chaos storytelling organisation to a chaos theory professor, he replied: 'they don't understand the dynamics of emergence in chaos theory'. The appeal to the scientific legitimacy of chaos theory can romanticise the experience of chaos, overwhelm the lay person's experience of chaos, marginalise how people experience the suffering in chaos and cover any tragic rifts in the existential fabric of complex organisation (Kauffman, 1993). Ironically, what chaos theorists offer is the same boon the bureaucratic and quest narratives hold out, to keep chaos at bay and, once encountered, to neutralise the effects of its interruption to order, coherence and purpose. Chaos theorists restore faith in the modernist project by offering a narrative of emergent chaos-control that promises more efficiency from acts of randomness and emergence. Such stories therefore 'represent the triumph of all that modernity seeks to surpass' (Frank, 1995: 97–8). This is not to deny that 'edge of chaos' narratives are at odds with the bureaucratic storytelling processes. It merely points out that the stories of those living in the chaos can not be told in quest or bureaucratic storytelling control processes or in the language of chaos theorists.

In summary, while the chaos storytelling organisation offers the possibility of marginalised stories being heard, the use of chaos theory by dominant actors can lead to employees' and customers' personal narrative experiences being romanticised or overwhelmed.

The postmodern storytelling organisation   This type of storytelling organisation is characterised by the reduction of the customer's, employee's and manager's life space to fragmented stories that become circulated throughout administrative networks. Thus, as in the chaos pattern, there are fragments of memory overwhelmed by situated occurrences that do not settle into the coherence of a meaningful journey or bureaucratic order. However, unlike in the chaos story, there is a conscious act by the storyteller to gain sovereignty over his or her experience and a more active role is given to retrospection, self-reflection and reflexive action.[5] These acts of self-reflection can create the time and space to give the appearance of slowing down events.

This can mitigate against the overwhelming sense of uncertainty as to what is being received. Another key aspect of the postmodern storytelling organisation is the deconstruction of experience and in some cases the telling of the story itself. This retrospective sense-making involving reflexivity and deconstruction is accomplished collectively through a dialogue between storytellers and story listeners. However, this is not the dialogue about which Senge writes, in which stakeholders seek some type of narrative consensus. In the postmodern storytelling organisation, no grand narrative is woven but a polyphony of narratives are told. As such, the life experience of the individual is not subsumed by a collective narrative account and the personal experience narrative can be recovered in the telling and making of narratives. Yet, the fragmented nature of the postmodern storytelling organisation can engender a sense of uncertainty in what is being told and listened to. This chronic uncertainty may, in some circumstances, be perceived as threatening and thus the postmodern storytelling organisation may not be experienced as a liberating structure.

In summary, it can be seen that in the four storytelling organisation processes outlined, the personal experience narrative is inadmissible, reshaped, fragmented or surrendered. For example, the bureaucratic storytelling organisation is scarcely able to imagine chaos as anything beyond disorder, much less hear stories of chaos as anything but calls to tighten the iron cage of rationality. A quest narrative gives a pedagogical role to chaos, so that one can return from the edge of the abyss with some useful lessons. However, today's complex organisations do not simply reflect one type of storytelling organisation but will probably include an intertextual and interpenetrating collage of the types depicted in Figure 2.1. There are monovocal narratives of bureaucracy and quest competing with polysemous narratives of chaos and postmodern, and this constructs the very complexity of complex organisations. Indeed, as Ritzer (1993) points out, modernity did not succumb to postmodernity. Disneyfication and now Las Vegasisation is everywhere, as is chaos and fragmentation. Yet, despite this, in the storied arena of complex organisations, the employee's and customer's life space is still more than various storytelling processes can register and retell. Part of the problem lies with the way that managers are forced into storytelling processes that substitute a more sanitised and restricted account of their identity and that rob both customer and employee of their life story. Only on rare occasions in organisations do employees and managers author their story in charged moments of personal experience storytelling (Frank, 1995: 5; Newton, 1995: 105). How then, might managers engage differently in the storytelling process and be more sensitive to others' personal experience narratives? My premise is that managers need to take advantage of the multiple, intertextual and polysemous (many meanings) strands of storytelling organisation processes. A further need is to engage in a interplay between the different types. Such a concern echoes Best and Kellner's (1997) call for a more 'moderate' postmodern turn in which there is interplay between grand

and more local narrating. These theory moves hold out the possibility that a modernist and postmodernist can dialogue in non-polemic ways. Thus, the need for managers is to develop a more coauthored and intertextual construction of narratives, to be aware of the problems of storytelling processes and to develop a more hybrid form of storytelling process that can draw on and enact the four ideal types. I now turn to a discussion of the interstory storytelling organisation.

The interstory storytelling organisation   In order to explore interstory storytelling processes, I will describe a play called *Tamara* that enacts a true story taken from the diary of Aelis Mazoyer. It is Italy, 10 January 1927, in the era of Mussolini. Gabriele d'Annunzio, a poet, patriot, womaniser and revolutionary who is exceedingly popular with the people, is under virtual house arrest. Tamara, an expatriate Polish beauty, aristocrat and aspiring artist, is summoned from Paris to paint d'Annunzio's portrait. In *Tamara*, a dozen characters unfold their stories before a walking, sometimes running, audience. You do not sit in a seat and watch the play, but have to decide which actor to follow from one scene to the next, knowing all the while that you are missing story fragments played out in the rooms you elected not to go to. Thus, the audience fragments into small groups that follow characters from one room to the next, following and cocreating the stories that interest them the most. No audience member gets to follow all the stories since the action is simultaneous, involving different characters in different rooms and on different floors. Characters also morph from stage to stage, and unless you follow a given actor you will not see the transformation of, for example, the chauffeur to the aristocrat pretending to be a chauffeur to the spy who pretends to be in love with the maid. I thus experienced a very different set of stories from someone following another sequence of characters.

In *Tamara*, the story consists of many stories, with each story masking a multiplicity of stories and each a particular framing of reality being followed by wandering and fragmented audiences. We can see that there is an interplay between the grand narrative and the many local narratives and between the story of the author and the different fragmented stories created by the audience. The possibility also exists that the audience could not make any sense at all of the play they saw, and were presented with a chaotic or fragmented series of events. The play can be understood as a metaphor for the interstory storytelling organisation in which different types of stories might coexist and affect the telling of each other.

For the manager, particularly one seeking to be a practical author, I feel that it is important for them to move between different types of narrative in a never ending interpolation and entanglement of bureaucratic, quest, chaotic or postmodern stories – the creation of an interstory. This is important for a number of reasons. First, the use of an interstory represents a move away from a managerialist approach to storytelling in which one story fits all, be it bureaucratic, quest or chaotic. Such a managerialist approach makes the manager the expert, the God-narrator and the sole author or organisational reality. However, the managerialist story performed on a single stage in which the audience hears but one account appears too simplistic in a pluralistic world and a world where organisations are accountable to many constituents. On the other hand, the interstory admits that there are multiple layers to the storytelling organisation and that many stakeholders narrate the organisation in ways that do not agree with the 'official' story. Thus, the use of interstories enables the manager to be telling, hearing and encouraging different types of (non-dominant) story.[6] Thus, while some organisational members may chose to reproduce the bureaucratic and quest stories presented in popular texts or as told by the CEO, such tales will be confronted by others, producing a much more contested landscape. I also envisage that the different types of story would foreground different types of claims, and the manager's job, like everyone else's, is to make people aware of these claims, their legitimacy and how they might affect the claims of others. Interstories also enable 'the stage' to become many stages. The story performed on the single stage with one audience is but one account and becomes too simplistic and less legitimate. Although there is a danger in this collective process of dialogue that the individual's personal narrative becomes subsumed in the chaos and fragmentation, the interstory does provide a better opportunity for the multiplicity of voices to be heard and for a wider number to be involved in legitimating the knowledge (be it scientific or aesthetic) of the firm.

The process of telling interstories should, I believe, promote dialogue between organisational members. In this new story approach to storied dialogue, I am not advocating the consensus through dialogue of the learning organisation or knowledge organisation. Rather, through dialogue the organisation participates to tell stories, to listen to counter-stories, and to unfold coauthored tellings. In this way, and as in the Tamara play, the line between actor and audience becomes blurred.

A central issue in the creation of a participative storied dialogue, a process that is at the heart of the interstory, is how can this be done in ways that do not over-privilege any one narrator? This question thus foregrounds the role of narrative ethics (Newton, 1995), which is concerned with questions such as:

1   Whose story is being told by the organisation?
2   Who gets to tell a story to whom?
3   What narrative framework is being given authority?
4   How do those who resist dominant storytelling processes fare?

While the process of telling interstories might not hold the answers to such questions, it does help to sensitise managers to them. By doing so it means that such issues may be addressed and lead to material changes in the processes for controlling storytelling in ways that impinge on practices that affect labour conditions and the ecological environment.

Conclusion

We know that telling stories is an important part of organisational life. As we indicated at the beginning of this chapter, stories are used to exchange information, to instruct others how to act and to articulate a future. However, as I have tried to show, the type of stories told (bureaucratic, quest, chaos, postmodern) affects people's experience of how they relate to others in the organisation and how they understand their self. Indeed, I have argued that the four different types of storytelling organisation can have adverse effects. This is because a person's own story becomes hard to hear or is ignored, because a story over-rides the complexity of their everyday experience, or because they feel lost in a sea of uncertainty and fragmentation. In order to address these problems I have suggested that the manager as practical author needs to interpolate between these different stories, between the grand and the local narrative, and create an interstory in participative dialogue with others. Indeed, managers as practical authors can decide if they are to be champions of official organisation stories or whether they are able to listen to and respond to personal experience narratives of employees, customers and communities.

Notes

I would like to thank Annette Holman for her constructive comments on this chapter.

1 Story has a strange subordinated relation to narrative. 'The term narrative is a story retold in the voice of another person' (Anderson, 1998: 169).
2 See also Boje, 1991a, 1991b, 1994, 1995, 1999; Boje, Luhman and Baack, 1999; Boyce, 1995; Gephart, 1991; Kaye, 1996.
3 These types are derived from Frank's (1995) work on medical narratives and on work primarily in medical narrative ethics (Anderson, 1998; Nicholas and Gillett, 1997; Tovey, 1998). However, I have changed several labels, resituated the typology from medical ethics to the narrative ethics of complex organisations, and added the fifth hybrid type (inter-story).
4 To bureaucratic and quest narratives, the chaos narrative is not only improper because the storyteller uses 'and then this happened' and 'then that happened' without tying the events to some orderly plot, but the events are not ordered or grasped by some retrospective act of narrative reflection.
5 Postmodern narrating can be understood as a critical witness to modern times (Cooper and Burrell, 1988; Currie, 1998).
6 I am not advocating that consensus is the main aim of this dialogue, since consensus 'is a horizon that is never reached' Lyotard (1984: 61).

References

Anderson, G. (1998). 'Creating moral space in prenatal genetic services', *Qualitative Health Research*, 8 (2): 168–87.
Barry, D. and Elmes, M. (1997) 'Strategy retold: toward a narrative view of strategic discourse', *Academy of Management Review*, 22 (2): 429–52.
Bauman, Z. (1993) *Postmodern Ethics*. Oxford: Blackwell.
Bauman, Z. (1995) *Life in Fragments: Essays in Postmodern Morality*. Oxford: Blackwell.
Bergquist, W. (1993) *The Postmodern Organisation: Mastering the Art of Irreversible Change*. San Francisco, CA: Jossey-Bass.
Best, S. and Kellner, D. (1997) *The Postmodern Turn*. London and New York: The Guilford Press.
Boje, D.M. (1991a) 'The story telling organization: a study of story performance in an office-supply firm', *Administrative Science Quarterly*, 36: 106–26.
Boje, D.M. (1991b) 'Consulting and change in the storytelling organisation', *Journal of Organisational Change Management*, 4 (3): 7–17.
Boje, D.M. (1994) 'Organisational storytelling: the struggles of pre-modern, modern, and postmodern organisational learning discourses', *Management Learning*, 25 (3): 433–61.
Boje, D.M. (1995) 'Stories of the storytelling organisation: a postmodern analysis of Disney as "Tamara-land"', *Academy of Management Journal*, 38 (4): 997–1035.
Boje, D.M. (1999) 'Is Nike Roadrunner or Wile E. Coyote? A postmodern organisation analysis of double logic', *Journal of Business and Entrepreneurship*, Special Issue (March) 2: 77–109.
Boje, D.M., Luhman, J.T. and Baack, D.E. (1999) 'Hegemonic stories and encounters between storytelling organisations', *Journal of Management Inquiry*, 8 (4): 340–60.
Boyce, M. (1995) 'Collective centering and collective sense-making in the stories and storytelling of one organisation', *Organisation Studies*, 16 (1): 107–37.
Cooper, R. and Burrell, G. (1988) 'Modernism, postmodernism, and organisational analysis: an introduction', *Organisation Studies*, 9: 91–112.
Currie, M. (1998) *Postmodern Narrative Theory*. New York: St. Martin's Press.
Czarniawska, B. (1997) *Narrating the Organization: Dramas of Institutional Identity*. Chicago, IL: University of Chicago Press.
Frank, A. W. (1995) *The Wounded Storyteller: Body, Illness, and Ethics*. Chicago: University of Chicago Press.
Gephart, R.P., Jr (1991) 'Succession sensemaking and organisational change: a story of a deviant college president', *Journal of Organisational Change Management*, 4 (3): 35–44.
Hallstein, D. and O'Brien, L. (1998) 'A postmodern caring: feminist standpoint theories, revisioned caring, and communication ethics', *Western Journal of Communication*, 63 (1): 32–56.
Kauffman, S.A. (1993) *The Origins of Order: Self-organization and Selection in Evolution*. New York: Oxford University Press.
Kaye, M. (1996) *Myth-makers and story-tellers*. Sydney: Business & Professional Publishing Pty Ltd.
Lyotard, J.F. (1984) *The Postmodern Condition: A Report on Knowledge*. Minneapolis: University of Minnesota Press.
Newton, A.Z. (1995) *Narrative Ethics*. Cambridge: Harvard University Press.
Nicholas, B. and Gillett, G. (1997) 'Doctors' stories, patients' stories: a narrative approach to teaching medical ethics', *Journal of Medical Ethics*, 23 (5): 295–9.

Ritzer, G. (1993) *The McDonaldization of Society: An Investigation into the Changing Character of Contemporary Social Life*. Thousand Oaks, CA: Pine Forge Press.

Stacey, R.D. (1996) *Complexity and Creativity in Organisations*. San Francisco: Berrett-Koehler.

Tovey, P. (1998) 'Narrative and knowledge development in medical ethics', *Journal of Medical Ethics*, 24 (3): 176–81.

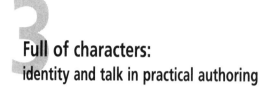

3 Full of characters:
identity and talk in practical authoring

David J. Holman, Jeff Gold and Richard Thorpe

Consider the following story.

Andrew is the recently appointed manager of a group of researchers in the R and D section of a chemical company. Until his promotion, Andrew had been a highly respected member of the research team. But now he is 'the manager', at least that is what the announcement on the R and D noticeboard states. On his first morning, he arrives at the laboratory and attempts to do some managing. He goes to the Monday meeting of the section, takes the chair and begins to follow the usual agenda. Over the weekend, he had prepared for the meeting as 'a manager' and his plan was to establish his position right from the start. However, it soon becomes apparent to Andrew that the rest of the team is somewhat resentful of his change of identity. Andrew feels that his team is refusing to respond in the appropriate manner, i.e., the manner expected by 'a manager'. Instead, the responses are those of one team member to another, and of a friend to a friend. Andrew is still seen by others as Andrew, 'the research team member', and it soon becomes clear that this is a pattern that the rest of the team wish to sustain. This begins to concern Andrew; it was not what he expected after having been identified as the right kind of person for management in an assessment centre last year, especially during the simulation exercise where his performance was classified as 'highly effective'. He also attended a management development programme, provided by a prestigious business school, which senior managers in the company feel is essential for those who are recommended for management positions. After a brief consultation with another manager, Andrew decides to assert himself. Needing some vital data, he approaches one of the team, Mary, and makes a request for the data. He is astonished when the request is denied. 'But as your manager, I *insist* you provide me with the data', Andrew asserted. He was even more astonished when Mary replied, 'As a manager, I do not wish to give you the data, but I will happily provide it for you *as Andrew*.' Astonishment soon gave way to confusion, however, when a week later Mary and another team member approached Andrew with the following: 'Some of us are becoming more anxious about the future of the section, we don't know what the company is trying to do and it's up *to you as our manager* to find out and tell us.'

This short vignette, distilled from a story told to us by Andrew, is, like much of our talk, full of characters. What is also evident is the importance of the identities of the story's characters to the telling and understanding of the story itself. These include, for example, Andrew as a manager, friend, ex-team member, and Mary as friend, team member and 'subordinate'. There are also other more peripheral characters who are identified primarily through a particular identity, e.g., senior managers, assessors, staff of a prestigious business school. Clearly, our need to know who we are, who others are and who others think we are, is essential to everyday life. Identity is at the centre of much of what we do and much of our talk is infused with the identities of oneself and others. Managers like Andrew have to devote much time to working on their identity and identity 'needs' play an important part in organisational processes (see also Stan Deetz, chapter 7). Indeed, as Watson points out, 'managers are portrayed [in the management literature] as essentially being concerned with *shaping* the organisation in which they are employed, and I am suggesting that we can only understand how they do this if we relate the way they carry out their management work to the ways that they shape themselves as individual human beings' (1994: 59).[1] This chapter then is concerned with identity. In particular, this chapter focuses on the 'character' of identity and the relational nature of identity. The chapter concludes by examining the implications of a relational approach to identity for the manager as practical author.

The narrative character of identity

Implicit within the idea of identity are the notions of similarity and difference (Jenkins, 1996). In other words, one way of understanding identity is to define it as the characteristics (e.g., physical properties, social practices, relationships, possessions) that a person shares with others and the characteristics that make them different from others. It is, perhaps, because of this that much of the literature on identity treats it as a category consisting of a particular set of characteristics (Turner et al., 1987). Consider the following extract drawn from an interview with Nick, a manager of a small company who had agreed to participate in a management development programme involving a series of meetings with a consultant.

> I did agree to an exploratory meeting with the consultant assigned to the project. Thus I was able to assess the appropriateness of the project to my situation before deciding whether to become a 'guinea pig'. Paul [the consultant]

on first impression appeared to be one of the 'old school', something of a salesman, marketing orientated but able to listen and willing to be flexible and to provide some practical hands on assistance. Generally I liked Paul's style, appearing to be more of the facilitative than prescriptive consultant.

In this extract we see that, although Nick has already labelled Paul as a consultant, he is trying to categorise (Edwards 1991) exactly what type of consultant Paul might be. The extract also shows that Nick is having some difficulty in categorising Paul, as Paul appears to be an 'old school' consultant, i.e., prescriptive, 'something of a salesman', but also a 'facilitative' consultant, i.e., able to listen, be flexible, etc. Nick even categorises himself, rather ironically, as a 'guinea pig', both as an expression of his uncertainty but also so that he can retain a view of himself as a manager with entrepreneurial freedom if the work with Paul does not succeed. Such a process of categorisation, although initially difficult, clearly helped Nick to understand Paul and to manage his relationship with Paul.

However, while it is possible to conceptualise identities as categories and to use such categories pragmatically, many writers have emphasised the important role that narrative plays in the experience and construction of identity (Czarniawska, 1997; Widdershoven, 1993). In the examples of Nick and Andrew, the stories they tell play a significant role in shaping a sense of their own identity (in Andrew's case) and that of another's identity (in Nick's case). Narratives, which include myths, legends, comic strips, pictures as well as stories, not only help to illuminate the important characteristics of a person and what 'category' of identity they might have, they also provide the context in which characteristics and categories become meaningful.[2] Furthermore, as narratives and stories are concerned with the temporal sequence of events and characters, they help to engineer 'a sense of connectedness and temporal unity to a person's life' (Ezzy, 1998: 245). For example, in Andrew's story, Mary's reaction to him appears to threaten the temporal coherence of his identity. Mary's reaction provokes a strong sense of discontinuity between Andrew's identity as a manager and his identity as a friend, as well as between his public persona and his personal self (Davies and Harré, 1990).[3] By telling this story, Andrew seems to be asserting that, even though he has a new identity, he is still the same Andrew 'underneath', that he is still the same kind of person as before. The story is used as a way of making sense of the dilemmas he faces and as an attempt to maintain some sense of temporal continuity and coherence in the way that he perceives himself. It is also worth noting that the use of narrative enables Andrew to articulate the historical context of his difficulties and to establish a connection with his past – something unavailable to him if he were to simply understand identity as a category. Narrative thus provides the organising and driving force in the experience and construction of identity. Indeed, identity without narrative would be superficial and lack meaning. It is because of the importance of narrative to identity that some writers talk about a 'narrative identity' rather than simply 'identity' (Ricouer, 1990).

The relational nature of identity

When we use a category to identify ourselves, when we tell a story about others' identities or when we make a claim about who we are, we are not just trying to convey an image of identity. Rather, such 'identity talk' has an important function in managing our relationships with others, namely, to impress on others how they should relate to the speaker as a person with this particular identity. Identity talk also functions to impress on the speaker how they should relate to others. Identity is thus fundamentally concerned with how we relate to each other. Drawing on John Shotter and Ann Cunliffe's opening chapter, we can understand identity as a way-of-being-in-relation-to others. Andrew's story is therefore not so much concerned with painting a picture of the nature of his managerial identity, nor is it just about getting others to simply recognise his managerial identity. Andrew's story concerns his efforts to establish a new way of relating to others (in particular to his ex-team members) and about getting them to relate differently to him. For Andrew, his newly assumed identity 'calls out' to him that he should engage in a different way-of-being-in-relation-to his ex-team members.

That Andrew has to engage with others to try and establish his identity as a manager highlights how identity is relational in another sense, namely, that identity is formed in the relationships between people. Being formed between people, identity is a social and practical accomplishment. In this ongoing social process, important tasks are to manage our way-of-being-in-relation-to others and to present one's identity to others. There is a significant body of work that has described the practices which people use to establish, maintain and alter their identities in social situations (Antaki and Widdicombe, 1998; Goffman, 1959). A central theme in this work has been to examine how individuals use interactional and linguistic resources to negotiate their identities with others. Goffman (1959), for example, focused on how individuals use their interactional competences to present a public image to others. The interactional competences by which this is achieved include dramatic style, expressive control, misrepresentation and mystification. Others have examined the linguistic resources that people employ and draw on to present their identity to themselves and others (Antaki and Widdicombe, 1998). Such work has focused on the stories, discursive repertoires, claims and categories that people use when trying to present their identity to others. In the first example above, Andrew uses what might be considered to be a 'managerialist discourse' as a way of presenting and justifying his actions and as a way of constructing and establishing an identity to himself and to others. While such 'identity work' may seem purposefully Machiavellian or manipulative, i.e., consciously presenting a false image of one's self, this is generally not the case. Rather, people habitually and routinely engage in identity work to present themselves as credible, to position themselves vis-à-vis others, to maintain their own identity of themselves and to add authority to their own actions and beliefs.

Interactional and linguistic resources are also organised locally and for specific purposes in particular contexts. If Andrew had related his story to friends in a pub or in a job interview, would he have told it in the same way, would he have drawn on the same linguistic resources? Would he have presented himself, his 'same' identity, in the same way? The answer is probably not and such actions are far from unusual. We have probably all been aware of the times when, retelling a story, we have changed it slightly by offering different justifications and dramatising some parts and not others. Likewise, when we present our identity to different groups we will use different interactional and linguistic resources. Again, this may be achieved by dramatising certain aspects of ourselves, bringing different aspects to the fore, etc. This shows that an identity is fluid and dynamic and that we are rarely restricted to just one story, to one reading of the plot. In this way, identities continue to unfold over time and are always open to further expression. As Polkinghorne points out, 'we are in the middle of our stories and cannot be sure how they will end; we are constantly having to revise the plot as new events are added to our lives' (1988: 150). Furthermore, we are rarely restricted to a single identity in any one context and, as Andrew's story demonstrates, we are clearly able to present a range of identities in our dealings with others.

The vast array of interactional and linguistic resources available would seem to offer the possibility of constructing an almost limitless range of identities. But while we may seek to construct and present a particular identity, this identity has to be accepted and validated by others. Most of the time, people support and collude in the identity work of others and much identity work is relatively painless and unproblematic. However, as we saw in the relationship between Andrew and Mary, this support cannot be relied on. Andrew believes, somewhat naively perhaps, that his identity as manager has been established because he has been assessed as the 'right person for the job' in the assessment centre and because he has been on a management development programme. Yet it is evident from the reactions of his former team members, and Mary in particular, that are they are not relating to him in the way that he thinks they should, i.e., as a 'manager'. Gergen states that, 'if others do not recognisably treat one's utterance as meaningful, if they fail to co-ordinate themselves around such offerings, one is reduced to nonsense' (1995: 37). Mary's acts of resistance do not coordinate themselves to Andrew's actions in the way that he wants. And, while Mary's actions do not reduce Andrew's identity to nonsense, they have clearly affected Andrew's sense of identity. This is probably the reason why Andrew engages in further, more explicit, identity work ('But as your manager, I insist you provide me with the data.').

The interaction between Andrew and his ex-team members illustrates wonderfully how identity emerges from the interaction between an individual's 'self-identity work' and the collusion, support and resistance of others.

Others may also seek to influence our identity by categorising, classifying and relating to us differently and in ways that may not accord with our own sense of identity (Becker, 1963). The work of a person on another's identity can be termed 'other-identity work' as its prime focus is to affect the identity of others rather than one's own. Our reaction to this other-identity work might be to agree, to collude, to take on a new identity or even to resist it, but it is unlikely that our identity will remain totally unaffected by the identity work of others. As identity emerges from our interaction with others, and we can never fully control these interactions, our identity is never fully under our control. Such a view challenges the idea that we are omniscient authors of our own lives, suggesting instead that we have multi-authored selves (Hermans and Kempen, 1993).

The reasons for Mary's resistance to Andrew's efforts to establish a managerial identity may be many. But, given her willingness to do things for 'Andrew', it seems reasonable to suggest that she is unwilling to be seen as Andrew's subordinate. It indicates that she still sees herself as equal to Andrew and not below him in any real or imagined hierarchy. Andrew seems unaware of the fact that in order to position himself as 'manager', he needs to position his ex-team mates and friends as 'subordinates'. Expressing an identity, a way-of-being-in-relation-to, can therefore implicitly or explicitly position another person and 'label' them with a particular identity (Davies and Harré, 1990). It can further be argued that there is a mutual inter-dependence between the two identities of manager and subordinate, i.e., that in order for Andrew to be a manager, he needs to invoke something or someone to be managed. A different way of saying this would be 'I need you in order to be me' (Shotter and Cunliffe, chapter 1). Other examples of how certain identities are mutually interdependent and imply different social positions include wife/husband, pop star/pop fan, dominatrix/slave, doctor/patient.

An important implication of a relational view is that it brings to the fore the moral character of identity and identity work, i.e., how we ought to relate to each other as persons of a particular identity. It does this in several ways. First, identity as a-way-of-being-in-relation-to exerts a range of moral obligations on the person about how to relate to others in a way that is more or less consistent with that identity. Furthermore, a person's identity will exert moral demands on others by impressing on them how to treat a person with this identity in a manner that such a person has a right to expect. Andrew thus acts in a manner that accords with his understanding of a managerial identity and expects others to act towards him according to this identity; although in this instance his ex-team mates resist the moral demands being exerted! Secondly, the assertion of an identity can position others as having a particular identity, and this may have positive or negative con-sequences for the recipient. Finally, identity work is intrinsically moral as the linguistic and interactional resources drawn on will simultaneously index a moral order of rights and obligations (Edwards 1991).

In our work conducting and researching personal development programmes for managers (see Gold et al., 2002; Gold et al., forthcoming), we try to provide a space for managers to consider their own authorship. In this work we are often struck by how much of the ways in which managers talk and write about their experiences are concerned with how they ought to act and how they ought to be treated. The relationship of this talk to identity is often made clear by the use of phrases such as 'as a manager I' or 'a manager should'. Take the following example concerning the work of Mike, a change agent working on a project concerned with encouraging interorganisation learning among a number of UK companies. The project involved a team of advisers working in close contact with the target companies. This team was managed by Dominic. Mike required the support of both Dominic and the advisers to make progress and he viewed his relationship with Dominic as problematic. Dominic also had difficulties with his team and Mike summarised the situation in the following manner:

> There is a feeling that support from his team for Project Y is mixed and at best qualified. There also seem to be hidden agendas working within the team, jockeying for position. I sometimes sense, although I have no evidence at all, that they are waiting for him to fail. Dominic's behaviour on the one hand would suggest that he has also picked up a sense of less than full support from his team. The body language from his staff when he is around is detached and disinterested, which in a way mirrors his own behaviour with the project.

Further discussion led Mike to foreground two aspects of this story. The first concerns Dominic's perceived failure to honour his commitments and his apparent lack of commitment to the project. As a result, Mike thought that Dominic failed to relate to him and his team with integrity and loyalty. The second relates to the observation that 'the team are waiting for him [Dominic] to fail'. Mike identified the team as not showing loyalty. What Mike appears to be doing in this story, and in the further discussions based on it, is setting out the moral obligations of the story's different actors, i.e., that being a manager involves exhibiting integrity, loyalty, etc. and that a team member is obliged to be loyal to the manager. His story also suggests that the team is disloyal because Dominic's actions have not impressed on the team members that he is a person who should be treated in the manner that a person with a 'proper' managerial identity should be treated.

Why then did Mike dramatise the story in this way, foreground these particular aspects and evaluate the story's actors according to the criteria of integrity, loyalty and commitment? Mike identified two possible reasons. The first was his own experience 'as a manager' of 300 workers in the mining industry where he 'supported his boss, had loyal staff and was loyal to them'. He emphasised the importance of group solidarity and support especially 'if things go wrong'. The second reason was his upbringing and the influence of his church-going mother. In this case, he identified the language of Christianity. From this we can also see that the dramatisation and moral evaluation of the story's actors (Dominic and the team members) is intimately bound up with Mike's own managerial identity, and in particular the moral character of a manager's way-of-being-in-relation-to others and how others should relate to a manager. Based on this new understanding Mike was able to make better sense of his difficult relationship to Dominic and plan out a way of addressing the difficulties faced. Mike was also able, for the first time, to appreciate some of the experiences and linguistic resources that helped to shape his own managerial identity. This example also illustrates the movement from vague feelings to more concrete linguistic expressions. It can be seen that in his initial orientation he could 'sense' that there was a problem and that he had no evidence for his statements apart from his 'feelings' and his observations of the body language of the team members and Dominic. It is through his conversations with himself and others and the use of narrative that he develops a more intelligible formulation (to himself, if not others) of the problem faced and his own identity.

Identity and the practical author

In the discussion above we have identified the following salient points about a relational approach to identity:

1   Identity is a-way-of-being-in-relation-to others.
2   Identity is an ongoing social and practical accomplishment that is formed, managed and altered through interaction with others. This implies that identity is not 'just there', is not given, is not pre-determined and that it is always open to reinterpretation and misinterpretation. An identity is not something that can simply be purchased and put on like a new hat!
3   Many different linguistic and interactional resources are used in identity formation and identity work. Identity can be thus constructed, expressed and dramatised in a variety of ways. This makes identity a multi-voiced, multi-faceted, fluid and dynamic phenomenon.
4   Identity work involves self-identity work and other-identity work.
5   Others collude with, support and resist our attempts at identity work.
6   Identity work will position others and there can be a mutual interdependence between certain identities.
7   Identity has a narrative character and the main way that we understand our identities is through narrative.
8   Identity has a moral character. Identity exerts moral obligations on the person about how to relate to others and exerts moral demands on others by impressing on them how to treat a person with this identity in a manner that such a person has a right to expect.

Understanding identity in this way can help the practical author to appreciate better their own and others' identities. Indeed, we have seen some of the problems that Andrew encountered by not seeing his identity as relational. For example, Andrew's eagerness to assert his managerial identity seemed to prevent him from recognising that an identity cannot be put on like a new hat, that his new identity would reposition others, and that his new identity exerted new moral demands on others. However, while the discussion above may sensitise us to certain aspects of identity, some of the ideas may initially appear to be too abstract to be immediately useful in everyday interaction and perhaps a little too distant from our sense of lived reality to be immediately relevant. What might be needed then are tools and methods that help bring a sense of lived reality to the understanding we have of our own and others' identities and which may help us to prepare to relate to others differently. Moreover, such methods should not only allow us to represent our own and others' identities, they should also allow us to orientate ourselves to others differently and to alter our day-to-day identity work.

In the opening chapter John Shotter and Ann Cunliffe outlined a number of methods, which they call social poetics, that might help achieve these aims. These methods are useful as they can provide us with the means to express 'the fleeting, flickering presence of new possibilities . . . in such a way that others can not only glimpse them too, but dwell on them long enough to make them items of public discussion' (Shotter and Cunliffe, chapter 1). Indeed, such methods may be particularly suited to identity as, although identity may have a continuing presence and effect throughout our everyday lives, its presence is only felt fleetingly and often only vaguely. Methods such as narrative, metaphor, contrast and analogy may thus provide the means with which a person can foreground and dramatise that which is felt vaguely and known only fleetingly.

Take the following example, in which we see Mike addressing a problem on the interorganisational project he was managing. It can be remembered that Mike was addressing this problem as part of a personal development programme. This programme involved managers writing a series of stories about problems they encountered at work (Roth, 1996). The managers were then asked to collate these stories and to look for significant and recurring elements in the plots of these stories. Managers were asked also to identify the claims they were making in the main plots of their stories and to then provide justifications for these claims (see Gold et al., 2002, for a fuller account of the programme). This process was aimed at helping managers identify the arguments contained in their stories (Toulmin, 1958).[4] Throughout this process managers were encouraged to reflect on the issues raised with other managers and the module organisers.

The issue that Mike identified was his relationship with Barbara, a key player in the interorganisational learning project. From Mike's stories about his interactions with Barbara, he was able to identify two seemingly contradictory ways that Barbara talked about the project. On the one hand she exhorted others to 'learn from each other' in a learning network and to use 'each other as mentors'. Such utterances evoked key themes in the project. On the other hand, she would also state that she should be selective about who she networked with and inferred that this was because she had a duty to protect her business interests. This view clearly challenged the ethos of the project as established by its steering group, of which she was a member. The contradictory talk was causing confusion and annoyance among the advisers, causing Barbara to be labelled as 'arrogant'.

From the stories he told, Mike was able examine the two contradictory claims that Barbara made about how to act. When he sought to understand how such claims might be justified, he identified a number of possible identities at work in her talk,[5] including:

(a) network participant
(b) steering group member
(c) project champion
(d) president of the Trade Association
(e) managing director

Each one of these identities implied a different way-of-relating-to others on the project. In particular, Barbara's talk indicated that her way-of-relating-to others as president of the Trade Association and steering group member should be open, cooperative and inclusive. As a managing director, her talk indicated that her way-of-relating-to others should be selective and exclusive. Barbara seemed unaware of the contradictory nature of her talk and how this was rooted in the multiple-identities she had. Mike made plans to talk to Barbara about these issues and intended to deal with the dilemmas caused by her multiple identities. The following text reveals what happened:

> As the meeting opened . . . the two identities of MD [managing director] and president, that I prepared for, were in evidence and I suggested that, of course she would have problems. The effect was immediate and startling. Here was someone who understood her dilemma, not only understood her dilemma but could articulate it for her. We talked about her priorities for her as president and as MD. We then talked through not which one she could do but how we could have both.

At the conclusion of the meeting, Mike was able to suggest that they 'could move the project positively' and that this had been achieved by 'addressing her identities'.

In this example we can see that Mike is able to dramatise what is vague and unsaid in Barbara's way-of-relating-to others. This dramatisation, and Mike's juxtaposing of Barbara's different identities, clearly moves Barbara ('the effect was immediate and startling'). Mike's understanding of the situation, that emerged primarily through the telling and analysis of stories, provided him with the means with which to articulate an intelligible and justifiable account of the situation facing him, Barbara and the other project members. More importantly, Mike's account 'enables those involved to make and to notice differences in their activities, thus affording them with opportunities to coordinate their activities' (Shotter and Katz, 1996: 222). This opens up, for the time being at least, new possibilities about how they can relate to each other. Mike can be seen to have authored an opening and rearranged the relational landscape through ordinary language use. This is a key point for practical authoring. For, while abstract theories may help us to understand or sensitise us to phenomena such as identity, their use in transforming everyday relations may be limited. It is in our everyday speech that we can find the methods for re-authoring our way-of-being-in-relation-to others (Wittgenstein, 1953). Shotter and Cunliffe have documented some of these (poetic) methods in the opening chapter (e.g., reminding, comparing, metaphors, analogies), so we will not repeat them here. However, we would also like to add that with regard to identity, narratives and storytelling would appear to be one other important method that can enable people to re-author their relational landscape with others. This is so because people use narratives and stories 'naturally' when talking about and making sense of identity.

Conclusion

This chapter has set out an approach to identity that is compatible with the idea of practical authorship and which could be labelled a relational approach to identity. It has set out how managers might become more aware, or more sensitive, to their own identities, to the linguistic and interactional resources used in constructing identities, to how their own identity work affects the identities of others and to the moral aspects of identity and identity work. The discussion above has also highlighted how identity is a dynamic phenomenon that is continually present, even if its presence is not always continually felt. We have also argued that, in managers' day-to-day activities, such theoretical accounts of identity may be of partial assistance and that managers may need to make greater use of what they possess already. We have suggested that managers can use methods such as social poetics and narrative in their identity work. These methods are useful because, as 'instructive methods' (i.e., do this, see that), they are the same methods that we use 'in gaining a practical kind of understanding in the first place' (Shotter and Katz, 1996: 227). This means that, in principle, they should be accessible to and useable by everyone. Social poetics, narrative and especially storytelling thus offer the possibility of dramatising what is vague and unsaid, of making the vague presence of identity more keenly felt, of providing intelligible and justifiable accounts of identity and, most importantly, instructing ourselves and others in new ways-of-being-in-relation-to.

Notes

1 Despite this, the important role of identity in action has often been overlooked in the literature on management.

2 For Gergen (1994), while stopping short of an ontological view of narratives, i.e., our lives are not actually stories, the key point is that narratives provide a conversational resource to make sense of our lives.

3 Such conflicts do not appear to be uncommon in 'novice' managers as they struggle to establish their identity (see also Watson, 1994). Attempts to establish a managerial identity are further complicated by the fact that management is in itself ambiguous and thus the boundary between manager and non-manager is never clear.

4 Toulmin (1958) has provided an approach to the examination of arguments as they take place in everyday life. Toulmin argued there were four basic parts to an argument. First, a view or a standpoint is stated; this is referred to as a *claim*. The importance of a claim is that it can be understood as an expression of someone's belief which others may contest. Therefore, a claim may require facts or evidence to support it; this is referred to as *data*. For example, in Andrew's story he is making the claim that he is a manager and that his data to support this claim is that he has the title manager and has been on courses which entitle him to be a manager. This can be expressed as:

> Claim: I am a manager.
> Data: I have a title of 'manager' and the courses I have completed entitle me to be a manager.

A third step, if the data is accepted as support for the claim, is to provide some means of connecting the data to the claim; this is referred to as a *warrant*. The warrant acts as a justification for linking the data to the claim made and, as suggested by Toulmin (1958) is 'implicit in the particular steps from data to claim', providing a kind of bridge (Van Eemeren et al., 1996) that explains why the particular data given is relevant to the claim made. For example, the following warrant might be implicit in Andrew's argument:

> Warrant: Managers are people who have the title 'manager' and who have been on management courses.

The warrant may also require some authority or *backing*. Why should the title 'manager' automatically imply that a person is a manager? Is this always the case? The backing in this case might come from tradition (because this is the way it has always been), from theory (X's theory of management education tells me this is the case), or from experience (all the managers I know have the title manager and have management qualifications).

5 On the module many of justifications for claims were concerned with the identity of the claim maker. This suggests that, as people often make a number of claims in a story, analysing arguments is one way of articulating and surfacing the many different identities present in talk. Ehninger and Brockeriede (1963) also point out that justifications, and in particular warrants, can provide other types of information. They point out that warrants tell us about: the way things relate to one another, i.e., a substantive argument; a person's desires, values and motives, i.e., a motivational argument; and, the reliability of the source of data and the authority of the speaker, i.e., an authoritative argument.

References

Antaki, C. and Widdicombe, S. (eds) (1998) *Identities in Talk*. London: Sage.

Becker, H.S. (1963) *Outsiders: Studies in the Sociology of Deviance*. New York: Free Press.

Czarniawska, B. (1997) *Narrating the Organization: Dramas of Institutional Identity*. Chicago, IL: University of Chicago Press.

Davies, B. and Harré, R. (1990) 'Positioning: the discursive production of selves', *Journal for the Theory of Social Behaviour*, 20 (1): 43–63.

Edwards, D. (1991) 'Categories are for talking', *Theory and Psychology*, 1: 515–42.

Eemeren, F.H. Van, Grootendorst, R., Henkemans, F.S. with Blair, J.A., Johnson, R.H., Krabbe, E.C.W., Plantin, C., Walton, D.N., Willard, C.A., Woods, J. and Zarefsky, D. (1996) *Fundamentals of Argumentation Theory: A Handbook of Historical Backgrounds and Contemporary Developments*. Mahway, NJ: Lawrence Erlbaum.

Ehninger, D. and Brockeriede, W. (1963) *Decision by Debate*. New York: Dodd, Mead.

Ezzy, D. (1998) 'Theorizing narrative identity: symbolic interactionism and hermeneutics', *Sociological Quarterly*, 39 (2): 239–52.

Gergen, K.J. (1994) *Relationships and Realities*. Boston, MA: Harvard University Press.

Gergen, K.J. (1995) 'Relational theory and discourses of power', in D.M. Hosking, H.P. Dachler and K.J. Gergen, *Management and Organisation: Relational Alternatives to Individualism*. Aldershot: Avebury.

Goffman, E. (1959) *The Presentation of Self in Everyday Life*. Garden City, NJ: Doubleday.

Gold, J., Holman, D. and Thorpe, R. (2002) 'The role of argument analysis and story telling in facilitating crtical thinking', *Management Learning*, *33*: 371–88.

Gold, J., Watson, S and Rix, M. (forthcoming) 'Learning for change by telling stories', in J. Stewart and J. McGoldrick (eds), *Researching HRD: Philosophy, Processes and Practices*. London: Routledge.

Hermans, H.J.M. and Kempen, H.J.G. (1993) *The Dialogical Self*. San Diego: Academic Press.

Jenkins, R. (1996) *Social Identity*. London, Routledge.

Polkinghorne, D.E. (1988) *Narrative Knowing and the Human Sciences*. New York: University of New York Press.

Ricoeur, P. (1990) *Time and Narrative*, translated by M. McLoughlin and D. Pallaver. Chicago: University of Chicago Press.

Roth, G.L. (1996) 'Learning histories: using documentation to assess and facilitate organisational learning', < *http://www.sol-ne.org/pra/* >, accessed 1/10/97.

Shotter, J. and Katz, A.M. (1996) 'Articulating a practice from within the practice itself: establishing formative dialogues by the use of a "social poetics"', *Concepts and Transformations*, 1 (2/3): 213–37.

Toulmin, S. (1958) *The Uses of Argument*. Cambridge: Cambridge University Press.

Turner, J.C., Hogg, M.A., Oakes, P.J., Reicher, S.D. and Wetherell, M.S. (1987) *Rediscovering the Social Group: A Self-Categorization Theory*. Oxford: Blackwell.

Watson, T. (1994) *In Search of Management: Culture, Chaos and Control in Managerial Work*. London: Routledge.

Widdershoven, G.A.M. (1993) 'The story of life', in R. Josselson and A. Lieblich (eds), *The Narrative Study of Lives, Vol. 1*. Newbury Park, CA: Sage.

Wittgenstein, L. (1953) *Philosophical Investigations*. Oxford: Blackwell.

Visual media and the construction of meaning

Richard Thorpe and Joep Cornelisson

From a social constructionist perspective, language is, in the first instance, a medium of *social action* rather than simply a code for representing thoughts and ideas (Shotter, 1995). For the study and practice of management, one of the particular attractions of this view is derived from the understanding that managers need to act pragmatically when faced with complex and ambiguous situations characterised by confusion, contradiction and a potential disagreement on exactly how a situation should be defined, approached and solved (Schön, 1983; Weick, 1995). Managers clearly would gain little from simply trying to represent such situations. Rather, managers must use language to advocate and legitimate particular world views and associated courses of action (Shotter, 1995). An additional point is that certain complex and ambiguous situations may not be amenable to the kind of 'rigorous' techniques associated with scientific and technical approaches. Instead, and as advocated throughout this book, other tools and approaches that explicitly focus on the use of dialogue and language may be of more use.

However, while dialogical and linguistically based tools may offer benefit, it is also worth considering how many times we resort to visual tools (e.g., pictures, photographs, maps, diagrams) and metaphors when we are trying to understand, discuss or describe a problem. Indeed, problem setting and problem solving quite often involve the interpolation between linguistic and visual tools.

Visual tools are useful in the problem setting process as the deployment, interpretation and understanding of an image is a creative endeavour. Thus, alternative images may be deployed as a means of representing or summating a situation, while the interpretation of an image not only involves deciphering an encoded content, but will also involve generating and discussing what the image means and what it invokes. The ensuing discussion can enable managers, particularly in group situations, to argue for different positions, to explain their views, to redefine issues in ways relevant to their interests, to clarify situations and resolve ambiguity, and, to help consider multiple frames of reference. What is more, this can be done without recourse to large amounts of data.

Images, and the visual media through which they are produced, can therefore play a pivotal role in managerial sense-making activities (see Weick, 1995), not only because of their vividness, depth, clarity (enhancing the interpretability which in turn strengthens a manager's grasp of key concepts) but also because of their inherent ambiguity and the way they are able to convey different meanings for different people (Astley and Zammuto, 1992). In such a sense, visual media and the meanings they evoke can enable managers to facilitate practical action and be used to develop a position around which a course of action can be argued for and implemented, i.e., authorship. Visual tools can be an integral mediating devise with which to shape organisational life.

Our focus in the rest of this chapter is partly theoretical and partly applied. It begins by offering a framework that suggests when particular types of visual tool may be most useful. It then goes on to illustrate, with empirical descriptions, the use of a number of visual tools and illuminate their relationship to practical authorship.

A framework for the understanding of organisational problems, information requirements and communication media

Although there has been little if any direct work on the potential value of pictographic tools and visual media in mediating managers' construction of meaning in ambiguous situations, Daft and Lengel's (1986) work provides a starting point. Daft and Lengel suggested that organisational situations can be characterised by uncertainty, caused by the absence of information, and/or ambiguity, caused by equivocality. Uncertainty is seen to lead to the acquisition of information about the world to answer specific questions. Equivocality leads to the exchange of existing views among managers to define problems and resolve conflicts through the enactment of a shared interpretation that can direct future activities. Chiming with Shotter's (1995) emphasis on the social context in which managers construct their world views, use language and act, Daft and Lengel further argued that uncertainty and ambiguity are caused by the relational characteristics of individuals or groups in the form of the relational differentiation (the extent to which an individual or group has developed its own functional specialisation, skills, time horizon, goals, frame of reference and jargon) and the interdependence between them (Lawrence and Lorsch, 1967). An implication of this is that various media, differing in their richness, are more or less suitable to

High	**1.** High Difference, Low Interdependence *Structure:* a) Rich media to resolve differences b) Small amount of information *Examples:* occasional face-to-face or telephone meetings, personal memos, planning, self-contained units, *photographs, projective tests, visual metaphors*	**2.** High Difference, High Interdependence *Structure:* a) Rich media to solve differences b) Large amount of information to handle interdependence *Examples:* full time integrators, task forces, matrix structure, special studies and projects, confrontation, *repertory grids, cognitive mapping*
Low	**3.** Low Difference, Low Interdependence *Structure:* a) Media of lower richness b) Small amount of information *Examples:* rules, standard operating procedures, reports, budgets	**4.** Low Difference, High Interdependence *Structure:* a) Media of lower richness b) Large amount of information to handle interdependence *Examples:* plans, reports, update databases, formal information systems, budgets, *process charts, diagrams, photographs*

Difference between individuals or departments (vertical axis, High to Low)

Low   High

Interdependence between individuals or departments

Source: Adapted from Daft and Lengel, 1986: 565.

FIGURE 4.1

The relationship between media use and the degree of difference and interdependence between individuals or departments

reducing the uncertainties and/or ambiguities surrounding management situations. Figure 4.1 shows this diagrammatically. A high degree of differentiation is seen as causing ambiguity to be resolved by arriving at a common definition of the situation, that is by having 'rich media' such as face-to-face meetings and visual tools that offer the possibility for discussion of multiple frames of reference and to process complex, subjective messages. A high degree of resource dependence between individuals or groups causes uncertainty as the action of an individual or group requires another to adapt, in turn requiring the distribution and sharing of a large amount of information through media of a lower 'richness' such as plans and reports.

This framework gives some indication as to the issues involved and how organisations might handle the dual information needs for uncertainty and a reduction in equivocality, for both obtaining data and for exchanging views. The concern of this chapter lies mainly within the upper quadrants of the framework, the media that enable ambiguity reduction, and with quadrant four, where a number of management writers have experimented with media of low richness and high pictorial value. The chapter develops Daft and Lengel's (1986) work in that it suggests that management tools that employ visual media (e.g., cognitive mapping, visual metaphors, photographs and repertory grids) gain additional value when used in conjunction with a range of learning devices and situations where the purpose is to reduce ambiguity, such as group meetings, action learning sets and so on. The following sections describe a number of visual tools. This is followed by a discussion of the ways in which they relate to social constructionist perspectives of management, including practical authorship.

Charts and diagrams

Charts and diagrams are examples of media that are generally low in richness and can be used where there is likely to be low difference and high interdependence, a large amount of information to handle and a common view of how the organisation should conduct its operations. Over the years, maps or charts of processes or critical paths of activities have been the preserve of industrial engineering, methods investigators, systems analysis or management service practitioners. Those using them have almost exclusively seen them as providing the *facts* of a particular situation not as a means of engendering multiple perspectives and debate. Their stock in trade has been various: charting techniques typically showing the flow of materials or people through a process or the layout of facilities; multiple activity charts which relate activities to a common time scale; or relationship charts that show the connectedness or interdependence of functions or activities. In the days of hand assembly of components, charts were also used to show how intricate assemblies operated, for example, two-handed charts or simultaneous motion charts.

Photographs, visual metaphors and projective techniques

The use of photographs, visual metaphors and projective techniques are useful in situations where there is often a small amount of data to start with, where the generation of rich ideas is proving difficult and where a means is needed to engage individuals in a discussion of issues that are viewed as contentious or problematic.

Photographs   Buchanan (1999), assessing the role that photography has played in organisational research, found that while photography has enjoyed a rich tradition in disciplines such as sociology and anthropology (Banks, 1995; Collier and Collier, 1986: Harper, 1994), it has been used far less outside management services traditions mentioned earlier. He planned his research therefore to use still photographs as part of a hospital process re-engineering project, both to enhance his collection of data and to assess the usefulness of using photographs. He argued that if something of relevance can be seen, it can be discussed and possibly altered. Buchanan's purpose was to collect detailed records of social reality that would give him a holistic representation of processes within the hospital. His method was to collect 35mm slide photographs in order to record complex scenes and processes that could provide 'non reactive' records and observations. He found that the photographs greatly helped the study. The use of photographs clearly triggered informants to talk much more about the ideas they had around the images and this helped to develop a more complex understanding of the chains of activity that occurred. Photographs of the process also contributed to a more accurate sequencing of the process as well as to a more detailed written analysis of the process. Once accomplished, the sequence was shown to a number of groups within the hospital and again additional complex details were added in the discussions and debates that they engendered. Drawing on the notion of social poetics, it can be suggested that the pictures offered the opportunity for a situation to be 'held captive' (Wittgenstein, 1953) such that it allows the possibility for new connections and relationships to emerge that would otherwise remain hidden from view, and that, once recognised, the new connections can help set a course for managerial action.

Other ways of visually using photographs include cyclographs and chrono-cyclography. Cyclographs are used to determine the paths of movements. In industry they can be used to determine hand movements on a particularly rapid task as they show the paths of movement. Using images in this way enables great complexity to be represented but once this has been achieved, their analysis has often been accompanied by a strong belief that all members of the organisation would share common interests and objectivities – usually, a desire for greater efficiency and improved performance.

Visual metaphors   One approach used to illicit the views of individuals or groups is to work with the notion of metaphors and to ask individuals to draw issues of concern or events as they currently see them or how they might like to see them in the future. Pictures or drawings are the media that is often used. This use of pictures, this time created by the individuals or groups themselves, can be a powerful way developing understanding and for groups to move forward with a vision for the future.

In research conducted in a large multi-national, one of Richard's research colleagues (Simpson, 1997) used this approach to explore how the senior staff viewed their organisation. The research was conducted using a series of focus group interviews. At each session, the group members were asked the following questions:

1   If the organisation was a parent, how do you think it would relate to its children?
2   If you were asked to write an honest character reference for the organisation, what would it say? Some guidance here included, how well it

FIGURE 4.2
Metaphor of management

performed in its most recent job, its achievements, anything else that individuals thought was important.

3 Try to imagine the company as an old friend whom you have not seen over the last ten years. How would you judge if their personality had changed?

4 Finally, individuals were asked to draw a picture of the company as the 'person' is today.

The questions produced very rich data indeed, which was taped and analysed, but perhaps the most interesting aspects of this metaphor approach were the drawings individuals produced and their interpretation. An example of one is shown in Figure 4.2.

The way the group discussed the drawings was as follows:

F. He's a man again is he?

P. Yes . . .

D. Yes I think he is a man.

A. It's impossible to get away from that I think.

F. Tell us about your picture, what does your picture show for us?

A. Shall I defend this? Since I drew it I got the shorter straw! Well, I was thinking of the bumbling uncle type person, perhaps not the sharpest person in the world, but at least you might get your pocket money off him. Next time you met him he'd got 30 years young, he'd got a flat top, a nice suit and a BMW. What I was trying to show [indicating hand on the drawing] I'm not much of an artist as you can see, was basically just no! It looks like on yer bike, which is just as appropriate.

S. What's that in his other hand?

A It's a mobile phone, it's trying to show he's a yuppie, flat top hair, double-breasted suit, trendy glasses, small chin.

S. It's interesting about the hand thing, because we thought there'd be a lot of gesticulation rather than the sort of verbal interaction it's sort of hi and over there . . .

C. We were going to put him with a bag of money in one hand . . .

S. But the portable phone gets that across.

F. So he's gone from being a friendly uncle to a yuppie . . .

A. Yes . . .

F. . . . And younger instead of older?

A. . . . Yes. Yes.

F. . . . Perhaps we should all find out what he's on then!

A. Didn't that also happen to the bloke who sold his soul to the devil . . .

F. I don't know.

A. . . . What's the film called, it's a baseball film, basically it's about an old guy who sold his soul to the devil, it's the Faust legend – and became a young baseball player – I don't know what happened to Faust, whether he got younger.

The above interpretations of the changes that had occurred revolved around the symbolism of a more business like future, the more conservative style of dress – the double-breasted suit and a more frantic (even harassed) appearance – and symbolised the increasing pace of organisational change and activity. An overall theme of the pictures from all the groups was the recognition of the change there had been from a friendly, caring, calm demeanor to an aggressive impersonal characterisation of the organisation. This example illustrates how, by making comparisons, in this case with something *invented*, a metaphor or picture can help people to articulate their hopes and fears in a relatively non-threatening, non-confrontational and even humorous manner. It also allows people to literally paint a new landscape that can be shared with others. Drawing pictures and drawing metaphors in groups may also enable employees to create a shared landscape, to which they all have contributed and to which they all can see their contribution and role.

Projective techniques   The rationale behind projective tests is that individuals will reveal hidden levels of consciousness in reaction to different types of stimuli, such as drawings or photographs. The stimuli are usually designed to be ambiguous with the intention that respondents will 'project' their own meaning and significance onto the drawings. By so doing they will declare aspects of their innermost motives and feelings and reveal hidden aspects of personality. This can then be used to help the individual begin a dialogue about aspects of their life or personality. The techniques have generally been confined to specific applications, particularly in psychotherapy and personality research, but they have been widely used in market research (Jobber and Horgan, 1987) in an attempt to establish deep-seated feelings about such things as the basic motivation to buy or not to buy, consumer reaction to colours, size and shape of packaging or names of products, and so on.

A common form of projective test is the thematic apperception test (TAT). This approach asks individuals to simply write a story about a picture; the researcher's task is then to find themes in what people say. This technique has been used by McClelland (1967) as a means of measuring the strength of an individual's need for achievement. McClelland found that a distinctive achievement motive could be isolated and stimulated. The strength of the motive could be measured by taking samples of a person's spontaneous thoughts, such as making up a story about a picture which they had been shown, then counting the frequency of mentions about it, for example achievement and task accomplishment.

Repertory grids and cognitive maps

Repertory grids and cognitive maps are visual and linguistically based tools that are pertinent to situations where individuals and groups are highly interdependent but different (see quadrant two, Figure 4.1). One of the main strengths of these tools is that they enable the simple and relatively immediate presentation of complex information.

Repertory grids   Based on personal construct theory (Kelly, 1955), a repertory grid is a representation of a manager's perception of their world that can be used to understand a person's view of a situation or problem. A grid contains elements (objects of thought, often people but they can be anything from dogs to kitchens) and constructs (the qualities to describe or differentiate between elements). They also contain linking mechanisms, the ways of expressing how the constructs and elements are associated. To elicit constructs, a person is asked to consider the ways in which two or three constructs differ or are similar (e.g., how is John, who is an unskilled manager, different from or similar to Anne, who is a skilled manager?). By analysing the relationships between the constructs, between the elements, and between the elements and constructs, a picture can be developed of a person's understanding of, for example, what they understand to be the skills of a manager. However, a grid offers more than simply a record, as it can also be used to communicate the perceptions thus derived to others; and it is not simply a method of representing what is already known, as the process of developing a grid can spur new understandings and new acts of sense-making (Easterby-Smith et al., 1996). In this context, the authors have observed that the grid is not only a graphical representation of an individual manager's concerns and beliefs, but also works in a reflexive manner (see Harper, 1989) where managers respond to the picture or map compiled. Grids can also help people to articulate with more precision those things only felt vaguely and to notice the previously un-noticed unique details of their circumstances. For example, Mackinlay (1986) used the repertory grid technique to illicit the values and perceptions that householders in a particular housing district had of different types of bathrooms and kitchens. Using photographs of different bathroom and kitchen colour schemes and layouts as elements, Mackinlay showed these to householders, and asked them to compare and contrast the different photographs and in so doing eliciting the 'constructs' they used to differentiate between the photographs and to reveal their likes and dislikes. The method proved extremely useful, with the photographs helping to resolve differences and deal with the complex issues involved in the notion of what people valued and preferred. This demonstrates that grids are a means with which to elucidate, as Shotter and Cunliffe in chapter 1 point out, what might not be immediately observable, so that new insights or perspectives can be gained. Repertory grids help individuals to look, not just at the words people use, but also at the wider constructs they use when making decisions and taking action. Often these are not even known to the individuals themselves, so representation in the visual form of a grid can be the beginning of a process whereby individuals learn more about the ideas they have, how they might have been formed and how they might be changed.

Grids can be used in group situations as a basis for discussion about how different people view the world, and they enable complex relationships to be represented for debate in groups with the objective of building up shared understandings (Easterby-Smith et al., 1996). The discussion of the repertory grid will obviously include the transmission of data, but it is also a way to overcome disagreement and thereby reduce equivocality about goals, the interpretation of issues, or a course of action. In the context of organisational development and change management programmes, where there is usually a lot of uncertainty and ambiguity, a repertory grid is a useful devise for triggering and enabling conversations so that new insights can be gained and problems (re)formulated and shared (Easterby-Smith et al., 1996).

Cognitive mapping   Based on the same personal construct theory as repertory grids, cognitive mapping is a modelling technique that aims to portray managers' ideas, beliefs, values and attitudes and their inter-relationships in a form which is amenable to study and analysis. A cognitive map represents the relationships between the constructs of a number of individual managers regarding a managerial issue or problem (Eden et al., 1983). A cognitive map is 'not supposed to be a scientific model of an objective reality in the way some influence diagrams are, but rather be a presentation of a part of the world as a particular person sees it – it can never be shown to be right or wrong, in an "objective" sense' (Eden et al., 1983: 44). Cognitive maps capture managers' professed theories-in-use, and their conceptual and symbolic uses of language.

In the process of cognitive mapping, groups of individuals, managers or employees collaborate together to share views and exchange opinions, and attempt to model the complexity of problems facing their organisation. One of the advantages of cognitive mapping is that the process enables a reduction of equivocality. Furthermore, the process of cognitive mapping enables those taking part to challenge the views and perspectives of others and it is often the realisation of differences between individual mangers and the following discussion which proves most useful by giving prominence to distinctions and making connections that might otherwise be overlooked (Eden and Ackermann, 1998). A final beneficial outcome of the cognitive mapping process is that it helps managers reach a collective judgement about issues that are ambiguous, complex and often of a contested nature.

Cognitive mapping has been found to be a particularly useful aid to the process of strategy formulation and the authors of this chapter have recently used cognitive mapping for this purpose. It involved the use of cognitive mapping in the strategy development process by managers of a local council in the United Kingdom. In recent years local councils and the UK public sector as a whole have been faced with an increasing complexity of management issues brought about by new government initiatives for performance management and for taking an integrated approach to the management of public services. The research process combined action learning (see chapter 9 by Mike Pedler), cognitive mapping aimed at strategy development and an intensive period of group discussions with the council's chief officer team augmented by documentary investigation and observational research through attending some subsequent team meetings. Rather than sketching a holistic picture of strategy development within the council, the case study presented here provides analytical insights (Yin, 1994) into how cognitive mapping (and management tools employing visual techniques in general) may be used within social acts of sense-making in ambiguous organisational situations. The cognitive mapping exercise reported here followed the methodology and process outlined for collective strategy development exercises in strategy-making terms (rather than individuals) by Eden and Ackermann (1998).

Working with the strategy-making team of the council, a cognitive mapping exercise was used to create maps of the team's collective and individual assumptions about the issues faced by the local council. In order to uncover their aspirations, views, beliefs and assumptions, each of the participating managers was asked to write down and share their views on two central questions:

(a) What is your vision of the borough in ten years from now?
(b) What does an effective and efficient council organisation look like?

The participants were then asked to identify enabling and constraining conditions inside and outside the council in relation to the views professed in response to the two questions. After each individual manager had articulated his or her views, these were then grouped and structured into a causal map on a black board, providing a synthesis of each participant's views upon the

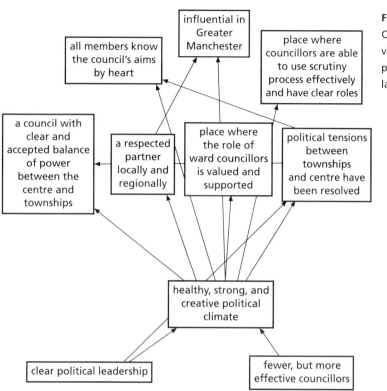

FIGURE 4.3

Cognitive map – vision of the political landscape

two questions. Simultaneously, managers were asked to discuss the suggested clustering of concepts and the content and priorities of the strategic issues. On the whole, the technique provided the group with the ability to surface quickly the strategic issues facing the council.

An initial group analysis and discussion of the content of the cognitive map (see Figure 4.3 for an example of a cognitive map) showed the complexity in terms of the multiplicity and diversity of social, economic and governmental issues facing the council, as well as the often conflicting views regarding the organisation and its environment. Despite the differences in perspective, it was observed that during the cognitive mapping process there were few difficulties in the interaction between the team members as they negotiated their way through the dynamics of reaching consensus on the key strategic issues presented in Table 4.1 (Churchill, 1990), which can be seen to indicate a collective form of organisational learning. That is, it appeared that the use of this technique with the chief officer's team, with each of them responsible for different parts of the organisation, enabled the team to experience the difficulties of other departments and to begin to understand how the council organisation functioned as a whole.

The main benefit of the cognitive map was to reduce the messiness and ambiguity that was thought to characterise the situation, by providing

TABLE 4.1
Themes and
strategy
development

Cluster	Selected Constructs	Suggested Strategies/ Organisational Development
Political landscape	Clear political leadership, effective councillors, clear definition of councillor role, balance of power between townships and centres	– Debate between council and politicians on roles and responsibilities
Efficient and effective organisation	Clearly stated priorities and strategies, valued for high quality services, appropriate balance of service providers and central services, meeting community needs, customer focus, effective financial planning process, multi-agency approaches to service delivery, committed staff	– Analysis of service delivery – Market research to identify customer needs – Market orientation (service orientation and staff development)
Staff development	Committed staff, staff development opportunities, can-do culture, inclusive workforce, flexible working practices, sense of identity and pride	– Develop staff development programmes – Review employee relations records – Develop human resources and hiring policy
Communication and delivery of services	Communication infrastructure (front-line staff and mediated communication), Information and Communication Technology (ICT), services available 24 hrs per day/on-line	– Establish communication infrastructure – E-government (including website) development – Acquire government funding – Train staff in modes of delivery
Reputation of council and borough	Services winning national recognition, positive image of council (as effective in service delivery) and borough (as place to live and work)	– Develop communications/public relations strategy – Revamp external relations unit – Invest in service delivery

groups with an ability to (a) manage the resultant complexity through the identification of emergent themes, and (b) prioritise the emergent themes for subsequent development into strategy and organisational development pro- grammes (see Table 4.1). To this end, the group discussion of the cognitive map included a transmission of information, but was also used as a means to overcome disagreement and thereby reduce equivocality about goals, the interpretation of issues, or a course of action. Again, this points to the man- ner in which grids work in a reflexive manner (Harper, 1989, 1994), where managers responded creatively to the picture or map compiled. This can lead to new maps or landscapes being developed and used to articulate a shared future. For example, Figure 4.3 presents a cluster of interrelated constructs involving managers' vision of a political landscape where the relationship between politicians and the council is a collaborative and mutually support- ive one.

This approach of cognitive mapping allies with action learning method- ologies, where managers open up their thoughts to the close scrutiny and critical comments of others and learn about the views of others (e.g. McLaughlin and Thorpe, 1993). Based upon a notion of experiential learn- ing (Kolb, 1984), where learning begins with action rather than theory and where managers must take responsibility for their own development in deciding what, when and how to learn, action learning is particularly suitable for dealing with issues of the management of change and organisa- tional development. In effect, the case study has shown that organisational development (through strategy development) and organisational learning co- evolve: as the organisation and strategy evolves, organisational learning is taking place.

Shotter and Cunliffe in chapter 1 discuss the importance of bringing issues into open view so that they 'become surveyable by a rearrangement'. They talk of the living experience of authorship and sense-making by exploring how meanings can be created between individuals both 'in the moment of speech' and 'after the moment of reflection upon it' – this is in part the process that takes place in the development of a cognitive map.

Conclusion

This chapter has outlined a number of visual tools that enable and facilitate debate and clarification within work groups, their aim being in part to lead to a reduction of ambiguity and equivocality by arriving at a common arguable formulation of a situation. In this regard the chapter has begun to articulate the role that visual media can play in promoting a social con- structionist approach to management processes and practical authorship. In particular, we feel that visual tools are important in highlighting the follow- ing three things. First, meaning is subjectively constructed in situ and, contrary to representational and more formalised forms of language, highlight the pragmatic use of language in constructing a symbolic landscape in which organisational life can be enacted and re-enacted (Astley and Zammuto, 1992).

Second, social constructionism is premised on a *group process of dialectic and conversational interaction*, and visual media used can play a pivotal role in capturing the verbalised and professed views of managers that shape and constitute their organisational life. In many ways the use of these processes as 'tools for thinking', links closely to the philosophy of action learning methodologies discussed by Mike Pedler in chapter 9, where learning begins with problems and dilemmas which remain unresolved and where managers are required to take responsibility for their actions and development.

Third, one of the central features of social constructionism and of practical authorship is the *openness of meaning*, and the process in which this meaning can be further specified or determined by a group (Alvesson, 1990; Astley and Zammuto, 1992). Visual media, unlike more formalised representations, can be particularly useful in promoting this process in the way they offer increased scope for interpretation and in the way they can potentially capture the unique indefiniteness of both managerial activity and managerial views (something that is not easily captured in an unequivocal way through formal accounts and processes) (Alvesson, 1990). Thus, on the one hand visual tools offer the scope for managers to create (through debate and discussion) new interpretations and 'landscapes' on which future action can be based. On the other, and unlike their more analytical counterparts, visual tools offer the facility to capture the ambiguity and complexity inherent in much organisational life. In other words, visual tools have a double action, they can open up new vistas and they can make the surveyable landscape become clearer. Furthermore, as this process is conducted in situ, it can help ensure that these views are placed within intelligible formulations of organisational life.

In conclusion, the crux of this chapter has been to show how visual tools can help managers think around problems to reduce the ambiguity of organisational situations. It has been argued that, from this, managers are able to create a landscape, from which they can argue for their position and take action.

References

Alvesson, M. (1990) 'Organization: from substance to image', *Organization Studies*, 11: 373–94.

Astley, W.G. and Zammuto, R.F. (1992) 'Organization science, managers, and language games', *Organization Science*, 3: 443–60.

Banks, M. (1995) 'Visual research methods', *Social Research Update*, 11. Guildford: University of Surrey.

Buchanan, D.A. (1999) 'The role of photography in organisation research: a re-engineering case illustration', *Journal of Management Inquiry*, 10: 151–64.

Churchill, J. (1990) 'Complexity and strategic decision-making', in C. Eden and J. Radford (eds), *Tackling Strategic Problems: The Role of Group Decision Support*. London: Sage. pp. 11–17.

Collier, J. and Collier, J. (1986) *Visual Anthropology: Photography as a Research Method*. Albuquerque: University of New Mexico.

Daft, R.L. and Lengel, R.H. (1986) 'Organizational information requirements, media richness and structural design', *Management Science*, 32: 554–71.

Easterby-Smith, M., Thorpe, R. and Holman, D. (1996) 'The use of repertory grids in management', *Journal of European Industrial Training*, 20 (3): 1–30.

Eden, C. and Ackermann, F. (1998) *Making Strategy: The Journey of Strategic Management*. London: Sage.

Eden, C., Jones, S. and Sims, D. (1983) *Messing About in Problems: An Informal Structured Approach to their Identification and Management*. Oxford: Pergamon Press.

Harper, D. (1989) 'Visual sociology: expanding sociological vision', in G. Blank et al. (eds), *New Technology in Sociology: Practical Applications in Research and Work*. New Brunswick, NJ: Transaction Books. pp. 81–97.

Harper, D. (1994) 'On the authority of the image: visual methods at the crossroads', in N.K. Denzin and Y.S. Lincoln (eds), *Handbook of Qualitative Research*. Thousand Oaks: Sage. pp. 403–12.

Jobber, D. and Horgan, I. (1987) 'Market research education: perspectives from practitioners', *Journal of Marketing Management*, 3 (1): 39–49.

Kelly, G.A. (1955) *The Psychology of Personal Constructs*. New York: Norton.

Kolb, D. (1984) *Experiential Learning*. Englewood Cliffs, NJ: Prentice Hall.

Lawrence, P.R. and Lorsch, J.W. (1967) *Organization and Environment: Managing Differentiation and Integration*. Boston: Division of Research, Graduate School of Business Administration, Harvard University.

McClelland, D.A. (1967) *The Achieving Society*. Princetown: Van Nastrand.

Mackinlay, T. (1986) 'The development of a personal strategy for management', Master of Science Degree, Manchester Polytechnic, Department of Management.

McLaughlin, H. and Thorpe, R. (1993) 'Action learning – a paradigm in emergence: the problems facing a challenge to traditional management education and development', *British Journal of Management*, 4: 19–27.

Schön, D.A. (1983) *The Reflective Practitioner: How Professionals Think in Action*. London: Maurice Temple Smith.

Shotter, J. (1995) 'The manager as practical author: a rhetorical-responsive, social constructionist approach to social-organisational problems', in D. Hosking, H.P. Dachler and K.J. Gergen (eds), *Management and Organisation: Relational Alternatives to Individualism*. Aldershot: Avebury. pp. 125–47.

Simpson, B. (1997) Unpublished MSc dissertation, Manchester Metropolitan University.

Weick, K.E. (1995) *Sensemaking in Organizations*. London: Sage.

Wittgenstein, L. (1953) *Philosophical Investigations*. Oxford: Blackwell.

Yin, R.K. (1994) *Case Study Research: Design and Methods*. London: Sage.

PART THREE

Developing the author's position

The leader as a practical narrator: leadership as the art of translating

Francois Cooren and Gail T. Fairhurst

As long as lions will not have historians,
Hunting stories will glorify the hunters. (African Proverb)

This chapter examines leadership skills in terms of the capacity of some individuals to deal with the multiple dimensions of organisational life, and to generate the conditions of an acceptable narration that can be meaningfully enacted by all the organisational actors present. Based on Shotter's (1993) idea of the manager as a 'practical author', that is, a person who can 'restore a flow of action that had become unintelligible in some way' (1993: 157), this chapter illustrates how sense-making processes can be understood as acts of *translation*. Starting from the latest developments of semio-narrative theory (Greimas, 1987) and the sociology of translation (Callon and Latour, 1981; Latour, 1994, 1996), we will show that an effective and ethical leader can be depicted as an individual capable of acknowledging and respecting many different agendas while translating them into a single objective. Far from imposing only one definition of a situation, a good leader is someone who is able to create a narration in which different definitions of a situation become compatible in order to address the respective interests of the actors involved. Moreover, we will show that this ability to recognise the multi-dimensionality of organisational life can be understood as the essence of organisational ethics. This position will be illustrated by a case study in which a workforce restructuring manager deals with the downsizings in his organisation.

Organisations as narratives

Over the past few years, the relationship between communicating and organising has evolved considerably. At one time, organisations were seen as containers within which communication was a transmission. More recently, communicating and organising are seen as mutually constituting and/or simultaneous achievements (Boden, 1994; Cooren, 2000; Cooren and Taylor, 1997; Smith, 1993; Taylor and Cooren, 1997). With this evolution comes the corresponding notion of *leadership as organising*. The communication of leaders and their constituents is no longer just reflective of the organisation, it is constitutive of it. Taylor (1995) suggests that the leadership relationship appears quite different when viewed in this way. This is because we are no longer looking for the communicational in the organisational. We are looking for the reverse: what is organising about leader–constituent discourse?

There are, of course, multiple ways to answer this question (Putnam and Fairhurst, 2001). We begin with Weick's (1979) view that organising can be depicted as a sense-making activity. However, few studies try to address the central question that follows from this claim, which is, what do 'sense', 'signification', or 'meaning' mean?[1] Greimas and Courtés (1982) argue that 'although it is a property common to all the different semiotic systems, the concept of meaning is undefinable [. . .] nothing can be said about meaning, unless metaphysical presuppositions full of implications are introduced' (1982: 187). If 'sense', 'signification', or 'meaning' cannot be defined, one can try to analyse the conditions under which they can be created or made. One way to address this issue is through the universal phenomenon of narrativity. Weick is sensitive to this issue when he recognises that 'most organisational realities are based on narration' (1995: 127). However, although he and Browning devoted an article to this subject (Weick and Browning, 1986), narrativity is never presented as the basic mechanism of meaning production.

Other important scholars in the field like Boje (1991, 1995), Fisher (1984, 1985), and Mumby (1987, 1993) have also explicitly highlighted the importance of storytelling to understand the way people make sense of their organisation, but their accounts never really explain *how* people literally organise their universe by mobilising narrative structures. Only John Shotter seems to understand that 'managers may be best seen as actually involved "in the making of history" ' (1993: 149), a characteristic that he associates with the ability to provide 'an intelligible formulation of what has become, for the others in the organisation, a chaotic welter of impressions' (1993: 148). In other words, narrativity appears to be the basic process of organising, a hypothesis that, following Shotter, we would like to explore here.

Before beginning, it will be useful to recognise that human experience is composed of both 'stories lived' and 'stories told' (Pearce, 1994). According to Pearce, stories lived are the narratives as they are performed by social actors. They can be identified as observable performances and constitute an ongoing process at the mercy of contingencies (cf. 1994: 64). In contrast to stories lived, stories told are the narratives provided by the actors to account retrospectively for their performances, i.e., for the story they lived. They may bear little or no resemblance to the actual episodes, but they help actors make sense of what others are doing and guide their behaviour (see also Barge, 1998). Based on the goal orientation of actors, Greimas's (1987) narrative model provides a universal framework for mapping stories lived and, thus, a means to analyse stories told. We now turn to that model.

Greimas's narrative model

Following Taylor and Lerner (1996), Greimas's (1987) semiotic theory suggests an interesting narrative model that will ultimately show the way sense is made by leaders and their constituents.[2] This analytical model establishes a causal link between organising and sense-making, since it shows that it is the general organisation of events within a given initiative that produces signification or meaning. In other words, we find here the etymological root of the French word 'sens' (coming from the Latin 'sensus') that can be used to express both the ideas of 'meaning' and 'direction'. As we will show, when a situation, a discourse, a sentence or even a word makes sense, it is because one is able to insert it within a project, a quest, a goal or an initiative. This insertion thus creates an *articulation* (i.e., a linking) with other situations, other discourses, other sentences or other words, and produces conditions for a specific way of interpreting the sense or meaning of a specific event.

In this connection, Greimas notes that every narrative has a similar structure or narrative schema that can be depicted in four phases. The first phase, called 'manipulation', involves the creation of a tension between a subject and an object. A subject wants or desires an object because she accepts the task of finding or recovering it, or just because she decides by herself to get it in order to reestablish an order that was threatened (in that case, we say that the situation is asking her to do something to reestablish an order). Four roles, or actants, are introduced in this phase: the subject who accepts to fulfil the quest, the object that constitutes the point of the quest, the sender who asks the subject to complete the quest, and finally the receiver who is requested to complete the quest.[3]

The second phase usually involves a series of alliances and tests that the subject will have to respectively create and pass. This phase, called 'competence' by Greimas, will provide the subject with many skills and (human and nonhuman) allies that are all considered helpers. Conversely, some actants will be identified as 'opponents', since their roles consist of creating obstacles regarding the quest.

A third phase, called 'performance', constitutes the main action performed by the subject in her quest. In other words, it is what we usually call the climax or the culmination of the narrative, since it usually consists of the fulfilment of the quest.

Greimas identifies a final phase where the subject is rewarded for what she did. This is the phase called 'sanction', in which the initial sender rewards or thanks the subject for fulfilment of the quest. This phase is very important, since it consists of counterbalancing what has been done by the subject to the advantage of the sender. By thanking or rewarding the subject, the sender establishes an exchange.

To illustrate this point, imagine the following narrative. Sandra is the manager of a small organisation that produces web pages for big companies in the United States. She started her business alone with one computer at home, but the success of her company led her to bring about some changes in her organisation. With the help of a bank loan, she rented a space in a building, bought a network of computers and progressively hired two designers, three programmers and a marketing manager.

Why does such a situation make sense? If we follow what Greimas tells us about the universal organisation of narratives, this situation can be retrospectively described as a 'story told' (Pearce, 1994), that is, as an account provided for reporting the articulation of behaviours involved in a series of communication episodes. Using Greimas's narrative model, we can note that Sandra appears as the subject and the primary object of her quest is to produce web pages for companies and, ultimately, to make a profit. Concerning the role of sender, it is actually a demand situation that led or pushed her to launch this project of a company and to offer her services. In other words, she is responding to a specific situation, a potential market. In this case, the market is the sender,[4] and she plays the role of both the receiver and subject.

The competence phase appears clearly in this case, since Sandra is progressively surrounded by a multitude of helpers who join her quest. Each association of allies can correspond to a narrative sub-schema. For example, when she is hiring a designer, this act can be depicted as follows: Sandra is making an offer to a candidate who accepts it (manipulation). Thanks to his personal skill and with the help of a computer (competence), the candidate – now employee – fulfils his contract (performance). Finally, he receives a salary for compensation (sanction).

As for the performance phase, we already know that it consists of building web pages for profit, but this has still to be narratively explained. In fact, building web pages and making a profit constitute the last two phases of Sandra's narrative schema. While building web pages is obviously the phase of performance, profit-making can be analysed as the direct compensation provided by the sender for the service, that is, the phase of sanction (for an illustration of this analysis, see Figure 5.1).

As we see, Greimassian theory provides us with a powerful narrative model that enables us to articulate the different activities inherent in an organisation. Far from being a marginal phenomenon in the organising process, we progressively realise that narrative structures appear to be a basic way to retrospectively make sense of an organisation (i.e., a story told). Moreover, it helps us better understand how the diverse activities of an

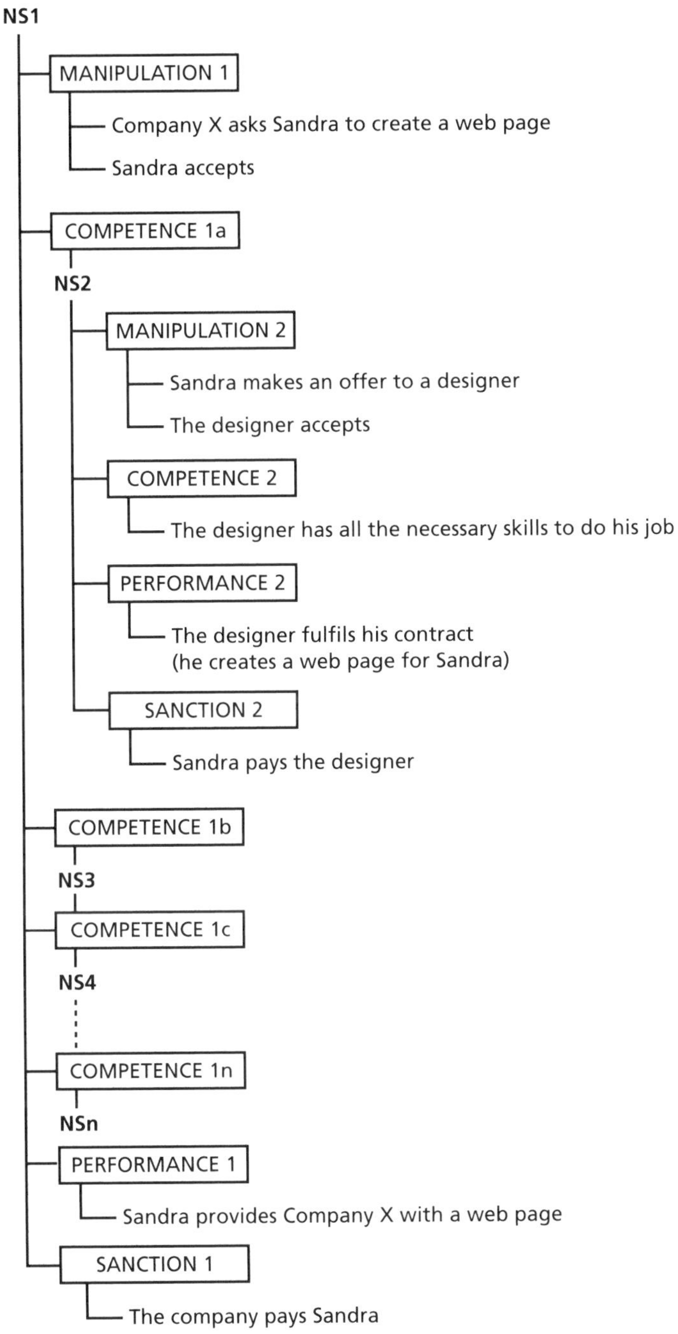

NS1

> MANIPULATION 1
>> Company X asks Sandra to create a web page
>> Sandra accepts

> COMPETENCE 1a

NS2

>> MANIPULATION 2
>>> Sandra makes an offer to a designer
>>> The designer accepts

>> COMPETENCE 2
>>> The designer has all the necessary skills to do his job

>> PERFORMANCE 2
>>> The designer fulfils his contract
>>> (he creates a web page for Sandra)

>> SANCTION 2
>>> Sandra pays the designer

> COMPETENCE 1b

NS3

> COMPETENCE 1c

NS4

> COMPETENCE 1n

NSn

> PERFORMANCE 1
>> Sandra provides Company X with a web page

> SANCTION 1
>> The company pays Sandra

FIGURE 5.1
Sandra's
narrative schema

organisation are inherently organised within a hierarchy that corresponds to the different levels of narrative schemata. This could be considered an interesting but useless theoretical point of view, without any practical consequences. However, we would like to show that the real implications of this model are to be found elsewhere.

Organising as translating

To fully understand what this model enables us to see, we need to consider Michel Callon's (1986) and Bruno Latour's (1987, 1996) work. Fathers of the so-called Actor-Network Theory, or Sociology of Translation, these authors have tried for almost 20 years to draw conclusions from Greimas's theory in the socio-technical field.

One of the most important contributions of Callon and Latour's theory is applying the concept of *translation* to explain the general functioning of organised systems. Consider Sandra and her designer. Given her goal of designing web pages for profit, she literally used the web page designer as a 'helper' in Greimas's terms. How do we recognise a helper? We recognise him, her or it, because a helper can become invisible to the analysis. In other words, a helper is someone or something that can be easily eliminated if we want to account for an action. Note that, at the end of the process, the client is not paying the designer for what he did; it is Sandra who is paid. What happened is actually a translation. Because of the contract signed between Sandra and her designer, what the designer will do counts as what Sandra does. An equivalency is established. For the company that is asking Sandra to design a web page, Sandra's organisation is a 'black box' in Callon and Latour's terms. As suggested by this metaphorical concept, the content of a black box remains unknown to us as long as we do not call it into question. One just knows what it is able to produce when asked to do something.

Organising would thus consist of a series of translations that enable one to articulate many different narrative schemata to each other. Each sub-narrative schema can thus be considered as a black box as long as it produces what it is expected to produce. If Sandra's designer does not achieve what he is expected to, his (non-)contribution will suddenly be revealed. He is no longer a simple intermediary whose action can be embedded or inserted within Sandra's main narrative schema (cf. Callon, 1991).[5] It is thus essential to understand that an actant can actually be labelled a helper only a posteriori or retrospectively (story told). As long as his, her or its contribution has not been assessed, it is impossible to know whether the translation occurred or not.

According to this approach, an organisation is thus nothing more than the temporary result of a series of insertions that can always be threatened or called into question as a story is lived. In a sense, an organisation is a kind of daily miracle, since it consists of mobilising a series of human and/or nonhuman actants who can at any moment fail to join in the narrative schema of the organisation (i.e., the narrative schema as told and anticipated by the managers). Note also that success or failure does not depend on the appropriation of the main narrative schema by the different actants. Since a black box remains closed as long as the expected output is produced, it is possible to be associated with a project or initiative without really knowing its ins and outs. For example, the designer does not necessarily need to know anything about Sandra's initiative to perform his task. Vis-à-vis Sandra's objective, he is reduced to an instrument (hence, his actantial role of helper) whose contribution can stop at the level of the output he is able to produce. The process of organising thus necessarily implies that, in one way or another, some actants be reduced to 'cogs in a machine'.

However, it is also important to note that such a reduction is narratively oriented. In other words, it is because the designer is submitted to or inserted within Sandra's initiative that he can be narratively and temporally reduced to the dimension of helper. Of course, a helper can never be absolutely reduced only to this dimension. Actants always exceed the dimension that a specific narrative or organisation ascribes to them, i.e., they are always multidimensional. This precision that could appear somewhat superficial actually undermines any functionalist approach that tries to reduce human or nonhuman actants to their mere instrumentality (Cooren, 1999). Historically dominant in the organisational sciences, the functionalist approach consists of representing or describing events from just one perspective, usually the managerial perspective (Deetz, 1992; Mumby, 1987). However, as Peirce (1932), Burke (1962) and Shotter (1993) remind us, naming or identifying a situation always amounts to offering a way to make sense of what happens under a specific definition of the situation. In this connection, Shotter writes:

> [. . .] although they must often function (as Marx said in general about people making history) 'under conditions not of their own choosing' – good managers, when faced with such unchosen conditions, can, by *producing an appropriate formulation of them*, create (a) a 'landscape' of enabling-constraints (Giddens, 1979) relevant for a range of next possible actions; (b) a network of 'moral positions' or 'commitments' (understood in terms of the rights and duties of the 'players' on that landscape); and (c) are able to argue persuasively and author-itatively for this 'landscape' amongst those who work within it. (1993: 149, our italics)

Thus, for Shotter, making a description amounts to producing a landscape/network that managers must be able to sell through persuasion or authority. Following Callon and Latour, we can illustrate this idea using the example of a company's rationalisation of a decision to downsize. As long as one tells the story from management's perspective, any attempt to reduce the number of its employees in the interest of profit is rational. However, everything suddenly changes if we tell the story from the employees' per-spective. What appears to be a rational act for management can actually turn into a financial, social and psychological disaster for the employees. That is exactly what we mean by the African proverb quoted at the beginning of the chapter: as long as lions will not have historians, it is clear that hunting stories will always glorify the hunters. A change of perspective consists of telling the story from a specific actant's perspective (a helper, an opponent, a sender, etc.), thus revealing the multidimensionality of a specific event.[6]

We can now return to the subject of leadership by noting that much of it consists of recognising the multidimensionality of organisational narratives. As transformational models of leadership suggest, the leader's job is to align everyone's interests (Bass, 1985; Bennis and Nanus, 1985; Shamir et al., 1993). As exchange based models of leadership also suggest, the leader must reconcile them in a way that is minimally acceptable to all relevant parties (Dansereau et al., 1975; Fairhurst, 1993; Fairhurst and Chandler, 1989; Waldron, 1991). However, to our knowledge, there is very little literature to explain the semantic mechanisms by which such an alignment is produced and sustained except to note in a very general way that an appealing vision, or appeals to individual and group identities, can enrol large numbers of organisational participants. As we will try to show, a leader is an actant who must constantly mobilise as many different human and/or nonhuman actants as possible toward the completion of a set of identified tasks, while taking into consideration that any type of mobilisation is always subject to a form of (implicit or explicit) moral contract. This is what Shotter calls the 'rights and duties of the players' (1993: 149). This is what we propose to explore now.

Leadership as the art of translating

If these approaches prove to be relevant in depicting how an organisation works, we will show that a good leader is someone who is able to cope with the multidimensionality of a 'landscape of enabling-constraint' (Shotter, 1993: 149). As Pondy (1978) and Fairhurst and Sarr (1996) argue, leadership is a 'language game' whose main characteristic is the 'art of framing'. But what does 'framing' mean here? Fairhurst and Sarr identify this skill by defining it as 'a quality of communication that causes others to accept one meaning over another' (1996: xi). This idea highlights the capacity of a leader to make sense of a given situation by articulating or relating it to different objectives that can sometimes appear conflicting (Bennis and Nanus, 1985; Schön, 1983). Since this skill consists of influencing people to accept one meaning over others, the art of framing seems very close to what Callon and Latour describe as the process of translating. Influencing people to accept one meaning over another actually amounts to enrolling them in a given initiative, a technical term used by Callon and Latour to describe an essential step in the process of translating. Defining the term 'enrolment', Callon writes that 'it designates the device by which a set of interrelated roles is defined and attributed to actors who accept them' (1986: 211). In other words, managing meaning would consist of showing that a given initiative is acceptable because it appears to minimally fulfil every actant's objectives or interests, whatever they are. In Shotter's words, it becomes 'relevant for a range of next possible actions' (1993: 149). By framing, one actually defines a situation – tells a story in potentially multiple ways, each way corresponding to a different portrayal of the organisational landscape.

Shotter reminds us that the meaning or sense of a given situation is always overdetermined. In other words, no description will ever exhaust its inherent complexity and multidimensionality. There is never only one way to make sense of a project or an event, but multiple ways. There is no one story, but multiple stories and frames that a leader can use to provide an 'intelligent formulation' (1993: 157) that will eventually enroll the different organisational actors and 'restore a flow of action' (1993: 157). We will now illustrate this idea by using a case study of a workforce restructuring plan called 'managed attrition' that emerged in a downsizing organisation.[7] This case is especially interesting, since it shows how a workforce restructuring manager succeeds in aligning the interests of many different actors (wage and salary employees, government regulators, unions, senior management, etc.) while respecting their own landscape of actions. After describing the case, we will show how our narrative approach explains what occurred.

Case study: downsizings at an environmental remediation site

The site for this study was a United States Department of Energy (DOE) facility that produced uranium metal products for the nation's defence programmes between 1953–89. These products were used in production reactors to make plutonium and tritium at other DOE sites. In 1989 uranium metal production was suspended after a series of controversies concerning off-site contamination. Like many organisations within the complex of government-owned, contractor-operated facilities, the site began environmental remediation to deal with its legacy of toxic and radioactive waste. At the time of the study, the site was in the midst of a protracted, multi-year closure. While the first contract to do the clean-up was awarded to another firm, the contractor who commenced the downsizings took over in 1992 and has remained. Over a seven-year period, three downsizings were conducted, with many more planned, in order to achieve site closure by 2006. The three downsizings are described elsewhere in greater detail (Fairhurst et al., 2000). The data reported here were collected at the start of the third downsizing.

The previous two downsizings had been especially traumatic. The first was an involuntary downsizing marked by an abrupt dismissal of over 200 employees and a recognition that the construction industry culture of the contractor, where abrupt dismissals were routine, was clearly at odds with the old manufacturing culture of the site and employees' psychological contract over continued employment (Rousseau, 1995). The second downsizing was voluntary and marked by the presence of the National Defense

Authorization Act for Fiscal Year 1993, Section 3161 (hereafter 3161) in which the US Congress conferred a windfall of education, health and cash benefits on the country's cold war workers at defence facilities such as the one under study. Given 3161, the voluntary downsizing programme was framed as a 'positive opportunity' that on the surface distinguished itself from the first downsizing. However, employees were also told that if they did not voluntarily leave and take advantage of 3161, they would be involuntarily separated (Fairhurst et al., 2000). Unexpectedly, too many employees sought to leave the site such that many had to be turned down.

Also at the time of the second downsizing, a workforce restructuring (WR) manager was put in place to meet with employees. As a result of these meetings, the WR manager became a change agent for a new plan for the third downsizing. This new plan was known as 'managed attrition'. The goals of managed attrition were: a) unprecedented openness in sharing human resources planning information as it became available leading up to a window of up to two years before one's job is restructured or eliminated; b) the provision of a variety of clear paths to alternative employment and/or education that would lead to such employment; and c) the provision of benefits well before site separation that could be shown to be more cost effective than usual severance packages.

A series of interviews was completed by the authors with different members of the human resources (HR) team responsible for this programme as well as with management, DOE officials, union representatives, and employees at the site (Fairhurst et al., 2000). We also attended several meetings organised by this team to introduce managed attrition to employees. For the purpose of this chapter, we will focus our analysis on an interview with Matthew, the main person responsible for the plan[8].

Thinking outside the box

When Matthew began his meetings to address the concerns of separate employees during the second downsizing, he faced a difficult environment. Here is how he described the atmosphere when he started to meet the employees to announce to them that their jobs would be terminated:

> Was I nervous? Absolutely. Because these were people who worked at this facility – some of them for 28 years – who were literally within hundreds of days of retirement, full retirement, who had just been told either voluntarily leave the facility or we're going to lay you off. We had people who had sick children in the hospital, who had wives who were sick, who had husbands who had lost their jobs. It was a very threatening time . . . That probably was the most gut wrenching time of my entire life . . . I got the stories, I got the heartache from the employees, and it was tough. To look at those people, especially in those small groups, and the thing that probably ripped me up more than anything was I knew most of them . . . They were all quality individuals. They performed and did a good job for this company. But because of budget cutbacks and the slide and the cleanup effort, those kinds of things, somebody had to look at them and talk to them openly and honestly and say, 'This is not your fault. It's not

something you did, it's not something you said.' And I went home, with my guts in knots, with the dry heaves and the whole works, and . . . I shed some tears privately about that issue. What I decided at that time . . . is, my God, there's got to be a better way to do things. We've got 2000 more people to go at this site. We can't be doing this. There's got to be a better way to handle this kind of downsizing effort.

Through this excerpt, we see how Matthew was confronted with other narratives. By meeting with employees, Matthew 'got the stories'. People started to tell him what downsizing meant for them, i.e., they told the stories from their perspectives. A process that might have appeared initially as one-dimensional progressively became more complex. Matthew heard narratives about children who were sick, of husbands who had lost their jobs, etc. To use Callon and Latour's (1981) vocabulary, the box that could have remained closed and black was suddenly opened by the employees. We are not following the company's narrative anymore, but its helpers and their own pathways.

By listening to the employees, Matthew realised that there might be another way to deal with the situation, a way that would take into account the different narrative courses involved in the process. What appears to be two conflicting or contradictory objectives in the organisational landscape – the downsizing process and the employees' aspirations for job security – could be transformed into a common cause where all of the actors' objectives could be minimally addressed. Thus, Matthew decided to transform a potential source of conflict (since the narrative courses first appear to be incompatible) into a rallying point. To be sure, this decision to change the process was also determined by other factors. As Matthew said:

I think we got a few lawsuits from the people who were denied the opportunity to leave because there was a $15,000 lump sum settlement plus severance and some other benefits that went with that. And we had a list of almost 200 people who wanted to leave, and we said 'no' to them. We thought we'd be hard pressed to get 400 to volunteer . . . almost 700 people applied. Now the message was getting out – even at that time – [that] this place was scheduled for closure. Now one of the things we found of the 200 people who applied, it's much like any corporation when you have a situation like this. If you don't control it to some degree, you're going to have your best people leave. Why? Because they can find jobs tomorrow. And the 200 or so people who [were] left [back] were individuals whom the company didn't feel they could afford to lose.

While the workforce transition process previously appeared to be advantageous for the company and disadvantageous for some workers, the situation was completely reversed for other employees. This time, the organisation was threatened with losing its best helpers who had decided to dissociate themselves from the site. Aware that the plant would close in the near future and that they could easily get a new position elsewhere, some of the company's most qualified employees decided to take the lump sum option and voluntarily leave. Thus, another story appears: some actors who were initially considered to be helpers progressively dissociated themselves from the managerial narrative (i.e., the story lived dissociated progressively from the story told). The translation does not work anymore, since the contract seems too flawed for several employees who prefer to leave.

Facing this challenging situation, Matthew then decided to formulate the new managed attrition plan for downsizing and workforce restructuring. Commenting on this new approach and how he presented it to other people, he said:

> Most everybody thinks inside a box. This box is 3161. I don't play computer games, but I saw a game on my son's computer one time called, 'Pong.' And there was a ball that just bounced around on the inside here, and it just left streaks and patterns and all that stuff. And I told them, 'You understand that this is all 3161, and all your ideas are bouncing against these walls, and these are parameters you built for yourself . . . Then bounce around on the outside because you got all this room to matriculate if you just look at it that way.' And then we began to share some ideas like, for example, separation benefits and those kinds of things. Don't look at these narrow inside walls. Look at what you got outside here. And one of the fellows who is the director for the Department of Energy down there said, 'Geeze, I didn't realise we could do that.' And I said, 'Well, I guess I'll ask the obvious question – Did you ask?' 'Well no.' So, 'OK, I'm going to tell you, you can do that.' Of course we had some Washington officials there, and they said, 'Yeah, there's no reason why you can't do that. You just never looked.'

Aware that he had to reconcile different interests that apparently seemed incompatible (or at least potentially dissociative), Matthew understood that he had to change the point at which the different narrative schemata were supposed to converge. That is exactly what Matthew suggests with his reference to 'thinking inside the box'. Thus, the opportunity consists of enlarging the landscape in order to find a potential rallying point through which every actant would be minimally ready to alter his or her behaviour for a common cause. The rallying point is described by Matthew:

> If you look at the program we have designed through [the] managed attrition approach . . . we will pay you [employees] to leave this facility – just simple normal severance. And again that severance is $7,000. Now the advantage, the trade-off to the employee, is first, you've got about a 2-year notification that your job is going away. Here, [speaking of the first downsizing] you are given a 60-day notification. OK, so you're looking a . . . 720 days as opposed to 60 days. Big difference. And if you look at the average employee per $10,000 income, it takes one month to find a job. For a $40,000 employee, they're going to be unemployed for 4 months. Here, they've got 5 times the lead to look for work. The trade-off is the employee says, 'Well, you know, I'm going to be involuntarily separated. I'm going to get the same benefit. Why would I want to wait?' Well, the difference is now you've got a 2-year opportunity to look for work with us assisting you with retraining opportunities and all kinds of things including [names of universities]. You've got some opportunities to take some skills with you so you can leave employed versus leaving unemployed.

Here, one sees how Matthew found a rallying point by taking into account both the employees' and the organisation's point of view. Though

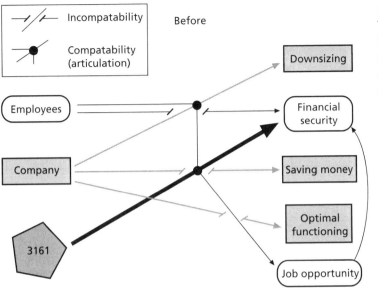

FIGURE 5.2
The situation before the implementation of managed attrition

the idea of finding a 'rallying point' is far from being new in leadership literature (for example, see Stokes, 1995), we see here how the establishment of this common ground is directly related to the capacity to make multiple narrative schemata compatible. Thinking outside the box amounts to offering a new landscape of action that everybody seems ready to follow. By implementing the two-year notification, along with severance and retraining benefits, Matthew was able to align the interests of employees with that of the organisation. Knowing that the first source of stress for employees is usually the uncertainty created by the loss of their jobs, he decided to help them prepare for this eventuality. One sees here how his approach consists of inserting his own narrative schema within the employees' schema. In other words, Matthew's narrative schema can now be considered as a potential helper by the workers, a resource that they can use to get job security and an education. To be sure, the initiative is viable because it also fits within the managerial narrative schema. By implementing this new approach, Matthew knows that it will not only save significant money for the company, but also avoid the brain drain that was threatening the optimal functioning of the organisation. In other words, this new narrative schema can also be considered instrumental from the perspective of the company. By reconfiguring the rules of the game, Matthew was able to insert his initiative within two narratives that initially appeared completely dissociated. One can represent this reconfiguration in Figures 5.2 and 5.3.

Figure 5.2 shows us how the different actors' narrative schemas – or landscape of actions – are initially incompatible. The downsizing process initiated by the company is perceived by some employees as a terrible threat to their job security, while other employees (identified as the best of the

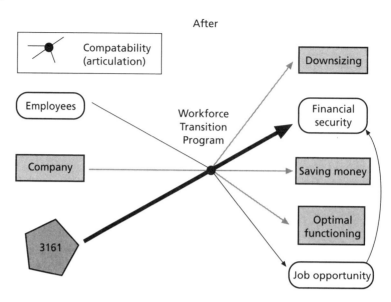

FIGURE 5.3
The situation
after the
implementation
of managed
attrition

organisation) are using this opportunity to find other jobs courtesy of 3161. The unintended 'brain drain' becomes incompatible with the interests of the company trying to maintain an optimal level of functioning until it closes down in 2006. Narratively speaking and taking the company's point of view, 3161 could be considered an opponent in Greimas's terms. This legislation contributes to the undermining of the company's financial health through the brain drain and a significant financial outlay. From the employees' point of view, the organisation could be considered an opponent, even a traitor, since it dissociates itself from their narrative schema of job stability. As for the most qualified employees, admittedly the downsizing process appears compatible with their own narrative schema, since it is viewed as an opportunity to find another position. For them, that is why a first articulation or linkage appears between their schema and the organisation's narrative schema of downsizing. However, this articulation becomes completely incompatible with another narrative schema of the organisation, since this brain drain threatens the optimal functioning of the site. The company refuses to separate these employees, becoming an opponent in the process. Thus, 3161 is used as a resource (or helper) by these employees (a second articulation) to sue the company.

After Matthew proposes managed attrition (cf. Figure 5.3), every schema appears compatible. This new plan appears as a potential helper for everybody, since it seems to fit within their respective narrative schemata. For example, all employees can now use it to prepare for the job market. With the new two-year window, the possibility of easily securing a new position is no longer reserved for an elite few (the employees who were identified as the company's most qualified). To use Greimas's model, Matthew's initiative appears as a competence phase vis-à-vis the employees' narrative schema that consists of getting a new job (performance) to restore their financial security (sanction). Moreover, the brain drain is now controlled, since the progressive lay off is now planned and scheduled according to the needs of the company. In other words, the dissociation is now potentially slowed down, since the best employees no longer have any interest in quickly leaving the site. Finally, 3161, intended to give financial security to cold war workers, is at least minimally compatible with the different stakeholders' narrative schemata.

Conclusion

Paradoxically, we may have contributed to 'glorifying the hunter' as referenced in the earlier African proverb. If this is true, it is a hunter who seems to respect the lions. Like the Cree Indians of Northern Canada who always apologise to the animals for killing them (Cooren and Taylor, 2000), Matthew seems to demonstrate a profound respect for the different stakeholders mobilised in his narrative schema. In John Shotter's terms, he is a 'practical-ethical author' (1993: 157).

In this case, ethics consists of taking into account the fiduciary contract that binds the employees to the company. As in any organisational or narrative process, the interactions between the different actants imply a series of exchanges that must normally be completed. Unethical behaviour would have consisted in simply getting rid of the employees, like in some forms of reengineering processes denounced so powerfully by Cheney and Carroll (1997) and Boje et al. (1997). To be sure, we are not suggesting that employees have a basic right to lifetime employment if hired by an organisation when their actual fiduciary contract typically says no such thing. An organisation has a right to downsize in order to stay afloat. Downsizing, reengineering, rightsizing, whatever we call it, is always stressful to employees, but it is an organisation's prerogative. What is the crucial point here is how many organisations achieve it. What we want to decry is not the dismissal per se, but abrupt dismissals and dismissals marked by subtle and not-so-subtle threats, as took place in the first and second downsizings respectively. Lacking ethics for failing to take into account the damage to the personal lives of employees, some reengineering efforts illustrate what Marx was denouncing when he was speaking of the reduction of persons to simple commodities or objects (Cheney and Carroll, 1997).

By implementing his multidimensional approach, Matthew succeeded in finding the rallying point that enables all the translations to operate. Because of this new initiative, workforce restructuring and downsizing for the employees means an opportunity to be trained and prepared for a job. It also means, for the company this time, an opportunity to save money and to stop the brain drain. According to Fairhurst and Sarr (1996), an effective leader is someone who is able to speak many 'languages' in order to achieve an objective. This capacity to speak different languages consists of showing how what is proposed can fit everybody's interests. It consists of arguing that the objective presented can be minimally inserted into everybody's schemata or aspirations. Thus, the art of framing or authoring becomes the art of translating, an art that amounts to concretely enacting what the language was able to frame. To use Pearce's (1994) terms, it consists of telling a story that can be livable for all the stakeholders. In other words, the art of translating appears to be the very foundation of ethical leadership behaviour, where the hunter finally translates (and does not betray!) the lion's perspective.[9]

Notes

1   We are aware that the concepts of 'signification', 'sense', and 'meaning' are sometimes considered far from being synonymous. However, to our knowledge, there is no consensus regarding the way these three terms should be differentiated. That is why we decided to use them indistinctly in this chapter.

2   Space does not permit a discussion of the differences that exist, for some scholars, between a manager and a leader, a difference that Shotter does not highlight. The terms 'managers' and 'leaders' are thus used interchangeably in this chapter. For more details about this debate, see Kotter (1990) and Zaleznik (1992).

3   In many narratives, the actor asked to fulfil the quest (the receiver) is usually also the subject, i.e., the actant who *accepts* the mission. Greimas establishes a difference between 'receiver' and 'subject' to account for some cases where the receiver does not accept the mission and never reaches the 'subject' status.

4   As you will notice, an actant does not need to be a human being or even an individual. In this case, the sender is a given situation. In other cases, it could be a nonhuman actant, like a text. What is important here is to attribute an actantial role to a given entity, whatever his, her or its *mode of being* is (individual, collective, nonhuman, human, animal, etc.)

5   Note that this analysis is similar to what Suchman (1995) is saying about the invisible work in organisations. For more details, see Taylor and Van Every (2000).

6   This idea is perfectly congruent with the critical approach that usually amounts to telling others' stories. For more details, see Deetz (1992).

7   For the purpose of this chapter, the names of the company and the employees have been changed.

8   The following analysis is only suggestive of a semiotic analysis of the text. Due to space limitations, a full semiotic analysis is beyond the scope of this chapter. For an example, the reader is urged to consult Greimas (1988).

9   As we previously noted, our chapter still starts from the hunter's (Matthew's) perspective. The limitations of the present chapter did not allow us to speak about the lions (the employees), but it is clear that the best way to view their perspective is to listen directly to their voices. This constitutes the subject of another article (Fairhurst et al., 2000).

References

Barge, J.K. (1998) *Storying Leadership as a Language Game*. Annual Meeting of the National Communication Association, New York.

Bass, B.M. (1985) *Leadership and Performance: Beyond Expectations*. New York: Free Press.

Bennis, W. and Nanus, B. (1985) *Leaders: The Strategies for Taking Charge*. New York: Harper and Row.

Boden, D. (1994) *The Business of Talk. Organisations in Action*. Cambridge, UK: Polity Press.

Boje, D.M. (1991) 'The storytelling organisation: a study of story performance in an office-supply firm', *Administrative Science Quarterly*, 36: 106–26.

Boje, D.M. (1995) 'Stories of the storytelling organisation: a postmodern analysis of Disney as "Tamara-land"', *Academy of Management Journal*, 38 (4): 997–1035.

Boje, D.M., Rosile, G.A., Dennehy R. and Summers, D.J. (1997) 'Restorying reengineering. Some deconstructions and postmodern alternatives', *Communication Research*, 24 (6): 631–68.

Burke, K. (1962) *A Grammar of Motives*. Berkeley, CA: University of California Press.

Callon, M. (1986) 'Some elements of a sociology of translation: the domestication of the scallops and the fishermen of St Brieuc Bay', in J. Law (ed.), *Power, Action and Belief*. London: Routledge and Kegan Paul. pp. 196–233.

Callon, M. (1991) 'Réseaux technico-économiques et irréversibilités', in R. Boyer, B. Chavance and O. Godard (eds), *Les Figures de l'irréversibilité en économie*. Paris: Editions de l'Ecole des Hautes Etudes en Sciences Sociales, 47: 195–230.

Callon, M. and Latour, B. (1981) 'Unscrewing the big leviathan: how actors macro-structure reality and how sociologists help them to do so', in A.V. Cicourel and K. Knorr-Cetina (eds), *Advances in Social Theory and Methodology. Towards an Integration of Micro- and Macro-Sociologies*. Boston: Routledge and Kegan Paul. pp. 277–303.

Cheney, G. and Carroll, C. (1997) 'The person as object in discourses in and around organisations', *Communication Research*, 24(6): 593–630.

Cooren, F. (1999) 'Applying socio-semiotics to organisational communication: a new approach', *Management Communication Quarterly*, 13 (2): 294–304.

Cooren, F. (2000) *The Organising Property of Communication*. Amsterdam/Philadelphia: John Benjamins.

Cooren, F. and Taylor, J.R. (1997) 'Organisation as an effect of mediation: redefining the link between organisation and communication', *Communication Theory*, 7 (3): 219–60.

Cooren, F. and Taylor, J.R. (2000) 'Association and dissociation in an ecological controversy: the Great Whale case', in N.W. Coppola and B. Karis (eds), *Technical Communication, Deliberative Rhetoric, and Environmental Discourse: Connections and Directions*. Stamford, CT: Ablex. pp. 171–90.

Dansereau, F., Graen, G., and Haga, W. (1975) 'A vertical dyad linkage approach to leadership within formal organisations: a longitudinal investigation of the role making process', *Organisational Behavior and Human Performance*, 13: 46–78.

Deetz, S. (1992) *Democracy in an Age of Corporate Colonization: Developments in Communication and the Politics of Everyday Life*. Albany, NY: State University of New York Press.

Fairhurst, G. (1993) 'The leader-member exchange patterns of women leaders in industry: a discourse analysis', *Communication Monographs*, 60: 321–51.

Fairhurst, G. and Chandler, T.A. (1989) 'Social structure in leader-member inter-action', *Communication Monographs*, 56: 215–39.

Fairhurst, G.T. and Sarr, R.A. (1996) *The Art of Framing. Managing the Language of Leadership*. San Francisco, CA: Jossey-Bass.

Fairhurst, G.T., Cooren, F. and Cahill, D. (2000) 'A structuration approach to management policy in successive downsizings', paper presented at the National Communication Association Annual Conference, Seattle, Washington.

Fisher, W.R. (1984) 'Narration as a human communication paradigm: the case of public moral argument', *Communication Monographs*, 51 (1): 1–23.

Fisher, W.R. (1985) 'The narrative paradigm: an elaboration', *Communication Monographs*, 52 (December): 347–67.

Giddens, A. (1979) *Central Problems in Social Theory: Action, Structure and Contradictions in Social Analysis*. London: Macmillan.

Greimas, A.J. (1987) *On Meaning. Selected Writings in Semiotic Theory*. London: Frances Pinter.

Greimas, A.J. (1988) *Maupassant. The Semiotics of Text*. Amsterdam/Philadelphia: John Benjamins.

Greimas, A.J. and Courtés, J. (1982) *Semiotics and Language: An Analytical Dictionary*, translated by L. Crist, D. Patte, J. Lee, E. McMahon II, G. Philips and M. Rengstorf. Bloomington, IN: Indiana University Press.

Kotter, J.P. (1990) 'What leaders really do', *Harvard Business Review*, May–June, 620–27.

Latour, B. (1987) *Science in Action: How to Follow Scientists and Engineers Through Society*. Cambridge, MA: Harvard University Press.

Latour, B. (1994) 'On technical mediation – philosophy, sociology, genealogy', *Common Knowledge*, 3 (2): 29–64.

Latour, B. (1996) 'On interobjectivity', *Mind, Culture, and Activity*, 3 (4): 228–45.

Mumby, D. (1987) 'The political function of narrative in organisations', *Communication Monographs*, 54: 113–27.

Mumby, D. (1993) *Narrative and Social Control: Critical Perspectives*. Newbury Park, CA: Sage.

Pearce, W.B. (1994) *Interpersonal Communication: Making Social Worlds*. New York: Harper Collins.

Peirce, C.S. (1932) *Collected Papers. Volume II Elements of Logic*. Cambridge, MA: Harvard University Press.

Pondy, L.R. (1978) 'Leadership is a language game', in M.W. McCall, Jr and M.M. Lombardo (eds), *Leadership: Where Else Can We Go?* Durham, NC: Duke University Press.

Putnam, L.L. and Fairhurst, G.T. (2001) 'Discourse analysis in organisations: issues and concerns', in F.M. Jablin and L.L. Putnam (eds), *The New Handbook of Organisational Communication: Advances in Theory, Research and Methods*. Thousand Oaks, CA: Sage. pp. 78–136.

Rousseau, D.M. (1995) *Psychological Contracts in Organisations*. Thousand Oaks/London: Sage.

Schön, D. (1983) *The Reflective Practitioner: How Professionals Think in Action*. London: Maurice Temple Smith.

Shamir, G., House, R.J. and Arthur, M.B. (1993) 'The motivational effects of charismatic leadership: a self-concept based theory', *Organisation Science*, 4: 577–94.

Shotter, J. (1993) *Conversational Realities. Constructing Life Through Language*. London: Sage.

Smith, R.C. (1993) *Images of Organisational Communication: Root-Metaphors of the Organisation–Communication Relation*. Purdue University.

Stokes, S.L., Jr (1995) 'Life after rightsizing, part 2', *Information Systems Management*, 12: 73–5.

Suchman, L. (1995) 'Making Work Visible', *Communications of the ACM*, 38 (9), 56–64.

Taylor, J.R. (1995) 'Shifting from a heteronomous to an autonomous worldview of organisational communication: communication theory on the cusp', *Communication Theory*, 5 (1): 1–35.

Taylor, J.R. and Cooren, F. (1997) 'What makes communication "organisational"? how the many voices of a collectivity become the one voice of an organisation', *Journal of Pragmatics*, 27: 409–38.

Taylor, J.R. and Lerner, L. (1996) 'Making sense of sensemaking: how managers construct their organisation through their talk', *Studies in Cultures, Organisations and Societies*, 2: 257–86.

Taylor, J. R. and Van Every, E.J. (2000) *The Emergent Organisation. Communication as Site and Surface*. Hillsdale, NJ: Lawrence Erlbaum.

Waldron, V.R. (1991) 'Achieving communication goals in superior–subordinate relationships: the multi-functionality of upward maintenance tactics', *Communication Monographs*, 58: 289–306.

Weick, K.E. (1979) *The Social Psychology of Organizations*. New York: Random House.

Weick, K.E. (1995) *Sensemaking in Organisations*. Thousand Oaks, CA: Sage.

Weick, K.E. and Browning, L. (1986) 'Argument and narration in organisational communication', *Yearly Review of Management of the Journal of Management*, 12 (2): 243–59.

Zaleznik, A. (1992) 'Managers and leaders: are they different?', *Harvard Business Review*, March–April: 126–35.

6

The logic of message design in organisational argument

Shirley Willihnganz, Joy L. Hart and Charles A. Willard

Between 21 and 24 March, 1918, the allies on the Western Front were stunned by a powerful German breakthrough. In three days, the Germans decimated the British 5th Army and drove a wedge between the British and French armies. Their big guns would soon be bombarding Paris and the British 3rd Army's flank was exposed. In three days, the allies lost territory it had taken them two years to capture, 40-odd miles.

The German breakthrough frightened the allies into creating a unified high command, ostensibly the unified command structure they'd needed from day one. The allies' choice as generalissimo was Ferdinand Foch, who likened himself to an orchestra conductor. Foch was in a vague position. He was by no stretch a Supreme Allied Commander as Dwight Eisenhower would be. It wasn't even clear who he was answerable to, French Premiere Clemenceau or the Supreme War Council. And his authority was virtually undefined. Should he issue blunt orders, or visit commanders and try to persuade them? Foch decided that 'persuasion is all powerful . . . categorical imperatives are useless . . . The commander must be able to inspire confidence and the spirit of co-operation in his followers' (Foch, 1931: x).

For the rest of the war, Foch raced from one HQ to another, cajoling, encouraging, smoothing ruffled feathers, and complimenting prickly, inarticulate and not-very-intelligent men, who were prone to red-faced shouting. Foch kept them as far apart as possible, and, managing by automobile, wheedled them into cooperating in a final successful offensive across all 500 miles of the Western Front in late 1918. It was the most vast and complex undertaking in human history to that time. It broke the German army and ended the war. Foch had achieved a managerial miracle.

The First World War was an extreme case of a common problem. Joint action can suffer from too much agreement or too little. Too much like-mindedness leads to 'group think', where groups confirm their prejudices rather than test their ideas. Too little agreement makes joint action difficult, if not impossible. Charting a course between these extremes relies on the rhetorical and argumentative skills of the people involved. Comparatively unskilled communicators are often reduced to shouting matches or coalition politics that simply out-vote rather than test ideas. Skilled communicators can often employ rational and dispassionate analysis. Thus, an organisation's intellectual capital lies in the rhetorical and argumentative skills of its members. The underlying sources of these skills are the subject of this chapter.

Whether simple or complex, all messages are based on a communicator's implicit theory of communication. That is to say that people communicate for a reason: to accomplish some task that requires cooperation from another, or to achieve some desired effect. People differ, however, in their assumptions regarding how communication should be rightly employed to achieve the goal and in their ability to produce messages that will accomplish the objective. Those communicators, like Foch, who exhibit what O'Keefe (1988) calls a Rhetorical Message Design Logic, believe the function of communication is to 'negotiate selves and situations'. Those with the skills required to construct messages that take into account both the instrumental goals – Foch's need to gain the cooperation necessary to win the war – and the interpersonal needs inherent in the situation – soothing the ruffled feathers of the other generals – truly have the ability to create new worlds and new possibilities for action through talk. In this chapter, we will explore a view that puts individual differences in rhetorical and argument skills at the heart of organising. We look to Barbara O'Keefe's Theory of Message Design Logic to argue that only rhetorical communicators have the argument skills and vision to be 'practical authors'.

O'Keefe's message design logic and argumentation

Though the comparison of organisational life with a war zone must not be pressed too far, whenever people take joint action they create at least the potential for argument, and the risk of collisions among explosive personalities. Because organisations rely on cooperative action, the argument potential is staggering. Organisational actors frequently lack shared common goals. The path to shared goals is often unclear. Some are unwilling to surrender turf or personal prerogatives for the commonweal. And others may engage in what Kenneth Burke called a 'blunt quest of advantage'. For them, it isn't enough to succeed but, as Gore Vidal quipped, 'Others must fail'. And in the minefields of worker diversity, changing technology and markets, unstable economies, and a plethora of other large and small 'webs of competing interests' (Morgan, 1986), the manager's role is to author texts that align these conflicting and competing perspectives so that joint action is possible, even desirable. In such an environment, those gifted in argument and rhetorical skills will feel distinctly more at home.

Such a view is embedded in a larger social constructivist perspective. If organisations should produce both satisfied individuals and a coherent community, coordinated action is the end result of a balancing act of accommodation and assimilation (Willard, 1989). Social structures emerge from interactants' shared perceptions, and as shared creations they then exist at least partially outside any individual's control. Through communication, then, we create social structure, help ourselves understand what we have constructed, and work out the tensions between what we have created in the past and what we want to create for the future. Each communicative moment holds both institutional constraints and creative potential (Eisenberg and Goodall, 1997).

Some people are better at creating possibilities through communication than others. Organisational structures privilege some – managers have legitimate power because the organisation allocates it to them. But there are also individual differences in the kind of conversational control interactants can exert in a situation. At least some people are forward-looking and explicate events in hopes of predicting and controlling them (Kelly, 1955). Even within the constraints of culture, individuals have local strategic goals they pursue in the hope of getting what they need from communicative encounters. They construct messages they believe will bring them closer to these goals.

Seeing message creation as a strategic shaping of means to ends has been standard in the rhetorical and argumentation lore since Aristotle. Argumentation accounts for the relationships between message characteristics and the assumptions people use to create them, and an argument is loosely constructed based on the premises one uses to speak meaningfully in a context, to decide on the effects one can achieve with communication, and to select the best means of achieving those effects (Willard, 1989). Arguments can be seen as strategic adaptations that conversational partners use to increase their chances of achieving goals and to adapt to the exigencies and constraints of situations.

That people argue and communicate is obvious. How they do it, and why some are more effective, is not as simple to see. When one does directly examine messages, whether written or conversational, they seem to emerge as claims buttressed by evidence with the expectations of others taken into account. However, what emerge as relevant claims and expectations vary by individual, and are grounded in local strategic needs (Willard, 1989). Arguments are social encounters that assume disagreement. Once we recognise that we are arguing, we employ cognitive schemas appropriate to dissensual interaction.

Competency in argument is a skill similar to other interpersonal skills, requiring adaptation of linguistic and social knowledge to specific persons and situations to produce effective communication. As such, argument requires the cognitive ability to organise and marshal beliefs and interpretations, and implies a grammar for translating intentions into effective messages. This cognitive-developmental view assumes that the ability to make and interpret complex arguments develops like any other cognitive skill, such as language comprehension and problem solving (Clark and Delia, 1977). Burleson's (1983: 597) summary of the main claims of this perspective were paraphrased by Van Eemeren et al. as follows: '(1) reasoning uses underlying cognitive structures, (2) cognitive structures are clustered in content domains, (3) because people differ in cognitive development (their cognitive structures differ) their performances (for instance, arguing) will systematically differ, (4) these individual differences affect the nature and substance of the arguments people make, and (5) individual differences in reasoning processes affect the outcomes' (1996: 198).

Cognitive structure exhibits itself in the arguments people make, and in how they differ. Based on myriad examinations of messages, O'Keefe (1988) proposed the Theory of Message Design Logics. The theory assumes that all messages are premised on a communicator's implicit theory of argumentation and rhetoric, and illuminates the cognitive scaffolding one uses to speak meaningfully in a context, to decide what one can achieve with communication, and to select the best means of achieving these effects. O'Keefe calls these implicit theories Message Design Logics (MDLs). She terms these design logics 'Expressive', 'Conventional', and 'Rhetorical' – labels representing not merely a classificatory device for deriving coding schemes, but a grammar explaining the production of particular message characteristics. Unsurprisingly, they comprise developmentally progressive stages (the more complex subsuming their simpler precursors) corresponding to constructivism's orthogenetic view of development (Clark and Delia, 1977). Each MDL is a theory of what communication is, how it works and what it can accomplish.

Differences in MDL are manifested in people's uses of systematically different communication-constituting concepts (distinct implicit theories) that yield different patterns of message organisation and interpretation. Thus it is possible for the facts about how communication works to be systematically different for different people.

Expressive design logic and argument

For Expressives, the primary purpose of communication is to clearly express thoughts and feelings: one communicates so others can understand one's views. Expressives seem literal in their creation and understanding of messages. They don't see that expression can serve multiple goals, and 'they interpret messages as independent units rather than as threads in an interactional fabric, and so seem to disregard context' (O'Keefe, 1988: 84).

From this perspective, what can communication accomplish? For Expressives, 'the only job a message can perform is expression' (O'Keefe,

1988: 84). 'The idea that messages might be systematically designed to cause particular reactions is foreign and mysterious to the Expressive communicator – messages are understood as simple expressions of beliefs' (1988: 84). Thus, only two possible relations exist between speaker intentions and messages. One is that the speaker is relating thoughts and feelings fully and honestly, or alternately, distorting such views, either by editing them or misrepresenting them by lying. Expressives see a stark choice between revealing the whole truth – the ethical choice for them – or concealing part of the truth. Recognising that some expressions may be too harsh, Expressives may edit messages rather than violate broad-scale politeness considerations. But because Expressives are concerned with honesty and prone to regard conventional etiquette as phony or dishonest, they often motor through organisational waters leaving a trail of fuming victims in their wake.

Expressive messages typically contain pragmatically pointless content (e.g., a lack of editing, lengthy expressions of the speaker's wants, even if the listener has already heard them or can do nothing about them, marked redundancies, noncontingent threats, and insults). Expressives often utter whatever thoughts they generate in response to events. As such, expressive messages are often 'idiosyncratic and subjective rather than conventional and intersubjective' (O'Keefe, 1988: 86). Their messages tend to be past-focused – one reacts, rather than creates.

Messages that convey one's thoughts openly and truthfully are often respected in our society, and we have a certain awe of those who risk all to 'tell it like it is', and who 'don't pull their punches'. At its best, the expressive logic mirrors a surface interpretation of Habermas's (1984) ideal speech situation – among those of good will, authentic expression of thought will lead to a meeting of minds that will bring understanding and good solutions. The organisational fool is an almost mythic figure – ignoring politics, niceties and self-interest to speak what is true. Like the child in the fairy tale who pointed out that the emperor was wearing no clothes, the expressive communicator can often cut through layers of ambiguity and go right to the heart of the argument itself. Because many expressive communicators frequently do say exactly what they are thinking, communication is relatively transparent.

When a good person thinks good thoughts and expresses them appropriately, this logic can work. But, if the thoughts are hurtful, or inappropriate, blurting them out can do lasting harm. What if a communicator wants to argue for self-interest, correct the behaviour of another, or impede another's goal but also maintain a positive relationship while remaining polite and considerate? What if truth is not singular, and there are multiple truths to be selected among?

Argument is essentially interactional, requiring co-orientation, and to have a successful argument one must first be in a relationship. Because 'arguments are not just scenes in which autonomous bundles of strategic repertoires are bumping heads' (Willard, 1989: 48), expressive arguers are often less successful than others because they are unable to do more than react to previous utterances, often ignoring the relational implications of what they are saying. Expressive communicators are thus prone to disagreeable confrontations and often don't know when to quit, pressing their points despite their interlocutors' attempts to disengage. If one person wants to argue and the other doesn't, this dooms the interaction from the start.

In addition to their inability to maintain the relational elements required of arguers, Expressives also face problems in situations where goals conflict or diplomatic communication is required. In those situations, most expressive communicators will try to avoid a confrontation, or will edit or distort a message (lie) in an attempt to manage the relational predicament. Although these tactics steer clear of immediate disaster, they also effectively close off any possibility of joint, creative action to solve the problem.

Nor do they always use fully rational strategies. For example, a common situation for managers is the need to correct a subordinate while maintaining the person's positive identity. So, imagine a fairly straightforward situation where a team is working to meet a deadline. One member of the team (generally called Ron in O'Keefe's studies) hasn't completed his part in time for the group meeting when final adjustments were to be made. What might a manager say to Ron to get him to complete his part of the project?

An expressive communicator might say, 'You idiot! Don't you know how critical meeting this deadline is? You're fired.' Or better, 'What happened? Remember we needed to get this out today? You've been really irresponsible and hurt the group and now I'll have to find someone else to get it done. This is irresponsible and immature to leave the team in a lurch.'

These messages do not do anything to get the person to finish the job, do not propose a remedy to the problem (other than to have someone else do it), and may make the relationship considerably worse. They do little to advance the position of the manager, create a new reality with new possibilities for action, or work on relationship building. They remain locked in the constraints of a communication system that cannot expand to take a new situation (the job isn't done) into account. Frequently, expressive messages are little more than litanies of complaints, extensive expressions of wants, and/or threats (O'Keefe, Lambert and Lambert, 1993).

Conventional design logic and argument

The Conventional Design Logic assumes that 'communication is a game played cooperatively, according to socially conventional rules'. In this view, 'language is a means of expressing propositions, but the propositions one expresses are specified by the social effect one wants to achieve' (O'Keefe, 1988: 10). One plays the game, obeys the rules and fulfils one's obligations. For the Conventional, communication is constituted by cooperation and assumes a cooperative interlocutor. For example, politeness norms might rule out expressing one's thoughts. Additionally, one's thoughts or feelings might not be deemed relevant for the particular context, other party's needs or interests, and the goal(s) present. To avoid inappropriateness, conventional communicators work to determine relevant social resource systems upon which to draw. Since conventional communication is rooted in the present it's important to define both situation and appropriate roles/identities within the situation so one can behave properly. Conventional communication is often critical to smooth interaction, in that such things as politeness, cooperation and the likely achievement of goals are rooted in conventions, such as those found in the 'rules' of varying organisational cultures. Saying thank-you, phrasing orders as requests or asking if someone can stay late to finish a project when we both know they will have to are examples of conventional communication.

In determining conventional messages, 'one generally looks for some clearly identifiable core action being performed that is easily characterisable as a speech act . . . In contrast to expressive messages, which are characteristically psychological and reactive in their relation to context, conventional messages bear a rule-following relation to context. If one asks of a conventional message, why did the speaker say this now, the answer is generally that this is the normal and appropriate thing to say under the circumstances' (O'Keefe, 1988: 87).

From a conventional point of view, argument is a cooperative activity for handling dissensus and most argument theory explicitly or implicitly assumes a conventional logic. This convergence is not accidental. Having an argument requires that arguers possess adequate communication competence to form comprehensible utterances, and that they know the rules of the conversational system. Seeing argument as interaction requires that we see it as a matter of 'conversational rules and structures, as a matter of substantive disagreements, as a matter of goal directed behaviour and as a matter of intersubjective accomplishment' (Willard, 1989: 47).

A good deal of conventional argument occurs in organisations. Although expressive communication undoubtedly takes place – social interactions at least sometimes are marked by angry outbursts and real, often heated, disputes – organisational participants more frequently make claims, produce evidence, lobby hard for positions that either foster their own or perceived organisational objectives, or both. Specific examples of organisational work that has emphasised the structure of discourse in organisational argument include Heath's (1988) study of how rational argument was used by organisations promoting public policy issues; Allen and Burrell's (1992) and Hirokawa's (1985) studies of the effects of rational argument on participants in dyadic conversations and small groups; or Putnam and Geist's (1985) study of rational argument in bargaining.

The apparent fondness for conventional-type argument in organisations is not surprising. Normal language conventions (e.g., Brown and Levinson, 1978; Grice, 1975; Searle, 1969) exhibit a strong preference for agreement rather than disagreement (Jackson and Jacobs, 1989; Jacobs and Jackson, 1982). In practical terms, this means that as soon as disagreement becomes evident, the language structure itself pressures participants to begin 'repair work' that will bring the conversation back to agreement as smoothly as possible. In this sense, an argument is 'a special sort of disagreement regulating mechanism related in various structural and functional ways to a wide range of activities involving conflict and disputation' (Van Eemeren et al., 1993: 25). As disagreement is externalised and incompatible standpoints are expressed and brought into confrontation with each other, 'one exhibits one's linguistic competence through a public performance that summons explanation and reason giving, attack and defense, and these provide glimpses of the tacit knowledge behind the routines. Arguments, and argument forms, prescribed by a culture describe the background and tapestry of assumptions around an event' (Willard, 1996: 219).

If linguistic and cultural forms provide the invariant field for organisational argument, the specific culture of the organisation functions as a dependent field. Rules, roles, values and linguistic structures provide both the grounds for organisational argument and conventions that guide its enactment. The culture holds both the for and against aspects of argument (Willard, 1996: 217), in that argument performances reflect both the essence of an organisation's culture, and are themselves a product of it (Bergquist, 1993). So, in a strong organisational culture, arguments function as scripted routines, where roles and rules for how an argument should be conducted are already set. Organisational argument in this view is a distinctly social process enacted through locally sanctioned language games. Once created, proper argument procedures would produce and reproduce themselves, and organisational values, by inculcating members into the proper decision premises.

In part, the conventional logic is popular because it works. Most organisational situations are routine, and best handled routinely. The conventional logic makes joint action relatively straightforward because the goal of the interaction is cooperation. The conventional logic is so rooted in larger linguistic and cultural forms that much of what is considered to be 'normal' talk and argument follow its dictates.

Conventionals are not likely to be practical authors. The Conventional MDL is largely a script. And while a good script will produce a good performance, there is little room for improvisation. Conventional communication is not generally personal, but operates in terms of social norms and rules, regarded as fixed and immutable (O'Keefe, Lambert and Lambert, 1993).

This scripted nature of the Conventional MDL means that non-routine situations are problematic. Many situations display a degree of complexity that makes the critical assessment, 'What is happening?' difficult. Is this a situation that requires regulation? Comfort? Conflict management? Conveyance of bad news? For the Conventional, this initial assessment is critical, because the situational definition itself triggers the deployment of the proper conversational schema that should be used to respond appropriately. In examining corporate advocacy appeals, Putnam and Fairhurst note that 'the way that organisations respond to crisis situations parallels work on conversational repairs by focusing on how companies make excuses, provide explanations and justifications and offer apologies and recompense' (2001: 103). Part of this process involves labelling the crisis as an 'accident, a transgression, a faux pas, or sabotage, depending on whether the public sees the event as emanating from internal or external forces and from intentional or unintentional motives' (2001: 103). Once labelled, the organisation can then select from an array of strategic message choices designed to appeal to various publics and restore the organisation's good image.

So, to continue the example we used earlier of the team member who hasn't done his part of a project, a conventional communicator runs through a repertoire of rules and determines which apply. In this case, the employee has not kept a communicative promise – to get the job done on time. Because a promise has been broken, a fundamental cooperative principle has been breached, and the manager has the right to be angry, as well as the right to invoke punishments or sanctions. The manager's job is to regulate the behaviour of the other, and this almost always involves criticism. However, the ultimate goal is to get the employee to finish the job, so conventional messages keep that goal in mind. Again, a very minimal conventional message might still express the manager's unhappiness, but would provide concrete direction regarding project completion. So, an example in this case might be, 'You know how important this is, and I'm disappointed that you've let us down. We needed your part of the project done, and we were depending on you. I'm sorry I can't give you more time. You'll need to stay as late as you have to tonight, so we can at least get it out tomorrow. I know you won't want to let the team down again.'

Our manager is constrained not only by the organisational context, but also by the rules of social interaction defining the 'proper' way to reprimand an employee. The conventional manager can use generally accepted politeness forms in the message, and can even try to create a positive image of the other, but such messages always involve an imposition on the hearer, since they contain directives. The conventional manager is often in the position of having to couch harsh messages in a polite way.

If both participants employ a conventional logic, argument is relatively straightforward – we can generally predict how the conversation will turn, and if we both follow the rules we can largely predict the outcome. In the above example, the employee knows that expected rules have been violated. A good employee will try to make amends. A good manager will push the proper buttons to elicit the requisite behaviour and the problem will be solved. A really good manager will have an arsenal of strategies for doing this so that the choice of the best one can be adapted to the situation. For example, a manager might respond differently to an employee who has been facing personal problems than to someone who has been consistently underperforming – as our social rules would support.

Rhetorical design logic and argument

The basic assumption of the Rhetorical MDL is that 'communication is the creation and negotiation of social selves and situations.' In this logic, conventional knowledge is subsumed within a view of selves and situations as mutable rather than fixed. One sees meaning in terms of 'dramaturgical enactment and social negotiation . . . knowledge of the ways in which communicative choice and language style convey character, attitude, and definitions of the situation is systematically exploited (on the one hand) to enact a particular social reality and (on the other hand) provide "depth interpretation" of received messages' (O'Keefe, 1988: 87).

The function of rhetorical messages is negotiation. Different speakers can adopt different voices and thereby talk different realities: 'The one thing Rhetorical message producers must accomplish in a social situation is the achievement of a consensus regarding the reality in which they are engaged . . . finding a common drama in which to play' (O'Keefe, 1988: 88). Whereas the conventional logic works to invoke the appropriate norms based on the situation (e.g., Who am I expected to be in this situation? What are the relevant rules for behaviour in this situation?), the rhetorical logic tries to invent identities which will facilitate goal attainment (e.g., Who should I try to be to accomplish my objectives? What sort of arrangement might allow us to fulfil our goals?) Or, as Weick noted in describing the social nature of organising, 'How can I know who I am until I see what they do?' (1995: 23).

The Rhetorical MDL puts a premium on interpersonal harmony and consensus, works to maximise all goals so far as is possible, and uses these criteria to judge the effectiveness of interaction. Often multiple, sometimes competing, objectives come into play. Indeed, when multiple goals are not present, rhetorical communication is usually not necessary. Using a rhetorical logic is hard work because it requires careful listening, psychological analysis, and adaptation to others in the creation of intersubjective understandings.

Rhetorical messages have characteristic connections to context. They are proactive rather than reactive. 'If one asks of a rhetorical message, what connects all these elements as a common theme, the answer is generally: These elements can be interpreted as steps in a plan or as moments in a coherent narrative or as displays in a consistent character (and usually all of these). In short, the internal coherence of rhetorical messages derives from the elements being related by intersubjectively available, goal-oriented schemes' (O'Keefe, 1988: 88).

In argument, the Rhetorical assumes that communication creates situations and selves – thus, solutions often transform identity. 'If one assumes that selves are socially constituted, then they are changeable through taking on a different character in social interaction. This is the rhetorical solution – to cast oneself or one's partner into a role in a new drama in which there is not conflict of interest or implication of shame' (O'Keefe, 1988: 91). Rhetoricals tend to 'ignore power and resource control as a means of conflict resolution; they persistently underestimate the force of social convention and routine and overestimate the individuality and creativity of themselves and others. They value psychological analysis and careful listening, for these form the basis for deep and individualised interpretations against which to test an emerging sense of intersubjective understanding' (1988: 88).

The Rhetorical sees situations and selves as pliable and emergent. For them, argument cannot be 'a monolithic description of a single discourse derived from a unitary human nature, but [must be] a picture of a pluralism of discourse animated by many voices' (Willard, 1989: 40–1). Willard's *A Theory of Argumentation* takes a rhetorical position by explicitly defining argument as interaction. He says,

> Argument is a *cooperative* activity involving joint action, intersubjective meanings, and accommodations to people and institutions; an *intentional* activity involving speakers who mean to say particular things; and a *creative* and *strategic* activity involving not only listener adaptedness and strategic repertoires but also a *translation* of one's perceptions and intentions into particular communication strategies. To *adapt* to persons and situations is to attribute characteristics to them and to assess the fit between these attributions and one's intentions. To translate these cognitive achievements into strategies is to use one's communication knowledge to capture a functional fit between one's goals and messages' (1989: 40–41).

During an argument, the ultimate resolution is accomplished through a process of mutual adjustment whereby meanings, agreements and disagreements are enacted through conversational moves that are largely improvisational and accommodated to the other. Arguments are emergent – 'we make them up as we go along. We improvise, change course, and adapt to developments. Our positions flex and strain as we modify claims, concede points and attack the claims of others . . . we adjust our goals, calibrate our stances, and fine-tune our claims' (Willard, 1989: 68).

As summarised by Putnam and Fairhurst (2001), work on organisational argument and unobtrusive control suggests that organisations foster a sense of identification through naming events, stretching old meanings into new ones (Meyer, 1996; Tompkins et al., 1975), appealing to common ground and the use of the 'transcendent' we (Cheney, 1983; DiSanza and Bullis, 1999), changes in training of professionals (Bullis and Tompkins, 1989), and manuals used in quality circles (Stohl and Coombs, 1988). These studies, and an extensive body of work on organisational metaphor, foster the idea that organisations are 'argument fields' (Keogh, 1987) where conversations, texts and memories create the playing field for change through transformative discourse. Putnam and Fairhurst note that this growing body of work shows how 'decision premises embodied in organisational texts and inculcated through rhetorical strategies promote identification and underscore the pervasiveness of organisations as arguments' (2001: 105).

This view of argument places organisational power in the discourse system, and largely in the hands of the rhetorical communicator. The Rhetorical MDL provides a way of reasoning and a set of message strategies that can mitigate incommensurability through acknowledging and reconciling competing agendas. Potentially, Rhetoricals can work against 'containment' – resisting entrapment in conventional predicaments and structures. Rather, the rhetorical communicator can bring argument to its fullest ideal as a 'dialectic procedure that has as its aim true resolution of disputes' (Van Eemeren et al., 1993: 64).

To continue the example of the worker who doesn't have his part of the project done, rather than try to control the behaviour of the other, the Rhetorical may decide that support and reassurance would be better moves and actually comfort the employee who missed the deadline. Or maybe the rhetorical manager will listen to why the project isn't done and realise that the push to finish will actually harm the organisation and use that realisation to come up with a new goal, or abandon the project completely. The key idea here is that the rhetorical communicator is not constrained by what he or she is initially presented with and is free to rewrite the text in as many ways as organisational constraints allow.

Assuming the rhetorical communicator accepts the situational definition – the employee needs to get the project done – he or she can still produce a message that will potentially transform both the interactants and the situation. So, the rhetorical message might clarify intentions and perspectives, verbally negotiate goal conflicts, and attempt to influence situations by altering beliefs and values regarding what is happening. The rhetorical manager might say, 'Well, if it's not done, it's not. Why don't you tell me what you've got, then you keep working on it and I'll explain to the group that your part is coming, and we'll start getting the pieces we've got ready to go. That way, when your part arrives we can get it incorporated and out quickly. I know we all want to make this the best we can, and if you need a little more time to be sure we've got good quality, that's the most important thing. Take it easy, we'll get it done.'

Notice the rhetorical communicator assumes that the other is a hard worker who will complete the project, attributes lateness to a desire for a good product rather than laziness or lack of commitment, and suggests that the deadline can be extended a bit so the employee can feel good about the final product.

The example we've used here is a fairly simple one, but the principle would apply to many organisational situations where a manager has to redefine a situation and transform, innovate, or think out-of-the box. Our argument is that practical authors who can do this must be communicators who have such control over the cognitive and structural elements of language that they are capable of generating genuinely new responses to situations they face.

The rhetorical communicator as practical author

The Theory of Message Design Logics presents a model of strategic choice, and it predicts that managers vary in their responses to the contingencies they face according to their perceptions, their implicit theories, preferences, values and power. Further, it sets forth some assumptions regarding how and why such choices might be made.

Of the three logics examined here, the rhetorical communicator seems best suited to be a practical author. In his work on leadership, Bryman (1992) describes critical abilities required to be an effective manager. They include the ability to manipulate symbolism, create a vision and control rewards. Because rhetorical communicators essentially value joint creation, manage in ways that make shared goals central, and have extensive control over the language system, they are in the best position to assume leadership roles. Work by O'Keefe, Lambert and Lambert (1993) has shown that workers judge supervisors who employ rhetorical communication strategies to be more competent than those employing conventional logics, suggesting that these constructs are not just theoretical ones, but accurately encode real organisational preferences. These observations lead us to believe that critical to leadership is one's ability to engage and energise followers in carrying out the leader's agenda. And this requires a reciprocal relationship between leaders and followers. Only the rhetorical communicator sees a duality of agendas to reconcile. Since expressive communication is largely subjective, an expressive manager reacts in ways that foster personal, immediate concerns – in other words, people should do what he or she wants done. The conventional communicator would be largely impersonal, assuming the social structure itself would mitigate incommensurability – people should do what should be done. Only the rhetorical position acknowledges that a critical function of communication is to create a shared space where incompatible agendas are acknowledged and reconciled – we should do what we want done.

Rhetorical communicators seem to intuitively understand that any structure is essentially dualistic. They are not unaware of real structural constraints that exist in organisational life – Affirmative Action laws, sexual harassment policies, chains of command, procedures for mass mailings, and a myriad of other seemingly insurmountable organisational rules and procedures do exert pressures that constrain action. But rhetorical communicators also understand that since these structures were created and are continually re-enacted by human participants, there is a good deal of room for creativity. Storytelling, metaphor, dialogue, argument and transformation are all processes that can change the way that structure is shaped in any given moment. As Eisenberg and Goodall (1997) have noted, through communicative dialogue we can balance the constraints that restrict the range of activity with the exigencies that allow room for change agents to act.

Because rhetorical communicators' critical interest lies in reconciliation of the interests of parties involved they continually seek ways to enact or create a social structure that is compatible with achieving this goal. To do this, they improvise and rhetorical communication highlights the 'performance' nature of organisational argument (Pacanowsky and O'Donnell-Trujillo, 1983). Performances are those interactions that are interactional, contextual, episodic and improvised. O'Keefe (1988) has argued that differences between the design logics are manifested most strikingly when people need to manage multiple, even conflicting, goals, e.g., cases where one wants to criticise yet offer face protections to another person. In such cases, given that those with an expressive orientation believe that the purpose of communication is the clear expression of thoughts, the options are be direct and completely honest or be less than frank. The Conventional will be polite by using off-the-record communications and conventional politeness forms such as apologies, hedges, excuses and compliments (Brown and Levinson, 1978). The rhetorical frame creates a new drama, or new characters, so as to minimise the conflict of interest (O'Keefe, 1988). In terms of argument, then, the rhetorical communicator may be able to reframe situations in ways that allow room for action, rather than impasse, and intersubjectivity rather than individualism.

This ability to manage social resources may itself be a source of considerable organisational power. Organisations are socially constructed and sustained through the 'knowledge, practical routines, and technical devices mobilised by social actors and their everyday interaction and discourse' (Reed, 1996: 42). The 'production, codification, storage, and usage of knowledge relevant to the regulation of social behaviour become strategic considerations in the mobilisation' of organisational power (1996: 42). If indeed, organisations are 'texts composed of connections among arguments' (Tompkins et al., 1989: 36) the rhetorical communicator may be instrumental in setting the agendas that bring incompatible positions into enough alignment to allow some action to be taken.

Rhetoricals, however, tend 'to ignore power and resource control as a means of conflict resolution' (O'Keefe, 1988: 88). Because their primary motivation is not partisan, but political, they are actually better able to manage the tensions and paradoxes inherent in most organisations. When multiple truths are all present and pressuring organisational actors in competing and/or conflicting directions, the Rhetorical can take whatever position and whatever identity is best suited to movement. Some theorists have argued that organisational learning and innovation rest on maintaining the tensions that occur between 'disorganising and organising, forgetting and remembering, increasing and decreasing variety, between the inside and the outside, the old and the new, determining and emerging, freedom and responsibility' (Clegg and Hardy, 1996: 683). Clegg and Hardy note that maintaining these tensions and, more importantly, acting with them, will require new skills from managers. While not a new argument, the realisation that communication is critical to effective management has gained momentum, and those leaders who can establish trust, listen, create meaning and empowering environments, and who emphasise flexible, adaptive systems will be much more effective than those who control and/or command. Because rhetorical communicators rely on cocreation of both selves and situations, they are likely to possess the skills needed to be effective leaders in a new organisational learning environment.

Rhetoricals can tolerate more tension because like all those who exhibit a high degree of cognitive complexity they manage inferentially incompatible information better than low complexity people. So, relatively low complexity Expressives see situations as fixed structures of constraints, positions as stable and absolute, messages as fixed structures of meaning, and other people as similar to themselves. Conventionals see the situation as given but look for the rules, roles and relations relevant to the projects and observe the proprieties and follow the recipes for adapting their projects to the expectations of others. Rhetoricals attempt to negotiate shared definitions that make their project possible.

We began with an example of a rhetorical communicator, General Foch, who staged a battle that won a war. It was a battle constructed along lines that hadn't been tried before: huge in scope, significant in consequences. He was a practical author. He was relationally responsive and exhibited practical understanding. He improvised, relatively unfettered by past history and able to create a unique sense of shared circumstances and shared sense-making. Indeed, in the best sense of what practical authors can do, he made history. In this chapter, we have argued that being a practical author requires rhetorical and argumentative skills unique to a Rhetorical Message Design Logic. Our central argument is that certain social and cognitive skills and orientations lead one to interpret the world in logically consistent ways, and that those who see argument as dialogue that can lead to transformation and freedom will be in positions to foster changed environments and outcomes.

References

Allen, M. and Burrell, N. (1992) 'Evaluating the believability of sequential arguments', *Argument and Advocacy*, 28: 135–44.

Bergquist, W. (1993) *The Postmodern Organisation: Mastering the Art of Irreversible Change*. San Francisco, CA: Jossey-Bass.

Brown, P. and Levinson, S.C. (1978) *Politeness: Some Universals in Language Usage*. Cambridge: Cambridge University Press.

Bryman, A. (1992) *Charisma and Leadership in Organisations*. London: Sage.

Bullis C. and Tompkins, P.K. (1989) 'The forest ranger revisited: a study of control practices and identification', *Communication Monographs*, 56: 287–306.

Burleson, B.R. (1983) 'Interactional antecedents of social reasoning development: interpreting the effects of parent discipline on children', in D. Zarefsky, M.O. Sillars and J. Rhodes (eds), *Argument in Transition. Proceedings of the Third*

Summer Conference on Argumentation. Annandale, VA: Speech Communication Association. pp. 597–610.

Cheney, G. (1983) 'The rhetoric of identification and the study of organisational communication', *Quarterly Journal of Speech*, 69: 143–58.

Clark, R.A. and Delia, J.G. (1977) 'Cognitive complexity, social perspective taking and functional persuasive skills in second- to ninth-grade children', *Human Communication Research*, 3: 128–34.

Clegg, S.R. and Hardy, C. (1996) 'Representations', in S.R. Clegg, C. Hardy and W.R. Nord (eds), *Handbook of Organisational Studies.* Thousand Oaks, CA: Sage. pp. 676–708.

DiSanza, J.R. and Bullis, C. (1999) ' "Everybody identifies with Smokey the Bear": employee responses to newsletter identification inducements at the U.S. Forest Service', *Management Communication Quarterly*, 12: 347–99.

Eemeren, F.H. Van, Grootendorst, R., Jackson, S., and Jacobs, S. (1993) *Reconstructing Argumentative Discourse.* Tuscaloosa, AL: University of Alabama Press.

Eemeren, F. H. Van, Grootendorst, R., Henkemans, F. S. with Blair, J.A., Johnson, R.H., Krabbe, E.C.W., Plantin, C., Walton, D. N., Willard, C.A., Woods, J. and Zarefsky, D. (1996) *Fundamentals of Argumentation Theory: A Handbook of Historical Backgrounds and Contemporary Developments.* Mahway, NJ: Lawrence Erlbaum.

Eisenberg, E.M. and Goodall, H.L., Jr (1997) *Organisational Communication: Balancing Creativity and Constraint* 2nd edition. New York: St. Martin's Press.

Foch, F. (1931) *Memoirs of Marshal Foch.* London: Batford.

Grice, H.P. (1975) 'Logic and conversation', in P. Cole and J.L. Morgan (eds), *Syntax and Semantics*, 3, *Speech acts.* New York: Academic. pp. 41–58.

Habermas, J. (1984) *The Theory of Communicative Action, I: Reason and Rationalisation of Society.* Boston: Beacon Press.

Heath, R.L. (1988) 'The rhetoric of issue advertising: a rationale, a case study, a critical perspective – and more', *Central States Speech Journal*, 39: 94–109.

Hirokawa, R.Y. (1985) 'Discussion procedures and decision-making performance: a test of the functional perspective', *Human Communication Research*, 12: 203–24.

Jackson, S. and Jacobs, S. (1989) 'About coherence', in J.A. Anderson (ed.), *Communication Yearbook 12.* Newbury Park, CA: Sage. pp. 145–56.

Jacobs, S. and Jackson, S. (1982) 'Conversational argument: a discourse analytic approach', in J.R. Cox and C.A. Willard (eds), *Advances in Argumentation Research.* Carbondale, IL: Southern Illinois University Press. pp. 205–37.

Kelly, G.A. (1955) *The Psychology of Personal Constructs.* New York: Norton.

Keogh, C.M. (1987) 'The nature and function of argument in organisational bargaining research', *Southern Speech Communication Journal*, 53: 45–58.

Meyer, J. (1996) 'Seeking organisational unity: building bridges in response to mystery', *Southern Communication Journal*, 61: 210–19.

Morgan, G. (1986) *Images of Organization.* Thousand Oaks, CA: Sage.

O'Keefe, B.J. (1988) 'The logic of message design: individual differences in reasoning about communication', *Communication Monographs*, 55: 80–103.

O'Keefe, B.J., Lambert, B.L. and Lambert, C.A. (1993) 'Effects of message design logic on perceived communication effectiveness in supervisory relationships', paper presented at the annual meeting of the International Communication Association, Washington, DC.

Pacanowsky, M. E. and O'Donnell-Trujillo, N. (1983) 'Organisational communication as cultural performances', *Communication Monographs*, 50: 126–47.

Putnam, L.L. and Fairhurst, G. (2001) 'Discourse analysis in organisations: issues and concerns', in F.M. Jablin and L.L. Putnam (eds), *The New Handbook of*

Organisational Communication: Advances in Theory, Research and Methods. Thousand Oaks, CA: Sage. pp. 78–136.

Putnam, L.L and Geist, P. (1985) 'Argument in bargaining: an analysis of the reasoning process', *Southern Speech Communication Journal*, 50: 225–45.

Reed, M. (1996) 'Organisational theorizing: a historically contested terrain', in S.R. Clegg, C. Hardy and W.R. Nord (eds), *Handbook of Organisational Studies.* Thousand Oaks, CA: Sage. pp. 31–56.

Searle, J.R. (1969) *Speech Acts: An Essay in the Philosophy of Language.* Cambridge: Cambridge University Press.

Stohl, C. and Coombs, W.T. (1988) 'Cooperation or co-optation: an analysis of quality circle training manuals', *Management Communication Quarterly*, 2: 63–89.

Tompkins, E.V.B., Tompkins, P.K. and Cheney, G. (1989) 'Organisations, texts, arguments, premises: critical textualism and the study of organisational communication', *Journal of Management Systems*, 20: 35–8.

Tompkins, P.K, Fisher, J., Infante, D. and Tompkins, E. (1975) 'Kenneth Burke and the inherent characteristics of formal organisations: a field study', *Speech Monographs*, 42: 135–42.

Weick, K.E. (1995) *Sensemaking in Organizations.* Thousand Oaks, CA: Sage.

Willard, C.A. (1989) *A Theory of Argumentation.* Tuscaloosa, AL: University of Alabama Press.

Willard, C.A. (1996) *Liberalism and the Problem of Knowledge.* Chicago, IL: University of Chicago Press.

Authoring as a collaborative process through communication

Stanley Deetz

Authoring is a complex process. The very description of the manager as an author may be misleading and less than prudent. In many ways it evokes an image of the manager as a writer, singular and in control of the process, crafting words for an awaiting audience. But authoring is deeply social.

The words, genre, routines, conventions and places of speaking/writing, while resources for the author, are socially produced, shaping authors, providing sayings beyond those known or intended by authors, making possible the very sight/insight of the author. Further, the call to 'writing' is always a response to real situations at best only partly the making of the would-be author. The author always speaks from and to a social/historical place of which the author is made as well as trying to make.

And authoring is social at the receiving end. The produced 'text' is always fundamentally ambiguous and determinable in multiple ways. The text floats away from the author, open to new meanings, open to endless reinterpretations, saying more and less than the author might have hoped. The text becomes a resource for other speakers to shape and use to multiple ends. And it returns to the author opening the author to rethinking, new self-understandings, to seeing possible meanings and implications hidden in the moment of production. To understanding authoring requires understanding the ambiguities and complex contests for meaning in the organisational site.

As the constructionists have shown, the world is not a place of fixed social divisions, events and interests that are expressed and prohibited from expression by social structures and routine decision-making processes. Social divisions, events and interests are produced and reproduced in actual practices. They are an outcome of social processes as well as a determinant of them. What we need to investigate is how authoring plays in these processes.

One of the invisible struggles of our time is the incorporation of new understandings of language and communication into our public discourse and social institutions. Much of our liberal democracy and public and private lives are founded on eighteenth century conceptions of language as representational and communication as the transfer of meaning (see Deetz, 1992, 1994a). Our newer constitutive theories recognise all of us as authors but authors without necessarily knowing it. Recognising authoring poses new possibilities for creativity and an enriched social life, new responsibilities, and new forms of potential disregard and unobtrusive control.

Human beings have always been authors but their authorship has often been limited to the simple reproduction of meanings created by others. When one grows up in a culture one unwittingly consents to that culture, its language and its political arrangements. One fails to recognise opportunity, responsibility or forms of domination. The more homogeneous the culture the more likely this failure. Such citizens express freely but have no voice.

The presence of unexpected and often undesired diversity creates a problem for that world, but also tremendous opportunity. In a diverse social context particular cultures are seen as only one type of social arrangement. Cultural consent is more clearly seen as one of several possible choices. Culture becomes seen as that which can be maintained through control or can be open to constant negotiation. Authorship becomes visible and contested. Actualising the negotiative opportunities requires a new conception of communication appropriate for the new situation and new practices within organisations.

This chapter promotes the alternative conception of communication by showing the emerging opportunities for negotiation in various aspects of organisational life. Recognising that which was once taken for granted is a social construction made possible by new found diversity. Authorship is understood as having this possibility, as producing rather than reproducing social life. And, hence, the contest of and for meaning is recovered as a core issue. Processes of keeping contestation vital can be better understood. And we better understand new and more insidious forms of control in the workplace.

Eroding consensus and new arenas for negotiation[1]

Arising from its relatively homogeneous context, traditionally Western society has been based on four foundation faiths or centres that have been assumed as unproblematic in most modern conceptions of people and organisations. These foundations have been assumed by both traditional economic/ managerial and most stakeholder models of corporations. In a sense they have served as a kind of consensual background, which meant that many things did not need to be negotiated. Communication could assume these things rather than be about them. They are based in values and support power arrangements but these were rarely considered problematic because if everyone accepted the same, they appeared as part of the natural order. In this way potential conflicts over them were deeply suppressed. These foundations are a belief in the existence of (1) unitary-autonomous psychological persons who know their interests and are capable of freely subordinating themselves in contractual relations, (2) a legitimate consensual-integrative social order, (3) an objective external world and proper methods of discovering it, and (4) a grand narrative of a material progress-driven cybernetic. But it is precisely these that can no longer be taken for granted in contemporary society.

Within a heterogeneous society, in every discussion four agreements must be accomplished that can no longer be assumed at the outset: who we are; what order there is to our social relations; what exists; what is good, right and worthy of pursuit. As authors we initiate these implicit negotiations with four expressive productions: (1) we produce who we are (our relevant identity[ies]) and who others are to whom this expression is or might be addressed, (2) we define the social order or normative conditions enacted in relation to the other, (3) we constitute knowledge, perception, or a claim of what we consider to be true and worthy of commitment, (4) we project a value-laden vision of the way we wish to live together.

These accomplishments are outcomes of both explicit and subtle processes. For example, I was in a meeting of managers the other day. Partly arising from a recent reorganisation and partly arising from multiple bases of authority and expertise, the possibility of contestation across these four areas is often likely. In this case, the discussion concerned ways of distributing more decisional authority to lower levels of the organisation. The topic alone provided an interesting meta-text. After a half-hour active discussion, the director who headed the meeting, said: 'I think we've heard a lot of good ideas. Why don't I sit down with Stan, and Jim [the other director] and come back with a plan.' The managers looked at each other, and one replied, 'I think we are in a better position to work it out here.' Tension in the room was clear.

What was authored and what contested? Clearly, the director was speaking as director, but he was also claiming 'directorship'. Disagreement could be due to the director's desires or his producing himself as director, and in the discussion it was hard to determine which was the issue. He narrated a form of order and responsibility but he also opened possible contestation of whose and which order, whose and which authority. He produced a differentiation of forms or types of expertise in making a plan, but also enabled questions of whose knowledge and justified in what way. He implicitly evoked values of efficiency and master narratives of process/progress, but also potentially undermined self-determination.

Since in a homogeneous society the content of each of these arenas might be assumed for the sake of interaction, communication could be conceptually reduced to information transfer, i.e., speaking as a director. In a heterogeneous society, however, we understand that personal identities, norms of interaction, knowledge claims (and the way they appear as factual information), and value-laden policies directing joint action are potential negotiated products that cannot be seen as simple shared cultural resources for expression. These negotiations cannot be avoided as we also try to negotiate pay, determine which products to make, and decide how we will handle the environment. The most basic and stifling forms of managerial control in organisations are the attempts to fix these contestable realms so that negotiation is limited to decisions regarding products and services evaluated by profitability under the guise of neutrality. Much management talk works to suppress contestation in these realms rather than to author actively and openly in it. Such activities stifle creativity, hamper organisational adaptation and learning, and leave organisations less able to meet the needs of multiple stakeholders.

As genuine diversity grows in the wider society, considerably more resources must be allocated if control is desired in these realms. Finally, we reach a situation like today where the costs of control exceed the costs of negotiation on purely economic grounds. But the real loss from controlling, rather than embracing, diversity is the partiality of decisions. The negotiation process if open can lead to increased diversity within each member's self conception, better organisational knowledge and the opportunity to represent broader interests in the development of goods and services. Let us look at each of these areas of potential contestation.

Identity negotiation

As many contemporary writers have demonstrated, the concept of the person as an autonomous agent is largely a fiction with major consequences. In a traditional world, identity was a relatively simple thing. One was a particular person, with a gender, class, geography, occupation and specific role ascriptions. These were integrated with minimal role conflict within the person and served as guidance for interaction with others. In primary institutional processes (family and community) one came to reproduce the principal scripted identities that would order the world and self for life. The person was expected to display coherence, continuity and value commitments integrated in a life history (Meyer, 1986). These were never as fixed as our psychological and sociological theories would have us believe, they only appeared fixed due to the redundancy of reoccurring but momentary reproductions in highly stable systems. This conception could be mistaken as an intrinsic characteristic of the self because of the lack of competing scripts or interactions wherein one would be conceptualised differently. In homogeneous societies this confusion is common. One's cultural practices are easily seen as arising out of nature.

The fiction of a fully formed autonomous person has important consequences for social political processes and for the way we do business (Meyer, 1986; Meyer et al., 1987). If the person's insides are independently formed, fully known, and non-conflictual, only the granting of freedom is necessary for self-representation and full participation in decision-making. In fact the contradiction between a political democracy and autocratic work organisations is based on the assumption of freely chosen subordination in the work contract. To the extent that we understand that the person and his or her insides are the outcome of asymmetrical social processes and/or that the person's needs and interests might only be partially known, freedom of expression is seen as less sufficient. The politics of self-formation and inter-action processes that aid in exploring one's insides, and the construction thereof, become of central concern. The self is not a singular noun but a complex verb. Active authoring is a temporary writing of self in relation to others, a writing that takes place in social/historical contexts.

Following the situation of the director discussed earlier, director in this new context is given no specific meaning by nature, the organisation or social relations. Directorship is to be worked out with others. The specific individ-ual in the director position has certain advantages in the narrating process owing to institutionalised structural and economic arrangements as sedi-ments of past narrations. But, those advantages are only actualised by suc-cessful evocation and active consent of others to their acquired complementary positions.

Mobility, occupational change, cross cultural contact and so forth pro-duce less stable interaction systems, show how tenuous identities are and make more visible the processes of social production. Identities in contem-porary society are increasingly fragmented as the sequestering of experiential realms is reduced (we are simultaneously workers, managers, parents, chil-dren, calculators and lovers) and the inadequacy of presumed coherent his-torically derived identities and category markers becomes more evident (Henriques et.al., 1984; Hollway, 1991; Knights and Willmott, 1985, 1989). As Kenneth Gergen argued regarding our contemporary situation, 'persons exist in a state of continuous construction and reconstruction; it is a world where anything goes that can be negotiated. Each reality of self gives way to reflexive questionings, irony, and ultimately the playful probing of yet another reality. The center fails to hold' (1991: 5–6).

Changing identities, role conflict and role negotiation has become a way of life for modern people. Management literature on diversity, however, continues to treat personal identity in organisations as essentialist, categor-ical, coherent, singular and normalised by the dominant group. But, as is clear from many more sensitive literatures, the contemporary person is sub-ject to so many identity producing discourses that personal fragmentation and identity conflict are common today (Berger et al., 1973; Gergen, 1991). Diversity in the workplace is not just the inclusion of many groups of people who heretofore were not there, but the presence of new and conflicting identities of even the traditional white male. Thus the unitary, autonomous conception of the person is not only weak as a base for representation and cooperative decision-making but is an increasingly hard to hold fiction. All identity is relational thus as the possibility of alternative relational forms develops, identities develop with them. Reciprocally, the relational quality of identity means that the development of particular identities always involves positioning others in particular identities. Identity development is never simply a self process or responsibility. Authoring is a social process with responsibility to and for others. Becoming a subject is always a subjugation as well as a move of agency and subjugates as well as gives particular agency to others.

The loss of this simple unified self on the one hand creates coordination/control problems for the managers of the corporation since identities that could be taken for granted as a consensual basis for meaning now have to be negotiated. But identity fluidity and diversity create opportunities for both furthering control or for furthering responsiveness in environments. Control can be enhanced since the individual without a fixed identity is more easily shaped and the competition with alternative institutions which provide identities is less (Hollway, 1991). In contrast, responsiveness can be enhanced since if the diversity is preserved more perspectives can be brought to play in making decisions, the possibilities for both personal and organisational learning and growth are enhanced. Strategic interaction fosters the former, dialogic communication the latter. Both could be considered as forms of authoring, only the latter provided for a world together.

Corporate managers have long been in the identity business even before identities became so fluid. It is not just a casual part of producing products and services. The presence of diversity helps us see just how critical this has been. Advertising explicitly promotes particular identities for consumers including life-styles and segmented images of age, gender and race. But the work process fosters more (see DuGay, 1997). Social divisions, for example, between management, technical staff, labour and secretaries, are not just economic divisions of labour, they produce (and reproduce) particular identities. Dress codes and expectations, use of space, pay differences and informal rules of association function more to symbolically reproduce identities than fulfil any work related need (Knights and Willmott, 1985). Work rules and meaning systems constitute different identities for men and women (Mumby and Putnam, 1992). Such things as day care policies can either suppress the identities of being parent and worker and the potential conflicts, or open them to productive negotiations (see Martin, 1990).

As corporate decisions have always been significantly influenced by 'identities' needs', the continued presence of authority relations often supports more a manager's need for feeling respected and in control than production needs. Image production and face-saving take up a significant portion of most managers' time and energy. As my own research on 'knowledge-intensive' organisations showed, as outside constraints of social class, religion or family diminish, the manager is more and more in a place that he or she can be whatever can be authored or negotiated with others (Deetz, 1994b, 1998). Since getting resources and evaluation of products is intrinsically interconnected with social identities, identity work may exceed any other kind of work that a person does. In fact, identity production may well be the most important product of most companies. Management's commitment of both financial and non-financial resources to this can be seen in choice of products to be produced, office design, pay systems and types of advertising. It does not take long watching organisational decision-making, until it is clear that in most cases the effects of decisions on identity production and defence far better account for the decisions made than any economic criteria. Economics is often the reason *given for* decisions in a legitimation process but is rarely the reason *for* a decision.

As Erving Goffman argued, 'a formal instrumental organisation does not merely use the activities of its members. The organisation also delineates what are considered to be appropriate standards of welfare, joint values, incentives, and penalties . . . Built right into the social arrangement of an organisation, then, is a thoroughly embracing conception of the member – and not merely a conception of him [*sic*] *qua* member, but behind this a conception of him, *qua* human being' (1959: 164). Most modern organisational decisions and practices reflect more the construction of appropriate individuals than the making of products, services or profits. If this is an important extra-economic social product, who should be involved in what is produced? All stakeholders have a right of authoring rather than simply being authored.

Identity work strongly influences corporate decisions and reciprocally which individuals get identities that give rights of decisional participation. And internal and external identities are leading products of corporate decisions (DuGay, 1997). Stakeholders, thus, have a significant interest in what happens in these processes. Managerial attempts to stabilise identities in the corporation through various forms of cultural management and employees' attempts to beat the game through strategic image construction and impression management exclude other stakeholders from this increasingly important process in society and weaken the capacity of corporations to effectively meet human needs.

Social order negotiation

Social order like personal identity is largely unproblematic in traditional or fairly homogeneous societies. The combination of consensual social expectations and accepted authority relations based in an assumed natural order provided high social legitimacy and much voluntary compliance. Sometime in the 1960s much of this began to give away; by the 1990s one was as surprised by the places where legitimacy, order and lawfulness remained as by where they were gone.

While the types of crimes and ways of dealing with the lack of accepted authority differed across social groups, no group seemed immune. Even the highest levels of management in the name of profitability lost a connection to the values and order of the societies in which they were chartered. No institution or its leadership could presume legitimacy any longer, it had to be continually renegotiated in a sceptical environment. Order today is understood as authored, thus removing its simple connection to a natural order and calling upon specific activities for its accomplishment. Neither employees nor consumers will ever be as naive and trusting again. The faith in authority has failed. The ITS director in the earlier example laments his lack of authority with especially younger workers and those who have ready employment alternatives. He wishes for more simple acceptance of his rights as the director even as he tries to push decisional responsibility down the hierarchy. He wishes there was more talk following the rules than about the rules.

The old move of trying to booster traditional social orders through contrastive logics (especially prevalent during the cold war years) does not work well in contexts without clear external enemies. The old social contracts in business appear gone and everyone becomes a free agent understanding personal responsibility for self-development and advancement. As the legitimacy of larger corporations has fallen, increasingly employees have sought autonomy through seeking employment in smaller organisations, through self-employment, or through the protection of two income homes, where there is either a greater sense of justice or ability to overcome perceived unfairness. Where the failing legitimacy was conceptualised as the fault of the individual or they perceived no proactive options, they have turned to drugs, exit or even mental illness (Martin, 1993).

Certainly the business world has responded to this. The Second World War style manager is becoming a thing of the past especially in professionalised settings. While at times is it surprising how many old time autocrats still exist in organisations, of much more interest are the new forms of authority imposition that hamper the open negotiation of social order. Historically, the workplace order arose out of common practices and values of the relative homogeneous wider society. Managerial control strategies as a form of parenting could be direct because of this consensual background. With the waning of this background and the growing difficulty in finding host communities that provided it, managerial processes have became concerned with the production of local cultures (Knights and Willmott, 1987). If local cultures could be produced in which experience was constituted in management terms, managerial control and widespread participation could happen at the same time. Authoring takes on a strategic sense in this move to the demise of open construction.

As Alvesson (1987) argued, participation and empowerment programmes are run often more for the legitimacy they give current managers than the power and freedom they give lower level workers. Strong cultures became a modern term of an integrated social order. But, like in the case of fragmented identities, most have tried to reclaim a new version of the past rather than confront the continued building of social order and relations among organisational members as an ongoing organisational process (see Pinchot and Pinchot, 1993). While discourses of simple authority relations and tyranny disappear, new forms of control appear. The coordination of the development and expression of interests in this new context often leaves the singularity of interest both more pervasive and difficult to understand and detect. Even in industries where social and intellectual capital far exceed economic capital as a basis for adding value, little genuine employee auton-omy exists. Control systems as consent have been reproduced by those con-trolled, they speak on behalf of a managerial logic of control (see Deetz, 1995, chapter 8, 1998).

The non-negotiative character of these settings is hard to detect and developing processes of negotiation in the face of unobtrusive, cultural or clan control is difficult. But these settings may not be as immune to negotia-tion as it might appear. We have to change our ways of talking about order in very basic ways. Traditionally order was treated as a natural state; it only had to be discovered or deviant people normalised and brought into line. We talked of organisations and organisational processes as real things that had foundations and structure, and that could fall apart. These were of course always fictions that led to important misrecognitions and identifiable con-sequence (Gergen, 1992; Sandelands and Srivatsan, 1993). The fear of them falling down or falling apart was a metaphorically driven justification for management utilising old fears of being attacked or losing territory (from a time when those were life experiences). But once we understand the repro-duction of these fictions our interests change. Disorder seems the natural state, the interesting question is how we maintain a faith in order and a particular order in the face of this? That is, how do we author and sometimes author together? What are the processes by which order is secured and people disciplined (see Deetz, 1998; Foucault, 1977)? And with that comes the question of who gains from a particular constructed order and gains from people fearing its collapse? In light of local narrative production and cultural management, Joanne Martin (1992) has shown that organisational cultures are more fragmented, and usefully so, than the searchers for excellence believed. Why did we think cultures were integrated? Who gained from the belief and the efforts to make them so? And as many of the model strong cultures flounder, what are the ordering processes within fragmented settings (see Deetz, 1994c)? How, finally, do we productively contest orders and author new ones?

Stakeholders need to be involved in negotiation of social order principles not so that they will get it right – so that an old-fashioned stability will return – but, as a way to get order to match their ways of being together. Policies, partnering arrangements, work groups, work routines and structures need to be open to constant renegotiation as a discussion among equals. Responsive and responsible corporations are not built at one time to be forever repro-duced through power arrangements, they must be seen as constantly open to renegotiation in the sense of a bounded democratic process (see Deetz, 1992, chapter 12). *Organising* rather than *organisation* (Weick, 1979) is not only a better conception of how corporations exist, such a conception helps remind us of the need for organising, in our sense here, authoring, to be a fully participative process.

New legitimacy for the internal work environment is not the only issue. Just as authority relations in corporations extended outward into education and child-rearing practices, new social relations at work provide a model for communities and non-work activities. Quality products, legitimate distributions of income and greater social responsibility from leading corporations can do more than image construction activities to gain the support of the public, facilitate better decisions and social relations.

Knowledge negotiation

Gradually public understanding has come to accept what scholars have known for some time, objectivity was over sold for the sake of prestige for clusters of elite researchers, journalists, teachers and owners of knowledge. Constructionist theories of knowledge show that every perception, every claim is positional (Shotter, 1993; Shotter and Gergen, 1994). Knowledge itself is always authored. Agreement as to knowledge requires agreement as to its means of construction. The recognition that experience and truth claims are more artifactual than factual (more textual than referential) forces a new sense of negotiation without recourse to the outside or a foundation or privilege. Truth has a profoundly social character that in a heterogeneous society must be realised in discourse. So called facts are produced from political social processes.

In addition, mediated experience (via any number of technologies and storytellers) increasingly exceeds any direct sensory experience in society and in the corporation. Virtual reality is a reality for most even without new technologies. The combination of the two assure that the social negotiation of knowledge claims and experience itself will have to follow lines in which the appeal to an objective outside will be seen as a particular rhetorical ploy. The question we have to deal with is not whether the facts are true or whose facts are to be believed, but can diverse groups be represented in choosing processes for the construction of the full variety of facts (see Harding, 1991)?

Corporations continue to operate with a rather naive notion of the facts, information and the bottom line. The presence of massive databases and information transfer systems often cover up these construction processes and makes open negotiation more difficult. Reminiscent of the epistemological tyrants of the last generation who lived the slogan, 'whatever exists, exist to some extent and can be measured' and who thereby dismissed and distorted large classes of human experiences and judgements, a new generation believes that anything that exists can be 'digitalised'. So it can, but not without losses. All representational systems, however, have political consequences. Information is a social production and there is a politics of codification. Experiences are lost, distorted and transformed in codification. Some are better expressed in some media than others. Suffice it to say that when the production activities are hidden behind the presumed to be neutral information artefact, control happens and negotiation is hampered. Authoring cannot in this case lead to contestation. The presence of diversity makes negotiation more likely and more important.

Clearly, the public really wants to believe in an independent reality. The general appreciation of an anti-rhetoric rhetoric and the fascination with amateur shows, docudrama and reporterless style news are all genuine attempts to get behind the social constructions. But they cannot. Unfortunately, the combination of a belief in a reality and cynicism is disastrous for productive authoring. Both arguments over objectivity and appeals to relativism which kill arguments, make it more difficult to understand negotiation and social determination (Deetz, 1990).

But the strength of the claim of objectivity will only continue to decline. As work becomes more service and knowledge centred it becomes increasingly difficult to base judgements on objects or products (Bergquist, 1993: 223). The production of massive knowledge industries makes issues of knowledge construction of great social interest. As value differences between cultures have become clearer, even accountants have been much more ready to discuss the value basis of standard accounting practices and to discuss how values shape the economic facts (Arrington and Puxty, 1991; Laughlin, 1987). In the design of information systems, increasing attention is being given to the construction of information artefact and less to its distribution (Boland, 1987; Zmud, 1990). At an even more basic level Sless (1988) has shown how the forms used to collect data carry additional value premises. In such an environment, stakeholder involvement in the construction of knowledge is critical both to adequate representation of diverse values and for the legitimacy of the knowledge produced.

Policy negotiation

In traditional societies policies were rare since dominant values and people served alongside nature as cybernetic centres directing the system along some course toward a future. Values were integrated along the line of 'grand narratives' which provided a construction of history, defined positions, structured dominant conflicts and promised a particular future. These provided grounds for legitimacy by narrative discourse interweaving a relation to the natural and sacred (Lyotard, 1984). As these collapsed with rapid change, diversity and technological changes, in their place arose numerous competing 'local narratives'. In the corporate site with the development of the state and organisational complexity, explicitly formulated policies replacing shared values were central to social planning. Organisational complexity gave rise to the policy centre, strategic planning and information control mechanisms of today (Beniger, 1986). As more new technologies are available and pluralism increases, we will have more difference of position and less voluntary compliance along the line of dominant values, hence, either control will grow or the need for explicit policy debate will become greater.

Consensus on dominant values to guide policy choices can rarely be assumed today. Even widely assumed to be shared values such as economic advancement and dominion over nature, the grand narrative of modernity, are likely to be more fully questioned as ecological crises become greater and more parts of the world expect equality. Women and African-Americans often hold values that differ greatly from dominant white male values.

Greater numbers of individuals appear willing to accept jobs with lower pay for the sake of other values. Growth is expected to be balanced more with proper care of the environment. Clearly more visions of the future are being authored.

In the space created by the demise of grand narratives and the competition of local narratives, new control systems have tried to set aside value issues. The pursuit of means is substituted for the pursuit of ends. In such systems means become treated as if they were ends, thus suppressing or concealing value debate. Policies related to the accomplishment of these new ends appear value neutral. The pursuit of performativity (heightened efficiency) and money become the clearest ends in these new systems (Lyotard, 1984). But neither is an end. Performativity only makes sense in regard to the pursuit of some social good (Carter and Jackson, 1987). Its value is derived from the value of that good. And money fulfils no need in itself, but is a means to need fulfilment. The instrumentalisation of people, life and work where everything is valued only in its contribution to increased means toward an unspecified end, not only raises moral questions in itself (Habermas, 1984) but allows for the massive dedication of social resources toward somebody's ends without active discussion or choice.

Perhaps this is clearest today in the discussions of the relation between technological innovations and competitiveness. When a technology is valued because of competitive advantages rather than social good, our thought is skewed in particular ways. First, competitive advantage is only secured by being there first and sustained by limiting the access of others to it, while social good would suggest spreading the technology as widely, as quickly, as possible. The competitive advantage is wiped out to the extent that social good is pursued. The focus on competitiveness as a value in itself always pits the corporation against social good. Secondly, the competitiveness discussion is a substitute for a discussion of social good. The questions do not concern the goodness or appropriateness of the technology or the cost and benefits of its various by-products. Competitiveness is treated as a meta-value, before and in place of other values. And, additionally, competitiveness constructs others as outsiders and antagonistic. 'Us' and 'them' are treated as unproblematic and the costs of 'us/them' thinking are disregarded.

To the extent that ends can be discussed, a greater number of positions on each social problem is likely as well as a greater number of differences in the definition of what is a problem. In this situation it is not surprising that many tried to depoliticise these issues through deregulation and a hope for a marketplace solution, an unauthoring author. Dollar (yen, mark) voting appeared preferable to policy debate. Clearly the marketplace solution has failed miserably in terms of representation and is highly value-laden (see Schmookler, 1992). Values always have been central to policy decisions and cannot be hidden behind performativity measures. The loss of consensus makes them visibly so. The questions that remain concern whose values and how open will be the process of negotiation. What social goods will be pursued effectively and with money? Expressed values of managers are changing towards more openness to employees, customers and the environment, unfortunately these have not yet transformed the basic conceptions of corporations or the basic practices of management (see Posner and Schmidt, 1992).

The potential value debates of greatest interest are not over espoused or easily known and conceptualised values (Schein, 1992). More fundamental values are of issue. These are usually embedded in linguistic distinctions, perceptual attention, decisional premises, routines and standard practices (Bourdieu, 1991). Many of these are so deeply assumed that they are difficult to discover and discuss. New communication concepts and processes are required. They are significant because they form the unproblematic ground for nearly all decisions in a thoughtless and innocent fashion. But when the way they differentially support different stakeholders is considered, they are anything but innocent. They frequently distort the interests of those enacting them in routine practices. Regular periodic reconsideration of policies, routines and standard conceptions is a first step to revealing these underlying values and initiating meaningful discussion.

A new authoring

If foundational faiths are gone, we are confronted with choices and responsibility which cannot be simply pushed to the outside by some grand causal force. *It is ours to choose the world and future, we are held responsible for it, and we must do it in conditions of fundamental uncertainty.* Individuals in the workplace face a double insecurity. Neither any thing nor any one will take care of them and they must make decisions without knowing for sure what is right. Often people settle for a contemporary type of waiting for Godot (see Shotter's, 1993, development). The hope and waiting itself gives meaning. I suspect that some of this supports the leadership fetish in the United States. Someone will come. But even if people individually prefer the burdens of subordination to the burdens of freedom, can we collectively survive without asking more of ourselves? Perhaps we have not yet learned well how to be free and secure. The response options to indeterminancy and insecurity are of central importance. The loss of stability can instead lead to more active negotiation with others, greater democracy and acceptance of responsibility. The pressure can be to make work more meaningful and reclaim the conflicts arising from multiple identities and needs leading to reform of the workplace.

Similar processes happen with knowledge of the world as happen with identity. The loss of secure foundations for knowledge is set aside with a preoccupation with large amounts of information. But the presence of information cannot make up for the fundamental uncertainty of knowing. Thus more information is sought and the individual heads down the road of increased disconnectedness from others and the world. The individual solves the wrong problem. The lack is not of objective, neutral, certain information of the world. The problem is the inability to produce knowledge with others in an uncertain and contested world. Information is a faulty defence against 'the unsystematic, unstructured nature of our experiences. [The] impersonal idioms we use in talking about them [these experiences] give us respite from the unmanageable flux of lived experience, helping us create illusory word-worlds which we can more or less easily manage because they are cut off from the stream of life. In this sense, objectivity becomes a synonym for estrangement and neutrality a euphemism for indifference' (Jackson, 1989: 4). Insecurity can lead to less and less engagement with others and the world and a disengaged understanding. The inability to make a world with others is an expected outcome.

So what do we do in a world that is opening up and requiring more constant negotiation and at the same time is producing an insecurity that leads people to close down and avoid negotiation? We are not going to get the old world back, so the answer rests in developing trust in making decisions with others. Nothing does more for this than making some good decisions together. Unfortunately, managers have acquired a keen sense for creating discussions where good decisions cannot be reached with others (see Argyris, 1986; Deetz, 1992, chapter 7). People cover up, and they cover up that they covered up. The undiscussable issues must be made visible and discussable if the cycle is to be broken. The constant production of crises and insecurity is an effective way to keep democracy from happening.

Giddens (1991) points us in the right direction when he suggests that we have spent too much time with actualities, trying to protect conceptions of self and world and have not focused enough on potentialities. Concern with how we prefer to live together should precede concern with identity and truth. Issues of morality and meaning cannot be avoided. As Gergen (1992) made clear, the final judge of any organisational theory is: does it lend itself to developing patterns of social life we like? Our task has to be the opening up of potentialities in apparently closed situations if insecurity is to give way to the comfort of respecting and working equably with others. Managers can start by breaking their own cycle of insecurity. One way is to complicate their view of subordinates by being around them, by learning more about their concerns, needs values, goals, competencies and environments. But further, communication training must aim towards skills in fundamental negotiation. This is a task that is difficult and finally must be a joint achievement of all stakeholders.

We begin by accepting our insecurity and the new spaces for negotiation both inside and outside, alone and together. If we cannot understand our own legitimate internal conflicts, which we either suppress or live with, we can neither understand the legitimacy of the difference of the other nor see conflicts as productive with him or her. Rather than segmenting our lives into historically given categories of private/public, home/work, emotions/reason, everyday/Sunday, we must accept these together as always part of us, as intertwined in our decisions regarding our needs and in those of the environment or others. And to the extent that we can be open to others we engage in the discovery of forgotten and lost needs, hopes and desires as well as the creation of tastes, thoughts and feelings not heretofore possible. A more advanced conception of communication processes is central to helping us overcome implicit consent to the false authority of foundations and discursive closures (Deetz, 1992) and facilitate being fully human – that is, author a world filled with thought, care and good humour (see Deetz and Stephenson, 1986).

Note

1   The remainder of this chapter draws on Deetz (1995).

References

Alvesson, M. (1987) *Organisational Theory and Technocratic Consciousness: Rationality, Ideology, and Quality of Work*. New York: de Gruyter.

Argyris, C. (1986) 'Skilled incompetence', *Harvard Business Review*, September–October: 74–9.

Arrington, C. and Puxty, A. (1991) 'Accounting, interests, and rationality: a communicative relation', *Critical Perspectives on Accounting*, 415–36.

Beniger, J. (1986) *The Control Revolution*. Cambridge: Harvard University Press.

Berger, P., Berger, B. and Kellner, H. (1973) *The Homeless Mind: Modernization and Consciousness*. New York: Random House.

Bergquist, W. (1993) *The Postmodern Organisation: Mastering the Art of Irreversible Change*. San Francisco, CA: Jossey-Bass.

Boland, R. (1987) 'The in-formation of information systems', in R. Boland and R. Hirschheim (eds), *Critical Issues in Information Systems Research*. New York: Wiley. pp. 363–79.

Bourdieu, P. (1991) *Language and Symbolic Power*. Cambridge: Harvard University Press.

Carter, P. and Jackson, N. (1987) 'Management, myth, and metatheory – from scarcity to post scarcity', *International Studies of Management and Organisations*, 17: 64–89.

Deetz, S. (1990) 'Reclaiming the subject matter as a guide to mutual understanding: effectiveness and ethics in interpersonal interaction', *Communication Quarterly*, 38: 226–43.

Deetz, S. (1992) *Democracy in the Age of Corporate Colonization: Developments in Communication and the Politics of Everyday Life*. Albany, NY: State University of New York Press.

Deetz, S. (1994a) 'The future of the discipline: the challenges, the research, and the social contribution', in S. Deetz (ed.), *Communication Yearbook 17*. Newbury Park, CA: Sage. pp 565–600.

Deetz, S. (1994b) 'The micro-politics of identity formation in the workplace: the case of a knowledge intensive firm', *Human Studies*, 17: 1–22.

Deetz, S. (1994c) 'Representative practices and the political analysis of corporations', in B. Kovacic (ed.), *Organisational Communication: New Perspectives*. Albany: State University of New York Press. pp. 209–42.

Deetz, S. (1995) *Transforming Communication, Transforming Business: Building Responsive and Responsible Workplaces*. Cresskill, NJ: Hampton Press.

Deetz, S. (1998) 'Discursive formations, strategized subordination, and self-surveillance: an empirical case', in A. McKinlay and K. Starkey (eds), *Foucault, Management and Organisation Theory*. London: Sage. pp.111–20.

Deetz, S. and Stephenson, S. (1986) *Managing Interpersonal Communication*. New York: Harper-Collins.

DuGay, P. (1997) *Production of Culture, Culture of Production*. London: Sage.

Foucault, M. (1977) *Discipline and Punish: The Birth of the Prison*, translated by A. Sheridan Smith. New York: Random House.

Gergen, K. (1991) *The Saturated Self: Dilemmas of Identity in Contemporary Life*. New York: Basic Books.

Gergen, K. (1992) 'Organisational theory in the postmodern era', in M. Reed and M. Hughes (eds), *Rethinking Organisation*. London: Sage. pp. 207–26.

Giddens, A. (1991) *Modernity and Self-identity: Self and Society in the Late Modern Age*. Stanford: Stanford University Press.

Goffman, E. (1959) *The Presentation of Self in Everyday Life*. Garden City, NJ: Doubleday.

Habermas, J. (1984). *The Theory of Communicative Action, Volume 1: Reason and the Rationalization of Society*, translated by T. McCarthy. Boston: Beacon.

Harding, S. (1991) *Whose Science? Whose Knowledge?* Ithaca, NY: Cornell University Press.

Henriques, J., Hollway, W., Urwin, C., Venn, C. and Walkerdine, V. (eds) (1984) *Changing the Subject*. New York: Methuen.

Hollway, W. (1991) *Work Psychology and Organisational Behavior*. London: Sage.

Jackson, M. (1989) *Paths Toward a Clearing: Radical Empiricism and Ethnographic Inquiry*. Bloomington: Indiana University Press.

Knights, D. and Willmott, H. (1985) 'Power and identity in theory and practice', *The Sociological Review*, 33: 22–46.

Knights, D. and Willmott, H. (1987) 'Organisational culture as management strategy', *International Studies of Management and Organisation*, 17: 40–63.

Knights, D. and Willmott, H. (1989) 'Power and subjectivity at work: from degradation to subjugation in social relations', *Sociology*, 23: 535–58.

Laughlin, R.C. (1987) 'Accounting systems in organisational contexts: a case for critical theory', *Accounting, Organisations, and Society*, 12: 479–502.

Lyotard, J.-F. (1984) *The Postmodern Condition: A Report on Knowledge*, translated by G. Bennington and B. Massumi. Minneapolis: University of Minnesota Press.

Martin, J. (1990) 'Deconstructing organisational taboos: the suppression of gender conflict in organisations', *Organisation Science*, 1: 339–59.

Martin, J. (1992) *Cultures in Organisations: Three Perspectives*. Oxford: Oxford University Press.

Martin, J. (1993) 'Inequality, distributive injustice, and organisational illegitimacy', in J.K. Murnighan (ed.), *Social Psychology in Organisations*. Englewood Cliffs, NJ: Prentice Hall. pp. 296–321.

Meyer, J. (1986) 'Myths of socialization and of personality', in T. Heller, M. Sosna and D. Wellbery (eds), *Reconstructing Individualism: Autonomy, Individuality and Self in Western Thought*. Stanford: Stanford University Press.

Meyer, J., Boli, J. and Thomas, G. (1987) 'Ontology and rationalization in the Western cultural account', in G. Thomas, J. Meyer, F. Ramirez, and J. Boli (eds), *Institutional Structure: Constituting State, Society and the Individual*. Newbury Park: Sage.

Mumby, D. and Putnam, L. (1992) 'The politics of emotion: a feminist reading of bounded rationality', *Academy of Management Review*, 17: 465–86.

Pinchot, G. and Pinchot, E. (1993) *The End of Bureaucracy and the Rise of the Intelligent Organisation*. San Francisco: Berrett-Koehler.

Posner, B. and Schmidt, W. (1992) 'Values and the American manager: an update', *California Management Review*, 34: 80–94.

Sandelands, L. and Srivatsan, V. (1993) 'The problem of experience in the study of organisations', *Organisation Studies*, 14: 1–22.

Schein, E. (1992) *Organisational Culture and Leadership*, 2nd edition. San Francisco, CA: Jossey-Bass.

Schmookler, A. (1992) *The Illusion of Choice: How the Market Economy Shapes our Destiny*. Albany: State University of New York Press.

Shotter, J. (1993) *Conversational Realities: Constructing Life through Language*. London: Sage.

Shotter, J. and Gergen, K. (1994) 'Social construction: knowledge, self, others, and continuing the conversation', in S. Deetz (ed.), *Communication Yearbook* 17. Newbury Park, CA: Sage.

Sless, D. (1988) 'Forms of control', *Australian Journal of Communication*, 14: 57–69.

Weick, K. (1979) *The Social Psychology of Organizations*, 2nd edition. Reading, MA: Addison-Wesley.

Zmud, R. (1990) 'Opportunities for strategic information manipulation through information technologies', in J. Fulk and C. Steinfield (eds), *Organisations and Communication Technology*. Newbury Park, CA: Sage. pp. 95–116.

PART FOUR

Rewriting the script, rescripting the author

Conversations and the authoring of change

Jeffrey D. Ford and Laurie W. Ford

There are two basic approaches for understanding the way in which organisation change is produced and managed. One approach is based in the objectivist, structural-functionalist tradition that there is an underlying, ordered pattern to the nature of reality, and that it is possible to come to know and represent this pattern (Burrell and Morgan, 1979). In this view, 'true' reality exists independent of the observer, and increasing one's knowledge of this objective reality is tantamount to increasing the accuracy and scope of one's ideas, models or representations of that reality. In this view, language is simply a tool for description in which words correspond to objects in the world.

In the structural-functional approach, the job of a change manager is to understand this reality and to align or adapt the organisation to it through appropriate interventions (French and Bell, 1995). Since gaining knowledge is seen as creating an increasingly accurate understanding and reproduction of an objective reality, it is assumed that the extent to which a manager's representations are accurate and correspond with that reality is the extent to which the change interventions will be successful. This means that ineffective or unsuccessful changes reflect a misunderstanding or misrepresentation of 'how things really work', prompting a search for bias in managers' misinterpretations of reality (Fombrun, 1992; Huff and Schwenk, 1990). Under these conditions, the management of change becomes a dual issue of the change manager's knowledge about the underlying reality and his or her ability to adjust the organisation for correspondence with that reality.

A second approach is based in a constructivist tradition in which the reality we know is interpreted, constructed or enacted through social interactions (Berger and Luckmann, 1966; Holzner, 1972; Watzlawick, 1984; Weick, 1979). In this view, our knowledge and understanding of reality is not a mirror of some underlying true reality, nor is knowledge a reproduction of that reality. Rather, knowledge is itself a construction that is created in the process of making sense of things. Since it is not possible for managers to know any true reality independent of themselves, what they come to know and understand as reality is an invention where the inventors are unaware of their invention and consider it as something that exists independent of themselves. In this case, change is not a response to a shift in understanding that corresponds more closely to some underlying truth, but rather is a function of a shift in the constructed reality.

In the constructivist approach, change managers use interventions not to bring about a greater alignment with a true reality, but rather to construct, deconstruct and reconstruct organisational realities, i.e., to author new realities. Since constructed realities provide the context in which people act and interact, shifts in these realities open new possibilities for action and the realisation of new orders of results. In other words, shifts in context provide for shifts in action which provide for shifts in the results that are produced. By the same token, continuation of existing realities means a continuation of corresponding actions and results. In this context, the job of change managers is to author realities in which people and organisations are more effective in achieving desired outcomes (Block, 1987; Senge, 1990).

The power of conversations

The reality of organisations that we experience occurs in conversation. At the most basic level, conversations are 'what is said and listened to' between people (Berger and Luckmann, 1966; Zaffron, 1995). A broader view of conversations as 'a complex, information-rich mix of auditory, visual, olfactory and tactile events' (Cappella and Street, 1985: 2), includes not only what is spoken, but the full conversational apparatus (Berger and Luckmann, 1966) of symbols, artefacts, theatrics, etc. that are used in conjunction with or as substitutes for what is spoken including emotion. The speaking and listening that goes on between and among people and their many forms of expression in talking, singing, dancing, etc. may all be understood as 'conversation'. People speak nonverbally through facial expressions, emotions and body movements, and with or without the use of instruments or tools. Similarly, listening is more than hearing, and includes all the ways in which people become aware of or notice themselves and the world. When conversations are considered in this broader context, 'one may view [an] individual's everyday life in terms of the working away of a conversational apparatus that ongoingly maintains, modifies, and reconstructs [their] subjective reality' (Berger and Luckmann, 1966: 172).

Conversations are omnipresent in organisations and can range from a single speech act, e.g., 'Do it', to an extensive network of speech acts which constitute arguments (Reike and Sillars, 1984) and narratives (Fisher, 1987). Conversations may be monologues or dialogues (Reigel, 1979) and may occur in the few seconds it takes to complete an utterance, or may unfold over hours, days or months. A single conversation may also include different people over time, as is the case with the socialisation of new people in an organisation (Wanous, 1992).

Although most of the conversations of which we are aware are explicitly spoken (verbally or nonverbally), much of the way in which they support the apparent continuity of a reality is implicit, by virtue of background conversations or what Harré (1980) calls latent structures and Wittgenstein (1958) calls the form of life. A background conversation is an implicit, unspoken back drop or background against which explicit, foreground conversations occur, e.g., 'its hopeless'. Background conversations are a result of our experience within a tradition that is both direct and inherited. They are manifest in our everyday dealings as a familiarity or obviousness that pervades our situation and is presupposed by every conversation. Yet, in spite of this pervasiveness, we are unaware of these background conversations and they remain unnoticed until there is a breakdown in which a background presumption is violated (Winograd and Flores, 1987).

Background conversations are already and always there (Harré, 1980), contributing to the intertextual links on which current conversations build and rely. It is this intertextuality of conversations, as well as an accumulated mass of continuity and consistency that maintains and objectifies our reality (Berger and Luckmann, 1966; Watzlawick, 1990). Objects exist for us as independent tangible things located in space and time and which impose constraints we cannot ignore (e.g., brute force [Searle, 1995]); they are manipulable, and we can do something with and to them (Holzner, 1972; Watzlawick, 1990). Although conversations are ephemeral, when they become objectified we grant them the same permanence as objects by assuming that they exist as some 'thing' independent of our speaking them. But this is not the case. Conversations have no existence or permanence other than when they are being spoken and it is we who speak them (Bergquist, 1993).

The realisation that conversations objectify and are themselves objectified is important to any manager interested in authoring new organisational forms because it means that conversations are both the process and product of objectification, i.e., conversations both create and become reality (Bergquist, 1993). What managers author when they author organisational changes, therefore, are linguistic products, i.e., conversations that are interconnected with or displace other linguistic products to form a new intertextuality of conversations we experience and talk about as organisation. And, what managers use in the process of authoring these new linguistic products are linguistic products. We use conversations to create, maintain or end conversations that create new contexts for action and results.

This process of authoring new conversations through conversations is evident in Barrett et al.'s study of the introduction of Total Quality Leadership (TQL) into a Navy Command (Barrett et al., 1995). As Barrett et al. point out, the introduction of TQL involved the introduction of a new language (set of conversations) through existing orders of discourse. Although everyone in the organisation was exposed to the same new language of TQL, their responses to it were different. Initially some people questioned the new language, pointing out inconsistencies, questioning the authenticity of those proposing it, and complaining. As both the number of people speaking the new language and the degree to which the new language was spoken increased, however, people began to invent and add new language (what Barrett et al. call 'nascent scripts'). This increase in TQL-related vocabulary provided a new background set of conversations that provided a basis both for sense-making and for taking new, novel forms of action. As the new vocabulary expanded, it replaced and transformed the older vocabulary, made new actions that were previously unimaginable possible and altered underlying assumptions and beliefs.

What is significant about the Barrett et al., study is that it clearly shows the progressive expansion of a conversation (TQL) within an organisation through the use of and invention of other conversations. It also shows, as Shotter (1993) points out, that strong feelings can be aroused when the introduction of new talk undermines our already established ways of talking. New talk can undermine our understanding of the world and the dynamically sustained context of the relations inside of which our life occurs. For this reason, new talk can be seen as dangerous and responded to accordingly. In the case of the introduction of TQL, the response was like a contest between the new language and the existing language as to which one would prevail. This contest was evidenced in the challenges to and complaining about the new language and whether or not it will take hold or be just another passing fad. However, as the TQL conversation persisted in being spoken, it began to spread and events were interpreted and explained using the new vocabulary. As new conversations were added ('nascent scripts') and people became habituated to the new language, a new context evolved inside which new actions that were previously unimaginable became possible and the background assumptions and beliefs of the organisation altered. At this point, the new vocabulary had successfully established itself within the network of conversations and the change was 'institutionalised'.

The power of conversations, therefore, rests in the realisation that they create our reality and the context inside which action is or is not possible. Conversations provide the context in which the world occurs for people, and their actions are correlated to those occurrences (Winograd and Flores, 1987). When these conversations shift (or are shifted in the case of organisational change), reality shifts and with it what can and can't be done. Conversations modify reality by virtue of whether or not something is talked about. Dropping conversations or adding them to a network of conversations will weaken some aspects of reality while reinforcing others. If something is not talked about for a long enough period, it ceases to be an integral part of the organisation's regular set of conversations. Certain management fads are an example of things that people once talked about but do no longer. By the same token, talking frequently about something makes it more real, particularly if a variety of different people do the talking.

When managers make 'declarations of change', they create new futures (realities) inside of which existing relationships alter, get redefined and unfold newly. Shotter (1993) gives an excellent example of this in his description of what happens when someone in a relationship declares 'I love you'. At that moment, a new reality is brought into existence and whatever relationship did exist is forever altered, following a trajectory given by the declaration. Although Shotter's example revolves around a reciprocated declaration, it is important to realise that regardless of the second person's response, the relationship is altered in the moment the declaration is spoken. Given this power of conversations, it is no surprise that declarations of change can evoke powerful reactions and resistance (Bryant, 1989; Hermon-Taylor, 1985). Managers engaged in authoring changes are not simply engaged in communicating change, they are engaged in declaring new realities that alter existing relations.

Organisations as networks of conversations

Within the constructivist perspective taken here, organisations are networks of concurrent and sequential conversations (Bergquist, 1993) that establish the context in which people act and thereby set the stage for what can/will and cannot/will not be done (Schrage, 1989). Planning, budgeting, hiring, firing, promoting, etc. are all conversations that constitute organisations and provide the context in which action is taken. Other constitutive conversations are conversations for and about authority, leadership, rewards, reengineering, competition, customers, resources and management, among others.

Organisations as networks of conversations do not mean that there are organisations and there are networks of conversations among the people within them. Rather, it means that conversations exist and a particular network of these conversations *are* the organisation. There is no organisation independent of that which is authored, maintained and referenced in conversations, including background conversations. If all the conversations for and about an organisation were to cease, there would be no organisation.

Many of the conversations in organisations engender commitments that can be fulfilled through special networks of recurrent conversations in which only certain details of content differentiate one conversation from another (Winograd and Flores, 1987). For example, recurrent requests for customer service create a predictable pattern of recurrent conversations within the organisation called 'customer service'. Recurrent conversations are particularly important in the authoring of organisations and organisational change because they are embodied in the offices and departments that specialise in fulfilling some part of the engendered commitments (Winograd and Flores, 1987). Indeed, jobs, offices and departments are existence structures for the conversations they embody, thereby ensuring that those conversations, and their correlates and derivatives, continue to be spoken and engaged with. In a very real sense, jobs, offices and departments are the protectors and purveyors of habitualised conversations and their commitments.

These recurrent conversations come to constitute a type of structural coupling between two or more participants (e.g., individuals, groups and departments) in which the participants work to maintain that coupling, i.e., their recurrent patterns of conversation, in the face of environmental perturbation (Maturana and Varela, 1987). Since structural coupling is always mutual, changes in the conversations that constitute the coupling requires a change in the conversations of all participants so coupled. In this sense, we exist in a network of structural couplings that continually weaves our conversations, linking them in a network of conversations (Maturana and Varela, 1987). The phenomenon of structural coupling underscores the fact that no organisation conversation can be treated in isolation, but only as part of a network. It also underscores that conversations and patterns of discourse hold other conversations in place, thereby contributing to what is experienced as resistance to change. Structural coupling implies that resistance in a network of conversations is not a function of individual attributes and conditions, but of the conversational context within which people are located. If this context can be revealed and shifted, resistance will disappear and change can move forward.

Not all conversations are the same

Although what can and can't be done, and what will and won't be done is a function of the conversations within an organisation, not all conversations are the same when it comes to the authoring of change. In our work, we distinguish two domains in which conversations may reside: committed and uncommitted.

Commitment, in the domain of communication set forth here, is not an experience, nor a deeply heartfelt sentiment, nor an obligation. It is a fundamental element in the acts of speaking and listening. Every language act has consequences for all participants, since by making a statement, a speaker is 'entering into a specific engagement, so that the hearer can rely on him' (Habermas, 1979: 61). This is what we mean by commitment, an intention to be engaged in certain ways in the future. Speech act theory recognises the importance of commitment as a first step towards dealing adequately with meaning (Searle, 1969, 1975).

Committed conversations

There is a minimal implicit commitment in every conversation which is granted by the commitment in the speech acts that constitute the conversation (Winograd and Flores, 1987). In some conversations, there is an additional level of commitment associated with the conversation as a whole, which commitment is senior to and inclusive of the commitments of the individual speech acts. This is a commitment on the part of one or more of the participants in a conversation to be accountable for the content of the conversation as well as the form and for having the conversation make a difference. This additional level of commitment is not necessary for a conversation, but, when it is present, the conversation is called a *committed conversation*.

Committed conversations are conversations *for* something, as compared to conversations *about* something, and include a commitment to accountability in speaking and listening. As a speaker, the participant is willing to be understood and related to as to their speaking, i.e., their word. That is, one is willing to be held to account for their speaking and its effects and impacts. As a listener, the participant is similarly accountable for what is heard or noticed in the conversation. In a committed conversation, both the speaker and the listener are engaged in and accountable for moving the action forward. Committed conversations, therefore, are conversations that create, direct and forward the action and for which the participants are accountable.[1]

Uncommitted conversations

Uncommitted conversations are conversations *about* something and are spoken by people who are not accountable for taking action or producing a result in the area in which the conversation is being held. For example, someone who complains 'They should do something about . . .', is talking about something that others should do and is not stepping up to or declaring themselves accountable for taking the actions needed to produce the result. In this context, uncommitted conversations are those conversations that offer commentary, opinion, evaluation, assessment or judgement about what is being observed with no intent of taking any action to make something different happen. If someone offers a criticism about a proposal, for example, but does not offer a way to improve or move the proposal forward, they are engaged in an uncommitted conversation.

Understanding the difference between committed and uncommitted conversations is critical to anyone engaged in authoring change. Committed conversations move things forward, make things happen and produce breakdowns or breakthroughs. Uncommitted conversations, on the other hand, slow things down or even stop the action altogether. We are all familiar with the person who raises objections without offering any constructive alternative, or who asks questions only to quarrel with the answer. Both are examples of uncommitted conversations that slow down what is happening, even though the speakers may insist that they are trying to help.

Oakley and Krug's (1991) work suggests that the rate at which changes are implemented is a direct function of the ratio of committed to uncommitted conversations. In particular, they suggest that as the ratio of committed to uncommitted conversations increases, so does the action and results associated with a change. Indeed, in both our educational and consulting work, we have been able to dramatically improve the effectiveness of hundreds of managers at implementing changes, including those considered impossible, with no change in other organisational conditions and circumstances, by having them shift from uncommitted to committed conversations. Shifting conversations has been effective even in those cases where people lack authority or other artefacts of position that are sometimes seen as necessary for change. For example, in one case a master's student was able to bring about a change in university parking policy and in another case a PhD student was able to get a new major approved and implemented.

The authoring of change, therefore, occurs in committed conversations. And, since managers engage in conversations every day, they have the opportunity in each and every conversation to choose between having a committed or uncommitted conversation.

Four types of committed conversations

In their work on organisational change, Ford and Ford proposed that there are four different types of committed conversations that managers use in the effective implementation of change. These are initiative, understanding, performance and closure conversations.

Initiative conversations

An *initiative conversation* is the call or proposal that creates an opening for change. In an initiative conversation, someone communicates that there is an opportunity for change with an assertion (e.g., 'We need to do something about the deteriorating situation in the East'), a request (e.g., 'Will you approve our undertaking a new programme to restructure the department?'), a promise (e.g., 'We will reduce the budget deficit by 25 per cent this year'), or a declaration (e.g., 'We will substantially increase the availability of health care'). The public promise of President Kennedy to put a man on the moon by the end of the 1960s was an initiative conversation sufficient to produce a massive change effort in NASA. The working components of initiative conversations are phrases like 'I propose . . .', 'Tell me what should we do about . . .?', 'We are going to . . .', 'It is time we undertake . . .', and 'What do you think about . . . ?'. Initiative conversations may arise in any of several different places: in informal meetings in which people discuss existing conditions and circumstances out of the visions that individuals have for what could be (e.g., Kouzes and Posner, 1993) or as a result of other change processes within the organisation. And, in any one interaction, several initiative conversations may arise, as in meetings where participants make multiple proposals, throw out multiple ideas or suggest multiple options.

While most initiative conversations die almost immediately, others are explored to a greater or lesser extent in conversations for understanding.

Conversations for understanding

Conversations for understanding are the conversations in which people seek to comprehend or understand what's behind the initiative conversation and come to a determination regarding what, if anything, will or could change. It is in conversations for understanding that participants work to make sense of and test initiative conversations by examining the assumptions, evidence, etc. that underly them, and to reflect on the implications of that thinking by questioning, challenging, supporting, etc. what is said. Through conversations for understanding, participants develop and add language to initiative conversations (Barrett et al., 1995), thereby creating a shared context (Ashkenas and Jick, 1992) that allows them to come to some understanding of the relative merits of a change, the reasons for it, and how they stand relative to it (e.g., support or resist).

Conversations for understanding are important in the authoring of change because they produce two important by-products. The first and most substantive by-product is the specification of the *conditions of satisfaction* for the change. Conditions of satisfaction give the measurable and observable conditions, requirements or measures (Kanter et al., 1992) that must be met in order for the change to be declared successful. Although there will almost certainly be miscellaneous, unintentional or unexpected outcomes, authors of change will want to specify the conditions that will exist when the change has been completed and the time frame within which these outcomes will be produced (Winograd and Flores, 1987). Generalities and ambiguity (cf. Eisenberg and Goodall, 1993), such as 'establish a new allocation process to improve performance' are insufficient if change authors expect to determine whether actions taken are effective.

A second by-product is some degree of *involvement, participation, and support* on the part of those engaged in the change. This by-product is particularly important because it provides people with a rationale, context or meaning for the change and an opportunity to express their concerns, ideas and suggestions (Kanter et al., 1992; Kotter, 1996). Where these conversations are missing or are incomplete, people may not understand what is happening or know their role in the undertaking, and may resist change efforts (Beer, 1980).

Authors of change will want to be aware that the foundational commitment of conversations for understanding is understanding, not action. Only conversations for performance (discussed below) are committed to making something happen. This means that no matter how well someone understands a change, they cannot be relied on to take action. And if they do act, understanding does not ensure that the appropriate actions (i.e., ones that forward accomplishment) are taken. For example, just because someone understands the organisation is moving to a team-based approach, and can cite all the reasons why, does not mean that they know to take action, what actions to take or when to take them. The failure to recognise that the commitment of conversations for understanding is understanding can result in change authors spending inordinate amounts of time trying to have people understand in the hope that once they understand, they will act. If managers are really interested in action, they will want to use conversations for performance.

Conversations for performance

Conversations for performance include what Winograd and Flores (1987) call 'conversations for action', which are networks of speech acts with an interplay of requests and promises spoken to produce a specific action and result. Requests ask another to take an action or produce a result by some deadline, e.g., 'Will you call my boss now and tell him I will not be at the meeting today?' Promises, on the other hand, specify the actions or results someone (including the speaker) has said they will produce by some deadline, e.g., 'I promise to have the sales figures for you by the end of today.' Together, requests and promises form the backbone of conversations for performance.

Conversations for performance call for a commitment to produce specific actions and results in time, not on the transmission of a request or promise, and not on their meaning. When someone makes a promise, or accepts a request, they are committed to taking the action or producing the result specified in the request or promise by the time specified. Conversations for performance, therefore, are intended to make things happen by having people in action. This means that by increasing the frequency with which they use conversations for performance, change managers can substantially increase the velocity with which changes are implemented (Goss, 1996).

Conversations for closure

Conversations for closure (Ford and Ford, 1995) are characterised by the use of assertions, expressives and declarations to bring about an end to an event or happening. Bridges (1980) proposes that where changes have not been closed or completed, people are left dissatisfied with the lack of closure. All subsequent attempts to introduce change will occur within this 'conversational space' of incompletion and dissatisfaction. In a sense, the incomplete past defines and colours the future, and people are not really free to move on until closure has been brought to the past (Albert, 1983, 1984). Conversations for closure are committed to completing the incomplete past, with all its attendant expectations and interpretations of failure and fulfilment. Closure allows the past to remain in the past, which makes possible a new recognition of what is actually present, and thus a new opportunity to create what's next (Goss et al., 1993).

Closure is essential to change. It implies a sense of harmonious completion wherein tension with past events is reduced or removed and balance and equilibrium are restored (Albert, 1983). One important aspect of conversations for closure is acknowledgement. Conversations for closure acknowledge accomplishments, failures, what has been (was) and has not been (was not) done, thereby allowing people to complete their contribution to the change and the results of that contribution, favourable or unfavourable. Conversations for closure also acknowledge that, whether the change was completely, partially or not at all successful, there is now a different future available, which contains new opportunities and problems that were not available before the change.

Conversations and the authoring of change

Authoring change within a network of conversations calls for an alteration in our understanding of what constitutes change in general and a change in particular. Traditional, structural-functionalist perspectives talk about a change as if change managers were removing or replacing one object or object-like thing with another (Ford and Ford, 1994). Even if it is acknowledged that there are many parts, stages or components, the change is nevertheless represented as if it has object-like properties and clearly defined parameters that exist independent of the conversations in which it is embedded. At best, conversations are simply tools that are used to put the change in place (Ford and Ford, 1995). Within the context considered here, however, such a monolithic view of change is problematic.

A change, like the organisation in which it occurs, is not monolithic discursively. Rather, a change is more appropriately seen as a polyphonic phenomenon (Hazen, 1993) within which many conversations are introduced, maintained and deleted (Barrett et al., 1995; Czarniawska, 1997) in such a way that a particular outcome is realised (Ford and Ford, 1994). This perspective is evident in Czarniawska's (1997) study of Swedish government agencies where changes were constituted by a series of conversational episodes organised around particular themes (e.g., decentralisation or computerisation). It is also evident in Elden's (1994) observation that the transformation of Magma Copper occurred in a 'myriad of many, mostly small, local activities' initiated on a local level within a common commitment to a possible future. Barrett et al. (1995) have also found that the implementation of a change occurs through a myriad of local conversations in which new conversations are invented inside a specific commitment or theme; in their case, a commitment to the implementation of total quality leadership (TQL).

Within a conversational perspective, there is no *the* change, like an object, that is being produced. Rather, change is an unfolding of many conversations within a general theme (Czarniawska, 1997), new vocabulary (Barrett et al., 1995), or metalanguage (Elden, 1994), most of which cannot be anticipated and must be generated locally in the moment. Indeed, every time change managers introduce a conversation, they need to engage in a variety of conversations depending on who they are talking to, where and when. In this sense, change in a conversational context is like experimental theatre or improvisational jazz where the script (music) is being written while it is being performed (Boje, 1995; Czarniawska, 1997). Although there is an intended result or outcome that is to be achieved, the specific conversations that are needed, with whom and when have to be generated on a moment to moment basis. Indeed, as Barrett et al. (1995) have found, an entirely new language, the specifics of which cannot be anticipated, is generated as a change grows and spreads within an organisation. For this reason, managers and the people they work with are ongoingly engaged in authoring the context in which they will work, and as this context shifts, the work that can and does get done also shifts.

Because the conversations required for producing a new intended outcome (i.e., a change) cannot be anticipated, the production of any change involves the generation and dynamic unfolding of many conversations that interplay in different ways. The failure to recognise change as this unfolding of micro-conversations within a macro-conversation robs change agents of their power in conversations and shelters them from their responsibility for authoring the conversations. Indeed, it is the very inconspicuousness of individual conversational events that generate and sustain change, that makes their actual relevance little noticed and underestimated (Hatch, 1999; Lynch, 1996). Yet, as can be seen in the case of epidemics, transmission need not proceed conspicuously to amass an enormous host population or produce dramatic conversational shifts (Ford, 1999).

Where organisations are networks of conversations, authoring change becomes a matter of shifting (e.g., changing the content, type and focus) conversations (Pascarella, 1987). Shifting conversations is accomplished by abandoning the speaking of some conversations (e.g., 'Why we can't') and deliberately introducing and repeating new conversations (e.g., 'What needs to happen?'). For example, the executive of one organisation was able to overcome complacency and increase the competitiveness of a utility by introducing and sustaining a conversation for phantom competitors (Johnson, 1988). Even in the case of a mining company that appears to operate solely using tangible processes for taking rock out of the ground and turning it into metal, the reality of those processes occurs in the conversations of the organisation. To change the organisation or some process in it, the managers must shift the conversations in which the processes take place and are understood (Zaffron, 1995). Since conversational (constructed) reality provides the context in which people act and interact, shifting conversations shifts reality, thereby providing new opportunities for action and results. A key to making these shifts is to move from uncommitted to committed conversations.

Change managers always have a choice in what they talk about. They can be reactive, complaining about what they see as wrong, the obstacles they perceive as inhibiting or stopping them, or the way things really should be in some idealised world. They can also be proactive, talking about what they want to accomplish, what will make that possible, and how they can get it done. Since what change managers talk about reflects what they pay attention to, the choice of whether to speak complaints or possibilities will make a difference in the progress of change (Oakley and Krug, 1991). When the proportion of proactive, or facilitating, conversations increases against the proportion of reactive, or inhibiting conversations in an organisation, the velocity of change also increases (Grant 1995; Oakley and Krug, 1991). This suggests that if change managers use proactive and facilitating conversations in their authoring of change, while discontinuing the use of reactive and inhibiting conversations, there will be a shift in their effectiveness. Consistent with this observation, we have found in our own work that where managers focus on what is needed to make something happen, and then engage in committed conversations for having it happen, they are far more successful. Others have found similar results (e.g., Oakley and Krug, 1991; Scherr, 1989).

Conclusion

The authoring of change occurs within and via conversations (Ford and Ford, 1995) in which new contexts are created and new actions taken. Rather than simply a tool in the production of change, conversations are the medium through which the construction, deconstruction, and reconstruction of realities occurs. In a network of conversations, change is a recursive process of social construction in which new realities for effective action are created, sustained and modified in conversations (Ford and Backoff, 1988).

In this context, change managers are engaged in bringing into existence, expanding and managing new conversations until they become part of the organisation's network of conversations and are able to provide a framework for effective action. Rather than bringing about a new alignment with the environment, or a correspondence between the organisation and some true reality, change managers work to create and shift networks of conversations to produce intended results. The effectiveness of an organisation change is thereby a function of the change manager's ability to identify the network of conversations that is operative in the organisation, and to add, modify and delete conversations in that network until the desired outcomes are realised or the project is ended.

Note

1 While it is possible to hold anyone to account for what they say, regardless of whether it is a committed or uncommitted conversation, we are using account-ability from the standpoint of who the speaker and listener are *being* in the conversation. In uncommitted conversations, people are just talking with no intention of *being* accountable and if you call them to account, they are likely to be upset. However, in committed conversations, both the speaker and the listener are *being* accountable for moving things forward and willingly (intentionally) do so knowing that they can and will be held to account.

References

Albert, S. (1983) 'The sense of closure', in K. Gergen and M. Gergen (eds), *Historical Social Psychology*. Hillsdale, NJ: Erlbaum. pp. 159–72.

Albert, S. (1984) 'A delete design model for successful transitions', in J. Kimberly and R. Quinn (eds), *Managing Organizational Transitions*. Homewood, IL: Irwin. pp. 169–91.

Ashkenas, R. and Jick, T. (1992) 'From dialogue to action in GE work-out: developmental learning in a change process', in W. Pasmore and R. Woodman (eds), *Research in Organizational Change and Development*. Greenwich, CT: JAI Press. pp. 267–87.

Barrett, F., Thomas, G. et al. (1995) 'The central role of discourse in large-scale change: a social construction perspective', *Journal of Applied Behavioral Science*, 31 (3): 352–72.

Beer, M. (1980) *Organization Change and Development: A Systems View*. Santa Monica, CA: Goodyear.

Berger, P. and Luckmann, T. (1966) *The Social Construction of Reality*. New York: Doubleday and Co.

Bergquist, W. (1993) *The Postmodern Organization: Mastering the Art of Irreversible Change*. San Francisco, CA: Jossey-Bass.

Block, P. (1987) *The Empowered Manager: Positive Political Skills at Work*. San Francisco, CA: Jossey-Bass.

Boje, D. (1995) 'Stories of the storytelling organization: a postmodern analysis of Disney as "Tamara-land"', *Academy of Management Journal*, 38 (4): 997–1035.

Bridges, W. (1980) *Transitions: Making Sense of Life's Changes*. Reading, MA: Addison-Wesley.

Bryant, D. (1989) 'The psychological resistance to change', in R. McLennan (ed.), *Managing Organizational Change*. Englewood Cliffs, NJ: Prentice Hall. pp. 193–5.

Burrell, G. and Morgan, G. (1979) *Sociological Paradigms and Organisational Analysis*. London: Heineman.

Cappella, J. and Street, R. (1985) 'Introduction: a functional approach to the structure of communicative behavior', in R. Street and J. Cappella (eds), *Sequence and Pattern in Communicative Behavior*. London: Edward Arnold. pp. 1–29.

Czarniawska, B. (1997) *Narrating the Organization: Dramas of Institutional Identity*. Chicago, IL: University of Chicago Press.

Eisenberg, E.M. and Goodall, H.L. Jr (1993) *Organizational Communication: Balancing Creativity and Constraint*. New York: St. Martin's Press.

Elden, M. (1994) 'Beyond teams: self-managing processes for inventing organization', in M. Beyerlein and D. Johnson (eds), *Advances in Interdisciplinary Studies of Work Teams, Volume 1*. Greenwich, CT: JAI Press. pp. 263–89.

Fisher, W. (1987) *Human Communication as Narrative: Toward a Philosophy of Reason, Value, and Action*. Columbia, SC: University of South Carolina Press.

Fombrun, C. (1992) *Turning Points: Creating Strategic Change in Corporations*. New York: McGraw-Hill.

Ford, J. and Backoff, R. (1988) 'Organizational change in and out of dualities and paradox', in R. Quinn and K. Cameron (eds), *Paradox and Transformation: Toward a Theory of Change in Organization and Management*. Cambridge, MA: Ballinger Publishing. pp. 81–121.

Ford, J.D. (1999) 'Conversations and the epidemiology of change', in W.W. Pasmore and R. Woodman (eds), *Research in Organizational Change and Development Vol. 12*. Greenwich, CT: JAI Press. pp. 480–500.

Ford, J.D. and Ford, L.W. (1994) 'Logics of identity, contradiction, and attraction in change', *The Academy of Management Review*, 19: 756–85.

Ford, J.D. and Ford, L.W. (1995) 'The role of conversations in producing intentional change in organizations', *The Academy of Management Review*, 20: 541–70.

French, W. and Bell, C., Jr (1995) *Organization Development*. Englewood Cliffs, NJ: Prentice Hall.

Goss, T. (1996) *The Last Word on Power*. New York: Currency Doubleday.

Goss, T., Pascale, R. and Athos, A. (1993) 'The reinvention roller coaster: risking the present for a powerful future', *Harvard Business Review*, (6): 97–108.

Grant, G. (1995) *Strategic Quality Management: Creative Tension in Action*. Calgary, AL: Strategic Links Incorporated.

Habermas, J. (1979) *Communication and the Evolution of Society*. Boston, MA: Beacon Press.

Harré, R. (1980) *Social Being: A Theory for Social Psychology*. Totowa, NJ: Littlefield, Adams and Co.

Hatch, M.J. (1999) 'Exploring the empty spaces of organizing: how improvisational jazz helps redescribe organizational structure', *Organization Studies* 20 (1): 75–100.

Hazen, M. (1993) 'Towards polyphonic organization', *Journal of Organizational Change Management*, 6 (5): 15–26.

Hermon-Taylor, R. (1985) 'Finding new ways to overcome resistance to change', in J. Pennings and Associates (eds), *Organizational Strategy and Change*. San Francisco, CA: Jossey Bass. pp. 383–411.

Holzner, B. (1972) *Reality Construction in Society*. Cambridge, MA: Schenkman Publishing Co.

Huff, A. and Schwenk, C. (1990) 'Bias and sensemaking in good times and bad', in A. Huff (ed.), *Mapping Strategic Thought*. New York: John Wiley and Sons. pp. 89–108.

Johnson, P. (1988) 'Why I race against phantom competitors', *Harvard Business Review*, 66(5): 105–12.

Kanter, R.M., Stein, B.A. and Jick, T.D. (1992) *The Challenge of Organizational Change: How Companies Experience It and Leaders Guide It*. New York: Free Press.

Kotter, J. (1996) *Leading Change*. Boston, MA: Harvard Business School Press.

Kouzes, J. and Posner, B. (1993) *Credibility: How Leaders Gain and Lose It, Why People Demand It*. San Francisco, CA: Jossey-Bass.

Lynch, A. (1996) *Thought Contagion: How Belief Spreads Through Society*. New York: Basic Books.

Maturana, H. and Varela, F. (1987) *The Tree of Knowledge: The Biological Roots of Human Understanding*. Boston, MA: New Science Library.

Oakley, E. and Krug, D. (1991) *Enlightened Leadership: Getting to the Heart of Change*. New York: Fireside.

Pascarella, P. (1987) 'Create breakthroughs in performance by changing the conversation', *Industry Week*, 15 June: 50–7.

Reigel, K. (1979) *Foundations of Dialectical Psychology*. New York: Academic Press.

Reike, R. and Sillars, M. (1984) *Argumentation and the Decision Making Process* (2nd edition). Glenview, IL: Scott, Foresman and Co.

Scherr, A. (1989) 'Managing for breakthroughs in productivity', *Human Resource Management*, 28: 403–24.

Schrage, M. (1989) *No More Teams! Mastering the Dynamics of Creative Collaboration*. New York: Currency Paperbacks.

Searle, J.R. (1969) *Speech Acts: An Essay in the Philosophy of Language*. Cambridge: Cambridge University Press.

Searle, J.R. (1975) 'A taxonomy of illocutionary acts', in K. Gunderson (ed.), *Language, Mind and Knowledge*. Minneapolis, MN: University of Minnesota Press.

Searle, J.R. (1995) *The Construction of Social Reality*. New York: Free Press.

Senge, P. (1990) *The Fifth Discipline: The Art and Practice of the Learning Organization*. New York: Doubleday Currency.

Shotter, J. (1993) *Conversational Realities: Constructing Life Through Language*. London: Sage.

Wanous, J. (1992) *Organization Entry: Recruitment, Selection, Orientation, and Socialization of Newcomers* 2nd edition. Reading, MA: Addison-Wesley.

Watzlawick, P. (1984) 'Self-fulfilling prophecies', in P. Watzlawick (ed.), *The Invented Reality*. New York: Norton. pp. 95–116.

Watzlawick, P. (1990) 'Reality adaptation or adapted "reality"? constructivism and psychotherapy', in P. Watzlawick (ed.) *Münchhausen's Pigtail: Or Psychotherapy and 'Reality' – Essays and Lectures*. New York: W.W. Norton and Company.

Weick, K. (1979) *The Social Psychology of Organizations*. Reading, MA: Addison-Wesley.

Winograd, T. and Flores, F. (1987) *Understanding Computers and Cognition: A New Foundation for Design*. Reading, MA: Addison-Wesley.

Wittgenstein, L. (1953) *Philosophical Investigations*. Oxford: Blackwell.

Zaffron, S. (1995) 'Inventing Futures from the Future', paper presented at the National Academy of Management, Vancouver, BC.

All in a knot of one anothers' labours:
action learning as joint practical authoring

Mike Pedler

These days we all work in partnerships, networks and 'relational practices'. Is it something about this particular era, where we quickly deconstruct individual heroics and '[n]o one Company can go it alone' (Doz and Hamel, 1998: 1)? Or is it that this has always been a way of seeing it: that we live and work best, in Samuel Hartlib's words, 'All in a knot of one anothers' labours'? As a member of the seventeenth-century Office of Addresses in the heady, revolutionary days of the Commonwealth Parliament, Hartlib and his colleagues were great practical authors who worked so closely together that they published anonymously or collaboratively under one name. They held education to be the 'readiest way to reform both Church and Common-wealth' and sought to replace the existing and limited system of privileged private instruction with a comprehensive spectrum of alternative educational institutions by which 'all universities and eminent places of learning might be subtly undermined and made useless' (Webster, 1970).

When Reg Revans proposed action learning as the basis for the then new business school in Manchester, he had a similar idea in mind. Now as then, we will all be the beneficiaries if notions of action learning and practical authoring can help managers and other people to take their courage to generate new constructions that help bring about valued ends.

This chapter explores the notion of action learning in its possible connections and relationships with practical authoring. In some ways these practices seem highly compatible, although there are some differences in emphasis. An organisational and social change perspective on action learning raises questions of organisational learning and how this might be brought about. A discussion of action learning and practical authoring leads first to some questions for practice in the organisational and social context. These questions are illustrated by a case example of a group of neighbourhood facilitators acting and learning their way through a challenging task in Walsall, UK. The chapter includes thoughts about how local knowledge is accessed for the purposes of organisational learning and the construction of new organisational landscapes. The chapter concludes with some observations on the facilitation of action learning and practical authoring in the wider institutional context.

Action learning and practical authoring

What are the connections between action learning and practical authoring? How are they similar and how do they differ?

In action learning, managers and other people create plans and ways of going forward, take action, reflect on the experience and seek to learn. They do this as individuals and by generating a collective relationship that allows for conversations characterised by openness, support and challenge within the action learning set. Sets are often experienced as places where people can say things differently, and where they feel listened to in a way not possible at work or home. The set process could well be described as: 'opening up conversations about one thing or another to produce a binding promise to perform an act' (Spinosa et al., 1997).

Action learning shares with practical authoring the essential element of working from practice. Both require a direct acquaintance with doing and include the simple ethical injunction of practising what you preach. Both respond to the test – what is learned here that might improve practice? Both take a pragmatic view of knowledge: it doesn't matter whether theory is partial or incomplete, for all theory-in-action is, what matters is where it takes you and what is accomplished. Faced with issues not amenable to straightforward solution, the action learner or practical author's task is always one of re-inventing the wheel of your own practice (Casey, 1976).

There are many similarities between life in the action learning set and the concept of practical authoring as elaborated in the first chapter of this book. Here, the manager creates with others a unique but shared sense of task and circumstances which in turn enables individuals to act in ways understandable to each other. This is important because the world is no longer a single, mechanical, fixed order of connectedness but a living, fluid, complex unfolding which is changed by the very act of our attempts to make sense of it. In this view, reality is socially constructed through dialogue, joint sensemaking and 'relational practices', participants 'interanimate', understanding is 'relationally responsive', and the process generates unique 'organisational landscapes' that 'become known only to us from within our momentary, living involvement with them' (Shotter and Cunliffe, this volume: 19).

Although I have not seen these particular words used to describe action learning before, they are recognisable, they ring a bell. This is perhaps not so surprising because the family of 'action approaches' in which action learning can be located – dialogue, action research, action inquiry, appreciative inquiry and so on – have grown recently in popularity and variation in management education (Marsick and O'Neil, 1999). This development in practice is paralleled by a growing academic interest; action learning and other cognate ideas have become a proper topic for study. This is ironic given action learning's genesis as a protest against the universities' perpetuation of the ancient splitting of knowing and doing and the privileging of the former over the latter (Revans, 1980).

Action learning is more often described as an approach to individual, organisational and social development associated with the work of Revans who has stipulated three essential conditions: that people learn from their experience; that this experience should include both the diagnosis and treatment of a real problem, and that this problem is strategic, or concerned with the total enterprise in its economic and social setting (Revans, 1971: 29). Starting with people and the problems or issues they face, action learning places great importance on the set or self-directing group of six or so colleagues meeting regularly over time to help each other move on.

After training as a physicist in the 1920s, Revans became a manager and administrator and by the late 1950s was a professor of industrial administration. The idea of action learning developed out of his operational research in schools, hospitals and factories and his attempts to apply scientific method to their problems. His most formal attempt to theorise action learning brings together cycles of scientific method, project management and experiential learning (Revans, 1971). His recent disciples have tended to emphasise this last element. Action learning is often understood as a process of individual self-development via tackling problems and seeking to change an external world. Yet while much contemporary practice operates from this perspective, Revans consistently notes that action learning is for organisational, community and social change (Revans, 1982).

Personal knowing

> All meaningful knowledge is for the sake of action, and all meaningful action is for the sake of friendship. (Macmurray, 1961)

Managers as practical authors are not particularly concerned with externalised descriptions of what happened, with dead forms of reality (Shotter 1993). Instead, people concerned to act to improve things seek help with the particular and the local. In a living involvement with other people, helped immeasurably by these few friends, people create their own intricate, local sense so that they can get on with their work. Personal integrity comes when knowing is integrated with being and becoming in the doing. Arguably, the most important question to emerge from action learning is not 'What did we accomplish?' or 'What did we learn?' but 'What is an honest person, and what need I do to become one?' (Revans, 1971).

This personal integrity is bound up with the wider purposes of action. Action learning aims to heal the splitting of thought and action, which Revans suggests has long riven Western society by segregating labourers and scribes, scholars and smiths, the book and the tool. He espouses action learning as a medium to bring together these talents 'in the quest for national salvation' (Revans, 1980: 179). In similar vein, and much more recently, Reason suggests that the aim of action research is 'to develop practical knowing in the service of worthwhile human purposes' (2000: 2).

And organisational learning

> Thinking is easy; action is difficult; to act in accordance with one's thought is the most difficult thing in the world. (Goethe)

Yet these action approaches can only aspire to these wider, collective purposes if they have strategies beyond the achievements of personal knowing and practice. Action learning can be described as a collective process in which new social meanings and realities are constructed (Pedler, 1997). This view shares the social-constructionist assumptions of practical authoring, and makes the individual actors and their organisational tasks the backcloth for the collective achievement of the set, which becomes a 'community of practice' of shared activity, shared knowledge and shared ways of knowing (Drath and Palus, 1994: 11). In this interpretation, the action learning set, as a particularly useful social invention for our times, can legitimise regular joint practical authoring in an organisational context.

The organisational and social change focus prompts some questions about the pragmatics of practical authoring in this context. How do these relational processes and dialogues take place in organisations? Do they happen as a matter of course? Watson's managers, for example, seem often to hear their authentic voices only in their inner dialogues, or in interviews with the researcher (Watson, 1994); and these personal experiences are reinforced by Vince who has detailed the many excuses and avoidances which senior people employ in not listening to questions of equality in the workplace (Vince, 1994). The experience of being listened to seriously as part of feeling fully a person (Shotter and Cunliffe, this volume, chapter 1) does not seem to be a common one in organisational life.

If managers do not feel free to engage in authentic dialogue, how is 'organisational common sense' (Shotter and Cunliffe, see chapter 1) to be brought about? The literature on organisational learning is replete with, even characterised by, descriptions of 'learning disabilities', 'defensive routines', 'organisational blockages' and the like which interfere with or prevent the free flows of information, feedback, dialogue and learning. How do managers as practical authors deal with these issues?

Descriptions of how managers go on in this way sometimes seem rather heroic. This passage, for example, might, with slightly different words, come from the rugged Tom Peters:

> More than just 'giving us a picture' – which lies dead on the page – the good author-manager can bring us to experience a *living reality*, a dynamic landscape, which spontaneously offers us a set of 'action guiding advisories', a 'shaped and vectored sense' of where we are now and where we might (or perhaps should) go next. (Shotter and Cunliffe, this volume: 20).

Individualism remains an important aspect of managing, but practical authoring is actually about what individuals accomplish in the company of others. Yet, how should they do this joint work? How is it culturally supported? Can the approach and processes of action learning support the efforts of the manager as practical author? If there is much that is held in common by these perspectives, then the experiences of action learning in the organisational context might add value in understanding how the above questions can be addressed. In the case example below, a group of local government officers in Walsall worked as an action learning set to tackle a difficult piece of work. These 'neighbourhood facilitators' were charged with enrolling the residents of selected neighbourhoods in a development process to help bring about better local service delivery through a new system of local governance. They had no blueprints for this work, despite decades of valuable research on neighbourhood regeneration, and had no other course but to try and do it, and learn the way through this doing.

The Walsall neighbourhood facilitators' group

In 1996 the borough of Walsall set out to realise a radical vision coupling the regeneration of deprived neighbourhoods with the development of local democracy. As part of this ambitious plan, I worked with a group of seconded local government officers charged with empowering the residents in seven pilot neighbourhoods via Single Regeneration Budget (SRB) funding. By the time I arrived, these neighbourhood facilitators were actively engaged on this demanding task, and although this was a newly constituted group, there was some significant history, both personal and political, among the members. Most of them were working part-time, the local political situation was unstable, and many of them felt insecure about their day jobs.

I worked with the group on 15 days over 11 months, sometimes in 2-day meetings. In retrospect, the work can be described straightforwardly enough. It began with public meetings and then progressed via the assembly of local 'design teams' which organised 2-day 'big events' to which all the residents were invited. A key purpose of these events was to build up, from the diversity of people, groups and local interests, a collectively generated vision of the desirable neighbourhood of the future. After this, steering groups sought to continue the momentum in each locality until local elections could be held and neighbourhood committees established.

In action, there was no smooth progression; the experience was of a white knuckle ride – difficult, exciting, stressful, depressing and joyful in turn. When I was asked to write a few pages about what had been learned at Walsall, what emerged was a story of collective action and learning, a biography of this group's development in its engagement with a wider world.

Start-up

The work in Walsall was characterised by the urgent need for action. This imperative created a steep learning curve for individuals and for the group as a whole. My meetings with the group were called 'action learning' days but no one was very clear or even interested in what was meant by that. The first meeting was pressurised; trying to make sense of the whole while planning imminent start ups in Brownhills and Harden. Many other things were going on, including several conflicts emerging from the group's history. With severe competition for time, we were overloaded with information and conflicting feelings, trying to make sense of the situation. Many things were left undone, and I struggled to make openings for reflection. There were lots of seemingly alarming questions:

- 'I'm interested in community work but I've never been out of the council, will I cope?'
- 'What will happen when we stand up in front of local people who are angry with us?'
- 'My manager didn't want to release me and told me I had to carry the extra workload – how do we get them involved?'
- 'What happens if the National Front come to the start-up in Brownhills?'
- 'Who should be in a design team?'
- 'What's happened to the baseline audit (being carried out by an consultant); who are the people and the agencies in the neighbourhoods?'
- 'How committed is the council to all this?'
- 'What's happening with the partnership group?'
- 'What logistical support do we get?'

There was little time to dwell on these issues because of the pace of the project. By our second meeting, the anxious concern with start-ups had switched to a focus on design teams (the next stage in the process) and then big events (an ultimate goal at that time). By the fourth meeting two members had dropped out citing day job demands. But by now the group was less fractured and more balanced in terms of an inner and outer focus. Outwardly, attention had shifted again to a concern not to over-promise to residents; key questions now were – 'Can we deliver?' and 'How much is in the pot anyway?' Inwardly, meetings were more reflective, and we pondered the difference between learning and training.

Development

Action learning now began to mean something as the facilitators reported in each time on what had happened in their neighbourhoods since we met last. In contrast to the hectic nature of their other meetings, the listening to each other's accounts and learning to question them for further understanding gradually brought about a valuing of reflective time. People often recounted what seemed to me to signal quite considerable individual learning, and perhaps more striking still was the rapid development of the group as a whole. After four months, the group reflected on their development, noting the rapid progress from one urgent concern to the next, and the personal development resulting from tackling apparently formidable tasks, overcoming them and moving on. People noted that they only remembered what and how much they had done when they reported back and reflected on what had happened.

This development was demonstrated in a growing confidence and an awareness of a much wider perspective. One outcome of this maturing consciousness was a clash with the Walsall chief executive, who insisted, in the face of the facilitators' collective view, on sticking to the original timetable for the SRB delivery plan. As promised in the plan, which was scrutinised in detail by the government regional office, the big events, would take place in each neighbourhood and last for two days. Yet the facilitators' experiences suggested that sustaining a two-day meeting would not be possible for many local residents in their neighbourhoods. After several discussions, the full corporate board of Walsall MBC visited the group on 17 September, where they listened carefully and eventually agreed it was necessary to be more flexible. This demonstrated a willingness to learn on the part of the corporate board and also revealed the limits of their formal leadership in such complex, ambiguous and rapidly changing situations. As an outcome of their contact with residents, the facilitators had acquired local knowledge not available to the board, and it became apparent that they had a contribution to make to policy development as well as to the operational leadership of the Walsall initiative.

A second conflict took place later over the timetable for neighbourhood elections, with a similar pattern of resolution. The board wanted to stick to the promised May deadline, but the facilitators argued for it to go back to September. Eventually September was agreed. This discussion had the effect of redefining work of the group in a yet wider context, extending beyond community development and back into the organisation development of Walsall MBC, the other partnership agencies, and even further.

The drawing of pictures like Figures 9.1 and 9.2 were a regular aspect of life in this group. While members were always urgently engaged with the detail of their own assignments, time together was usually marked with

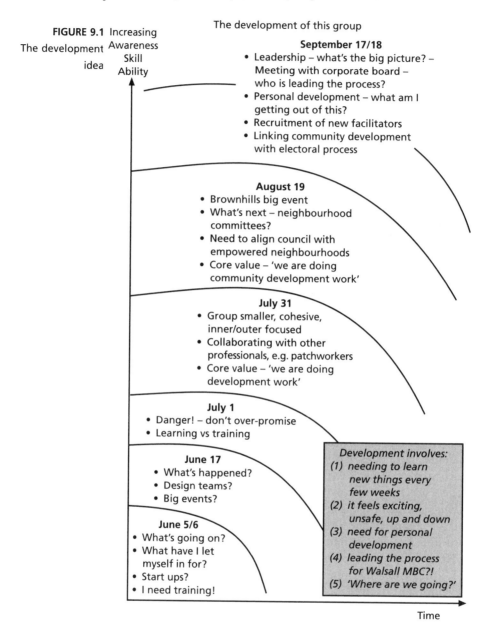

FIGURE 9.1 The development idea

The development of this group

Increasing Awareness Skill Ability

September 17/18
- Leadership – what's the big picture? – Meeting with corporate board – who is leading the process?
- Personal development – what am I getting out of this?
- Recruitment of new facilitators
- Linking community development with electoral process

August 19
- Brownhills big event
- What's next – neighbourhood committees?
- Need to align council with empowered neighbourhoods
- Core value – 'we are doing community development work'

July 31
- Group smaller, cohesive, inner/outer focused
- Collaborating with other professionals, e.g. patchworkers
- Core value – 'we are doing development work'

July 1
- Danger! – don't over-promise
- Learning vs training

June 17
- What's happened?
- Design teams?
- Big events?

June 5/6
- What's going on?
- What have I let myself in for?
- Start ups?
- I need training!

Development involves:
(1) needing to learn new things every few weeks
(2) it feels exciting, unsafe, up and down
(3) need for personal development
(4) leading the process for Walsall MBC?!
(5) 'Where are we going?'

Time

questions about the big picture and frequent and successive attempts to draw it. The need to contextualise the work, to 'helicopter' up from their own patch in order to see where they might be going, was one of the facilitators' consistent preoccupations.

Throughout this time the membership of the group was turning over. By May 1997, some key members were leaving, several new facilitators were poised to join and the group had a new convenor. The work was now shifting

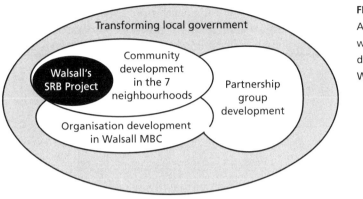

FIGURE 9.2
A big picture:
whole systems
development in
Walsall

to introducing new liaison officers and 'patchworkers' from other agencies to the neighbourhoods and their committees.

What was accomplished? At my last meeting I circulated an open-ended questionnaire, which was completed and discussed. From these responses it is clear that people had learned a great deal: acquiring new skills, under-standing more about how to work in organisational contexts and usually deriving some profound knowledge about themselves. Yet, in response to the question 'What happened?', the collective story seems as salient as any individual tale and it was the participation in the collective that enabled the often profound learning of the individual. This collective narrative was characterised by:

- 'absurd deadlines'
- 'just-in-time survival . . . several times the project looked like collapsing and resources arrived just in time'
- 'not trained professionals, but people willing to learn'
- 'individuals in a process of development – this was not a straight-line graph, but people were always learning and moving on'
- 'the corporateness of us . . . lots of different people, but supporting each other . . . it was said that this group was the most corporate thing about Walsall, not excluding the corporate board!'
- 'we handled succession well – key people were allowed to leave and new ones were welcomed and supported'
- 'What is attracting the newcomers? Because this *is* the way we want to deliver services. The concept, the vision of the people who have the services saying what they want – that's what I've always believed in. We all knew local government wasn't working.'

The focus here is not so much upon individual learning, but on the collective or joint accomplishments of the group. Here are some shared experiences and learning, and some joint values discovered. The pressure of deadlines, anxieties and threats to survival and continuity forged a 'comrades in adversity' spirit – even, as one person noted, with people you didn't like. It is this joint authoring which strongly informed individual actions and, as a collective voice, which contributed to a wider organisational learning in Walsall.

Creating the conditions for learning within the whole system

The illustration from Walsall demonstrates some issues for action learning and joint practical authoring in the whole systems context.

Accessing local knowledge

Although the Walsall facilitators were all professionals with specialist skills, their expert knowledge was only occasionally useful. In more general terms it was undermined by the awareness that 'we all knew local government wasn't working'. Instead, and in their dealings with Walsall's corporate board, it became obvious that the facilitators had acquired some *local* knowledge, which was important not only for operational decisions, but also for developing policy. The reason for devolving service commissioning to local level in Walsall was because the professionally directed, centrally provided services were not contributing enough to the regeneration of the borough's needy neighbourhoods. This realisation prompted an awareness of the limitations of professional knowledge and expertise. The problem of professional knowledge is that, as a generalised storehouse based on the resolution of past problems (known as P or 'programmed' knowledge in action learning), it may or may not be useful in this particular context. Professionals acting in isolation from local knowledge can produce borough-wide plans based on the rational allocation of resources and on sound technical judgement, which when implemented in this or that locality, make no good sense.

Local knowledge, defined by its locatedness in a particular setting, is produced by, and is essential to, effective action in this place. Like electricity, it does not travel well, is hard to store and best used as it is generated. What seemed to happen in Walsall is that the facilitators were acquiring local knowledge from their action and learning which, through them, eventually became available to the board, which would not otherwise have had access to it. Yet, as the case shows, it took some effort for the group to be listened to by the board. It did not happen as a matter of course.

Accessing this scattered, various and largely tacit local knowledge is one of the central problems in organisational learning. At least three conditions must be met for this to happen: first, it will only happen if people are prepared to share their knowledge; secondly, it can only happen if people are able to make their understandings explicit; and thirdly, this exchange is only useful, if those charged with decisions are willing and able to listen and hear what is being said (see Figure 9.3). Arguably, people's tacit knowledge, a notion which overlaps with that of local knowledge, is made more accessible if it is held in a community of practice such as an action learning set, rather than in the 'private office' of the individual (Dixon, 1997).

Nonaka and Takeuchi (1995) go much further in proposing that tacit knowledge can be systematically converted into explicit knowledge for the benefit of the firm. However, despite the somewhat alchemic 'knowledge creation spiral' which apparently makes this routinisation of 'double-loop learning' unproblematic (Nonaka and Takeuchi, 1995: 46), such claims should be regarded with appropriate scepticism. Experience in UK organisations as least suggests that the effort to derive organisational knowing from the local and tacit achievements of people as practical authors is likely to remain a demanding and exceptional, rather than routine, accomplishment, requiring good will and courage on all sides.

New organisational landscapes and drawing big pictures

A common shared experience in action learning is to feel suddenly that a new vista has opened up for someone. Suddenly, somehow, what this person has been struggling with looks different and something new has appeared. This is described in practical authoring as unique organisational landscapes 'that become known to us only from within our momentary, living involvement with them' (Shotter and Cunliffe, this volume: 19).

Just so. And in this moment there is some organisational common sense between the few of us gathered together bending our minds, bodies and wills to this purpose. In Walsall, we were always preoccupied with what was called 'the big picture', meaning the wider context in which we were working. What was the project about? Who was involved? Was it these few neighbourhoods or the whole borough? Was it really multi-agency or really just the council? These and other questions constantly jumped out when considering how best to act. Without understanding this bigger picture, how can you decide what to do next?

This picture changed every time we discussed it, which was at every meeting. The conversations with Walsall's corporate board made it radically different as group members glimpsed a landscape seen from a different perspective. Here is the regeneration discussed by Shotter where, in situations defined by ambiguity and dilemma, ways forward are found through understanding the positions of all the actors present and seeking a position which builds on these and articulates them.

In Walsall, the interactive discussion of the big picture was summed up by a colleague, as being a matter of 'widening circles of inclusivity' (Wilkinson, 1997). The Walsall neighbourhood facilitators first had to learn to work together as a group and accommodate various conflicts in so doing;

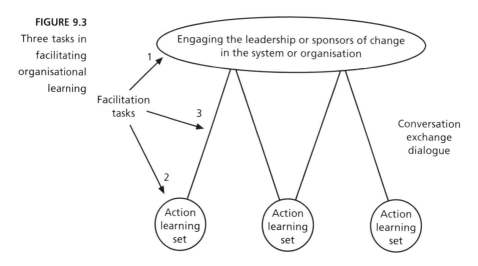

FIGURE 9.3
Three tasks in facilitating organisational learning

once this had been accomplished they could encompass a wider world. Discussions with the corporate board for example brought government regional office into the picture, along with the other agencies in the Walsall partnership group and they also glimpsed the chief executive's ambition for contributing something to the reform of local government nationally. When I left the project, the group was losing hitherto core members but was embracing the neighbourhood 'patchworkers' from the other Walsall agencies. Deciding how to go on at each or any of these points was always guided by the current big picture, the organisational landscape as we now saw it, or you could say, by 'a set of "action guiding advisories", a "shaped and vectored sense" of where we are now and where we might go next' (see Shotter and Cunliffe, chapter 1).

Facilitating action learning and joint practical authoring in the whole system

Unless the manager as practical author finds some way of joining with colleagues in different locations, it is difficult to see how this dialogical accomplishment can progress much beyond the local. Although action learning is often conceived of as a small group activity, and facilitation means the facilitation of the set; when it is seen as being concerned with organisational, community and social change as well as with individual action and learning, facilitation takes on a much wider and more challenging remit.

Revans (1999) is notably sceptical about facilitators, sensing a new opportunity here for experts to take over. His preferred role is the 'accoucheur' or midwife who assists with the birth and helps to bring a new thing into being. This distinction is worth making: facilitators are indeed there as assistants, but usually become managers of certain processes within organisational settings. It is all too easy to fall into a representation of the system or of the powerful groups outside the set and intervene on their behalf. Intervening is an 'outside-in' process, whereas what is needed here is something of the contrary movement.

In robustly questioning why managers need facilitators, when they can toast each other in cold water from the factory tap, Revans makes light of the difficulties of bringing about organisational development through action learning. Yet at the same time he bemoans the attitudes of top managers who block the best efforts of action learners (Revans, 1999). Earthiness is absolutely central to action learning, let our feet get off the ground of action and we need to be quickly pulled back; yet unless we are to go with Nonaka and Takeuchi (1995), how is a wider organisational learning to be accomplished?

In Walsall, it seems that there are three focuses or tasks for facilitation or midwifery: helping with the development of the group of action learners, assisting with the engagement of the leadership or sponsor group, and encouraging the conversation or dialogue between these groups. Without the engagement of the leadership, change in any system or organisation is unlikely to succeed. As with any effort at organisational development, change or transformation, action learning leading to learning at the organisational or system level needs sponsors who represent the whole system or organisation. It needs these people to help determine what problems or tasks should be addressed, to generally support the work including helping with evaluation and review, and also – crucially – to honestly seek their own learning in this process.

Finding such leaders ready and able to do this work is not usually easy. To begin with, in a complex system such as Walsall, it is often difficult to identify or recruit the leadership. The candidates for this role may not see themselves in this way and may not have worked with their colleagues to the point where they can operate as a leadership team. The problem of how to create leadership in a system is frequently encountered, for leadership must be accepted as well as taken. It is a relational concept, existing in the spaces between people and groups, a culture in which people generate the best conditions for working together. To build this sort of leadership often requires considerable development work, starting from what exists in terms of current power structures.

Even where leaders can be identified, it takes courage and an unusual willingness to risk and engage with people which is not as widespread as might be thought among people in the high offices. If we call this facilitation, then this work involves encouraging, challenging and coaching leaders who will stand for the whole organisation or system in dialogue with people who are seeking to learn from changing things. Yet without the development of a leadership group, the third facilitation task – of encouraging and moderating, from time to time as seems appropriate, a conversation between those engaged in local action and learning and those concerned with organisational direction and strategy – cannot happen.

This linking of micro and macro, of the operational and the strategic, is one way of understanding the problem of implementation. The implementation of change, from good policy to effective practice, is not brought about either by decree from above or by empowered energy from below, but only in a partnership of both. Once again this collaboration, which may well involve significant differences of views, and conflict over them, is a considerable practical achievement, not a simple recipe to be followed. This goes beyond understanding the micro-politics of organisation, which Revans sees as one of the important outcomes of action learning (Revans, 1999), to an active involvement in organisational politics in order to bring about desired change.

In the face of these challenges, it is common to make the mistake of assuming that proffered methodologies and reproducible processes such as Future Search (Weisbord and Janoff, 1999) can bring about whole systems change in any context. This is not only a chimera – such recipes cannot match the variety needed in the complex world of systems such as Walsall – but a flight from power, an attempt to devise a process which can bypass the messy, conflictual and unpredictable business of actually bringing about sustainable change that adds rather than destroys value.

Much current practice of action learning also displays this flight from power. The set acting in isolation of its organisational context falls back on personal development and lends itself to expert facilitation. This over simple interpretation of the action learning idea results in a formulaic which cannot engage with the politics of action and cannot bring about organisational change and learning. However, if these difficulties are accepted, then action learning in the whole systems context may offer the manager as practical author an organisational outlet for her and his efforts that might otherwise be published only in their private office.

References

Casey, D. (1976) 'The emerging role of set advisor in action learning programmes', *Journal of European Training*, 5: 162–73.

Dixon, N. (1997) 'The hallways of learning', *Organizational Dynamics*, 25: 23–34.

Doz, Y. and Hamel, G. (1998) *Alliance Advantage*. Cambridge, MA: Harvard Business School Press.

Drath, W.H. and Palus, C.J. (1994) *Making Common Sense: Leadership as Meaning-making in a Community of Practice*. Center for Creative Leadership, Greensboro.

Macmurray, J. (1961) *Persons in Relation*. London: Faber and Faber.

Marsick, V. and O'Neil, J. (1999) 'The many faces of action learning', *Management Learning*, 30: 159–76.

Nonaka, I. and Takeuchi, H. (1995) *The Knowledge-creating Company: How Japanese Companies Create the Dynamics of Innovation*. New York: Oxford University Press.

Pedler, M. (1997) 'Interpreting action learning', in J.G. Burgoyne and M. Reynolds (eds), *Management Learning: Integrating Perspectives in Theory and Practice*. London: Sage.

Reason, P. (2000) 'Action research as spiritual practice', paper presented at the University of Surrey Learning Community Conference, May.

Revans, R.W. (1971) *Developing Effective Managers: A New Approach to Business Education*. New York: Praeger.

Revans, R.W. (1980) *Action Learning: New Techniques for Managers*. London: Blond and Briggs.

Revans, R.W. (1982) *The Origins and Growth of Action Learning*. Lund: Studentlitteratur.

Revans, R.W. (1999) *ABC of Action Learning*. London: Lemos and Crane.

Shotter, J. (1993) *Conversational Realities: Constructing Life Through Language*. London: Sage.

Vince, R. (1994) 'The dynamics of learning about management: the impact of a psychodynamic approach with a local government management development programme', paper presented at International Consulting Conference, South Bank University, London, January.

Watson, T.J. (1994) *In Search of Management: Culture, Chaos and Control in Managerial Work*. London: Routledge.

Webster, C. (1970) *Samuel Hartlib and the Advancement of Learning*. Cambridge: Cambridge University Press.

Weisbord, M.R. and Janoff, S. (1999) 'Future search: finding commonground in organisations and communities', *Systems Practice*, 9: 71–84.

Wilkinson, D. (1997) *Implementing the Borough of Walsall's SRB: The Final Report on Empowering Local Communities*. Whole Systems Development: July.

10

A critical conversation between author managers and management authors

Dorothy Lander and Craig Prichard

Narrator: Craig Prichard and Dorothy Lander invite the reader into the middle of their continuing, intercontinental, critical cross-talk on management practice. This reflexive dialogue is between their identities as 'management author' and 'author manager' and includes their gendered, managerial and authorial selves. Craig's and Dorothy's dialogue could be said to take Shotter's dialogic constructivism (1993a, 1993b, 1993c, 1997) at its word. By this they attempt what John Van Maanen calls 'allegorical breaching' (in reference to Karl Weick's work) in breaching

> the generic recognizability of normal organizational theorizing with its relentless summaries of past research, propositional chants, pachyderm-like solemnity and off-the-shelf textual formats (i.e., introduction, hypotheses, methods, findings, conclusions). (1995: 136)

In the following excerpt from their on-going dialogue Dorothy and Craig discuss John Shotter's notion of the 'manager as practical author' (1993a; Shotter and Cunliffe, chapter 1). Their dialogue draws from various critical literatures, and extracts some empirical material from their own work. While it celebrates the challenge that Shotter's work offers to the monological rationality of 'normal' management science, it argues that the dialogical constructivism that underpins Shotter's manager as practical author does not go far enough.

Craig: [*interrupts*] Thanks . . . calling up an identity as 'management author' (Prichard, 2000; Prichard et al., 2000), 'I' bring to this dialogue a series of questions or problems with Shotter's 'manager as practical author'. One is that the links between this manager and broader capitalist relations of production and patriarchal gender relations in which the manager is already 'nested' seem unclear. I already anticipate that you, Dorothy, will have a different take on this, but for me such seemingly big narratives are not outside the seeming small talk about managing. Management as a process, whether conceived as a science of efficient coordination or as the delicate daily work of actually getting work done, is linked to and part of capitalist relations of production (Alvesson and Willmott, 1996; Braverman, 1974; Chandler, 1977; Hollway, 1991; Jacques, 1996). For example, mainstream management's contemporary interest in attempting to manage learning and knowledge in the workplace (Nonaka and Takeuchi, 1995; Zuboff, 1988) is 'small' and 'large'. Large in the sense that it links with core Taylorite scientific management, which is involved in wrestling control of workers' knowledge of how to work from what Frederick Taylor called 'traditional management'. Large in the sense that it can be read as part of constant skirmishing by a loose alliance of interests (including the state) which seeks to realise the full potential of human work in the creation of economic value. And small in that this process of realisation can involve supporting relationships between people in a bearable, dialogic fashion (McKinlay, 2000). Managers, and management as a set of practices, are engaged in realising economic value and with keeping the 'show on the road'. To speak of the manager outside of these broader relations is to miss some of the deeply embedded reasons why authors like John Shotter are induced to write about managers rather than say mothers. If these issues are left out, then my response to the notion of 'manager as practical author' is 'So what?' I feel that to survive a charge of being an ahistoric, apolitical and a conceptually challenged formulation, the limitations of this manager as 'dialogical author' of organisational landscapes must be addressed (see also Willmott, 1994).

Dorothy: So, our aim is to upset the grammar of the 'manager as practical author', to rearrange the syntax, to play the story otherwise, and to 'work the hyphens' – to use Michelle Fine's (1998) poststructural term – of author manager and management author?

Craig: Indeed, and I guess one way to 'work the hyphens' (upset the grammar/relations) – between manager–practical author – is to throw up other terms so the conjunction can be read otherwise. 'Manager as practical author' becomes

> corporate capitalism's managerial subject position set in counterpoint relations with other subject positions, e.g., the subject positions of 'professional' and 'worker'.

Dorothy: In the spirit of responsive, relational dialogue, do you think we might get into this conversation by locating ourselves in rhetorical relationship? And as a way of signalling that as we speak-write, we are addressing a whole range of readers in separate and parallel dialogues? For sure we are addressing our editors, David and Richard, but also managers, students of management, other management authors, readers positioned in oppositional narratives, and of course ourselves and each other.

Craig: Absolutely. This will also help us critically explore the dialogical foundation to Shotter's 'manager as practical author' (1993a). Shotter talks of everyday life as made up of a 'strange', 'relational-responsive' process based around the 'utterance'. He regularly draws on Harré's phrase that the 'primary human reality is persons in conversation' (1983: 58) and states that all human phenomena of importance are relational (Shotter, 1997: 348). Much of his philosophical, empirical and conceptual work addresses the primary question of how people relate together. So for instance some of the things that relate *us* together are: academic identities, PhDs and researching the work of managers. Of course such things are not things at all, given the broad methodological positions we adopted. So let's utter together about these 'non-things'.

Dorothy: I would like to pose some hitherto unsaid and unresponded-to non-utterances as well. I was new to the United Kingdom and new to academic research into the management practices of higher education when I first met you as a 'fellow' doctoral student in continuing education at the University of Nottingham in 1995. My particular research interest was the lived experience of quality in the university. I don't think I've ever told you my memory of our first meeting. When I first arrived on the academic scene, your ready command of critical management research – or so it seemed to me – on academic managers in further and higher education inspired me to learn this new language at the same time as it fuelled my 'imposter syndrome' (Brookfield, 1995). You were very welcoming to me so a big thanks to you. I had been away from higher education as a student for 15 years. I was an intuitive knower and author of management practices drawing on my 18 years of managing university student residences, cleaning services and contract food services at St Francis Xavier University in Nova Scotia. The coauthoring of quality was a preoccupation when I was a service operations manager and it has become my passion in my current work as an assistant professor and researcher in adult education. Over to you, but first I want to call your attention to my deliberately placing 'fellow' in quotation marks. This anticipates a theme in our dialogue: chatting reflexively about our texts *as texts* – that is, bending back our texts as fictional constructions and in flux – is not your everyday conversational reality. It is not my manager as practical author but rather my management author that is often reflexively 'struck by' (Cunliffe, 1999; Shotter, 1997) the gendering of language and what Judith Butler (1990) calls performativity – the idea that our talk has the capacity to produce what it names. It is my come-lately management author identity that responds to Czarniawska-Joerges' ideas of interrupting the text and 'refusing to accept a text's premises of gender construction' (1994: 230).

Interrupter (Curt, 1994): Excuse the intrusion in this text but when you say, 'It is not my manager as practical author but rather my management author that is often reflexively "struck by" ', I take it that you are referring to different identities that make up your past – the service manager and the academic writer on management who are in a sense evoked in different contexts?

Dorothy: Different contexts and different temporal space and different ways of authoring, but at times my identities and these histories and biographies get awfully confused. As a service operations manager, I mostly applied my spoken and written speech acts to operations. Although I lived the structural inequities embedded in everyday language, in my 18 years as a manager I was rarely 'struck by' the interweaving of patriarchal and managerial language or the appropriation of the higher moral ground of service (a feminist discourse) in the rhetoric of services as a commodity (a masculinist discourse) (see Lander, 2000a). As an academic author of management practices, I now rarely engage with the operational implications of language – say, the practical author who uses rhetoric to curb absenteeism. Nowadays, I am often 'struck by' management authors who rekindle my unsaid and hitherto unsayable experience as a service manager. I was awakened anew the first time I read Holmer-Nadesan's (1996) poststructural research and relived my service manager experience: 'patriarchal significations may seem "natural" when invoked by a less ubiquitous discourse such as managerialism' (1996: 56). By the way, I haven't forgotten that it was you that alerted me to Holmer-Nadesan's work. How could I? It is your copy of the paper that I still refer to, complete with your handwritten note, 'Dear Dorothy, a service worker in Universities paper I thought might be of some interest. Craig P'.

Craig: I think some readers might at this point find this discussion a curious way to proceed. It is! But it puts, by way of process, a serious set of questions: Why do writers who stress the dialogic, celebrate the conversational, and worry about the undecidability of joint action refrain from such processes when they themselves write? Why do they not let a little chaos reign? And why, if we understand the manager as practical author who works through localised rhetorical practice performed tacitly by situated bodies, don't the texts that they reference include the physical, geographical, relational locatedness of text production? And why also are readers not invited into the text in a dynamic way? And why if we follow Wittgenstein – as Shotter does – have we not thrown out the paragraph, the introduction and conclusion and started writing in numbered notes and perhaps asking readers to scribble responses in between these?

These questions might sound silly and the criticisms harsh and unforgiving. After all there are examples in Shotter's texts of 'alternative' practices being used to support his approach within the monological text. For instance Shotter and Bhaskar go head-to-head in the conclusion to *Conversational Realities* (1993a). And Shotter uses poetry and a speaking voice in some texts (1997). But these are side dishes to the main meal that is eaten from the table of standard academic set for the performance of monologue. What is perhaps even more surprising is that such disciplining practices hold sway in the midst of a critique of academic discourse (1997: 473). But perhaps this is too harsh. Perhaps what appears monological depends less on its form and more on how it is read. After all academic discourse could easily be considered dialogic. Policy documents and operations manuals also. In academic discourse referencing practices form the dialogic linkages which mark out zones of academic debate. While at its surface each piece of writing might seem disembodied, formalised and instrumental, to the initiated reader, each term, comment and assertion plays to a background of other terms, comments and assertions in that particular field, and each passage references the past, forms objections and anticipates future responses (Bakhtin, 1981). But now I think I'm talking about power; about the practices which exclude some (those without the cultural capital to participate – those silenced by the discourse) and include others to the dialogue of a particular zone. This is my problem with Shotter's Wittgensteinian musings about knowing in the third kind, and the manager as practical author. The work rails against the power practices that produce the monological representation zone of knowledge. It prescribes for the manager the rhetorical skills suited to a dialogic zone of knowing. Yet clearly the two zones, if we continue to assume a separation, are interdependent, and the latter – the dialogic zones – are infused with power relations of a more subtle and pervasive kind than those found in the rules and objectives of the representational order. But perhaps I'm stating the obvious?

Dorothy: I'd venture to say that it is often the power relations as they are reproduced in the dialogic zones that don't get uttered. As a long time manager I felt excluded from the category of 'good manager' in Shotter's chapter (1993a) on the manager as a practical author. If, as Shotter claims, a good manager is 'not an author of texts, but a "practical-ethical author", a "conversational author", able to argue persuasively for a "landscape" of next possible actions, upon which the "positions" of all those who must take part are clear' (1993a: 157), I *obviously* must have been a bad manager. As a manager, I was able to act transgressively rather than argue persuasively for a landscape of next possible *operational* actions; rarely was I clear on the *structural* positions of all those who must take part. I was not able to argue persuasively for a landscape that reconstituted the positions of all those in the structural milieu of patriarchy and capitalist production. When I did manage to challenge the structural milieu, it was quite often acts of authorship that were *not* conversational. I found that while I could not argue persuasively in conversations (assuming I could get into the conversation at all!), I would have no trouble being accepted in the position of secretary for any number of committees and here I managed to skilfully write the minutes as nuanced performativity. This is Butler's speech action – either written or spoken – that 'echoes prior actions, and accumulates the force of authority through the repetition or citation of a prior and authoritative set of practices' (1997: 204). Over my 18 years as manager, my minute-taking of committee conversations became a ritualised practice. I would deliberately 'position' students and workers of every stripe by juxtaposing their names to a **Required Action** and **Time Frame** – in bold, just like that. And yes, a transgressive textual ploy, or in Butler's terms a 'subversive repetition', that alters the conversational reality! I'm pretty sure that at the time I was more explicitly focused on operations than structural and gendered inequity. I wanted to make sure that the work got done – say for the special events around graduation weekend – and only secondarily was I concerned that the dirty work was distributed equitably among men and women, knowledge workers, service workers and students.

A digression! My point was that Shotter is not the only management author to normatively name the good manager and thus exclude from the good the living texts of a whole range of managers. Chia and Morgan's good manager is a philosopher manager, 'a critical thinking manager who persists in the vigilant deconstructing or "de-signing" of hitherto self-evident social and management concepts and categories in search of the deeper and bigger issues affecting the human condition' (1996: 41). This good manager refuses 'to be seduced by the dominant signifying systems [that] . . . serve to deceive our senses, disorient priorities, disable critical thought, and restrict vision in . . . the crucial practice of managing' (1996: 37). In Chia and Morgan's terms, I mostly got to be a good manager when I was the secretary. What vexes me is that management authors – of which I am now one – are so ready to name and normalise the good manager as this critical thinking manager without ever working the ground of everyday managing in chaotic settings. I don't think it is just 'postmodern researchers [who] sometimes distance themselves from those who experience and consume the phenomena around which they construct their academic endeavours' (Hardy and Clegg, 1997: S11). I am not convinced that I would have been a better manager, in the sense of serving others, and getting food dished up and students' rooms cleaned – which was after all the job at hand – whether patriarchy and capitalism reigned or not.

Craig: Before I forget and fail to do what we have charged others with not doing (dialogue that includes 'us'), I guess (if I can retrospectively author an identity as a PhD student in our little reading group in Nottingham) I'd have to say that I respected enormously what you had done and were doing and continue to do (e.g., through this chapter) to 'write' management otherwise. It was inspiring to hear you talk critically and openly about your 18 years as author manager, but it was probably more inspiring at the time to hear how this author manager was faring in her encounter in your PhD with narratology and feminist poststructuralism.

I guess some readers would find this open celebration of each other's work a little nauseating? My challenge would be rather than hide such relations in footnotes and referencing practices (the old joke about academics reading books via the bibliography), why not bring it into the text (Frost and Stablein, 1992)? This is where I think we align with Shotter – particularly as it links to Bakhtin – and celebrate his work. But we also 'see/hear' some limitations, and worry about the 'capture' of dialogue as managerial technique (Ellinor and Gerard, 1998; Isaacs, 1999). This capture is achievable in part because it is the process of dialogue over its content which is in the foreground. My point is that it is way deeper. For example, the relative success of our dialogic relationality is informed by our mutual positioning in colonial identities. As we have attempted to unpack elsewhere (Lander and Prichard, forthcoming), our joint positioning as English-speaking colonial subjects in Britain for PhD study (and our subsequent return with newly minted PhDs to the postcolonial periphery), together with our gendered and sexual identities form, if you like, the terrain against which it is possible to perform our responsive-relationality. The pleasure and support we gave/give each other via dialogue can be only fully understood by bringing these identities to the engagement.

Dorothy: [*aside*] Notice how our relationality immediately sounds less nauseating when you theorise on it – when you make it more abstract!

Craig: [*continuing*] The methodological challenge here is that we 'do' and read dialogue in depth. Of course there are allusions to these issues in Shotter's writing. But they seem hesitant and metaphorical. For example Shotter speaks powerfully via Wittengenstein's metaphor of language being like a disorderly city with: 'a maze of little streets and squares, of old and new houses and of houses with additions from various periods; and this surrounded by a multitude of new boroughs with straight and regular streets' (1953: no. 122.)

So while the 'city' of my discourse provides me with places to perform my gender and sexuality, for example my identity as petit-bourgeois kiwi bloke, so too the city provides positions from which the manager performs as boss or expert decision-maker or legitimator of the inequitable or the unworthy. For me, it is this history, and the city that it brings to bear on the position of the manager that is missing from Shotter's 1993 discussion of the manager as practical author (1993a). Dialogues can only be done with the materials, ideologies, knowledges or discourses that prefigure and enliven the dialogic encounter (as they have here in this one). There are, for example, certain ways to being a kiwi bloke or a business manager. Some are more economically and socially successful than others.

Of course I don't want to deny the potential of dialogue for reworking oppressive forms of knowing, but I also don't want to deny the power and intransigence of already constituted positions. These deeper structures are like icebergs and the dialogic engagement is the visible tip.

Dorothy: As a management author, I have used and reused a passage of conversation from my doctoral research (see Lander, 2000a). Why? It is dialogue that features a woman manager, Rose, who as hall manager responsible for university cleaning and food service does much the same job in the UK as I did in Canada. The dialogue is between Rose, the hall manager, Malcolm, the hall warden, Ross, the head chef, Jerome, a first year law student and first year rep, and me as the tutor and researcher into quality.

> *Dorothy*: Any quality moments that the students have that would be surprises to the rest of the group here?
> *Jerome*: I don't know if this is my imagination but I think that, I think that the food's got better. You know when I first came, I remember, the first day, we came down in corridors and we were told that we were going to go at specific times . . . and I remember getting my food and it was, you know, I eat quite a lot anyway, and it was orange juice, a main course with rice or something in it, and a pear. And I thought, 'You know, this is not really what I'm used to' but . . . There should be more stodgy puddings and custards and things like, that's usually what I like.
> *Ross*: I've got a difficult job here.
> *Jerome*: I know, that's what a lot of people have said.

Rose: Because equally there's somebody else who sits on the other side of the table who says, 'I can't eat stodgy puddings. I can't eat. . . .' So it's like a real . . .

Malcolm: The student wouldn't be aware [that] at the beginning of term actually, the kitchen staff were doing valued things with only Ross and me and the second chef. We were without, we normally have two assistant chefs as well. But one was on long-term sick leave, one had just resigned and had not been replaced so we were down to two staff out of a normal four.

Rose: And also the dining room side of it as well. Margaret [dining hall supervisor] has been from the start of term and still is at the moment varying the staff. She is doing a steady job, recruiting, badgering ladies to come back. Probably you'll find ladies washing your sink in the morning, peeling spuds at night as well, so you know sort of a lot of, you know cajoling, and persuading to get people to come back. It's time-consuming, not always a, a thankless task as well but you know.

Shotter's (1993a) ideas of the manager as practical manager are inspired by Bakhtin's dialogical imagination, the sense that 'our speech is filled to overflowing with other people's words' (1981: 337). I'd say that other people's words are your prefigured signifying systems as icebergs. I could hear myself saying practically the same words as Rose as a manager in my Canadian situation, and I could hear the male managers managing me out of the management discourse (see Boot and Tanton, 1997) in much the same way that Malcolm does in this passage. Bakhtin confers agency and intention on the speaker/writer whereas Butler is hostile to agency and places discourse rather than an embodied doer behind the deed and the utterance. Listen for Rose's liberal discourse on equality and democracy (giant icebergs!). Listen to Malcolm lay claim to the management function of replacing for sick time, which in actual practice is Rose's work along with the head chef, Ross, who reports to her. Listen for the silences: Rose does not challenge directly Malcolm's implicit appropriation of her work. This suggests to me that the narrative repertoire of liberalism, contractual arrangements and managerialism that Rose and Malcolm draw on are not 'populated with intention', indeed are closer to Butler's ritualised practices.

I also have concerns that the representation of the feminine-in-management as good management (Calas and Smircich, 1993; Poynton, 1993) repeats the history of valuing women on the basis of instrumental necessity while continuing to devalue women's ways of managing by representing these ways as attributes of biological woman rather than learned skills. The relational, caring, cooperative multi-skilling of managing and serving others tends not to be attributed to an embodied knower, tends not to be attributed to skill. It is not clear from what Rose says that Margaret reports to her. Although Rose recognises that persuading is involved in management work – 'cajoling and persuading people to get them to come back' – she does not 'argue persuasively for a "landscape" of next possible actions, upon which the [structural] "positions" of all those who must take part are clear' (Shotter, 1993a: 157). She does not use the language of managerialism. Malcolm's use of the passive voice in 'had not been replaced', avoids naming Rose in the reporting hierarchy and serves to give the impression that he himself is the manager. Rose is clearly the manager as practical author on an operational level, as her active, task-oriented verbs of 'varying the staff', 'badgering', 'cajoling and persuading' underscore.

Rose is not the cook who does this handwork. But she (and Margaret) do the dirty work and 'thankless task', in Ann Game's (1994) sense, of cleaning up for 'real' managers. As an illustration of Butler's (1990: 141) gender performativity, consider how Rose and I do gender, do our cook and secretary acts, as 'the stylised repetition of acts through time'. On the critical level of reauthorising the wo-manager as practical author, I never got to say the unsayable, to challenge patriarchy or perhaps with reference to Malcolm and Ross, to challenge 'fratriarchy'. Boot and Tanton (1997) oppose patri- archy based on the authority of 'wise old men' to fratriarchy which is 'altogether more insidious in that it is concerned with furthering the self- interest of the association of men itself' (1997: 134). It is as a management author that I get to 'write against Othering' (Fine, 1998) of patriarchy and fratriarchy and managerial discourses that commodify human beings as resource.

Rose's authorial response to Jerome's request for 'more stodgy puddings' relies on the big narrative of democracy and treating students equally; however, my research into quality literally catches Rose in the act of authorising quality moments where students and staff were treated partially, not impartially. Quality constituted as serving others 'way beyond the normal' is borne out over and over again in my research into the lived experience of quality of organisational actors of the university in the UK and Canada (see Lander, 2000b).

Craig: The conversational aspects of this piece are fascinating and important clues to the relations which are lived through dialogue. For me the key aspects are that Rose – in response to the student's critical comment about a lack of stodgy meals – uses snatches of dialogue from a fictional student. She is doing the dialogical manager by playing back to the student what another student might have said.

Dorothy: [*interrupts*] And what the fictional neo-liberal manager is scripted to say – your iceberg??

Craig: [*continues*] This, as you say, positions the manager in a discourse of equality of service which then defends the organisation's reputation and implicitly Rose's managerial identity also. Malcolm however brings quite different resources to bear on the problem. First, he interrupts Rose (in the midst of a sentence), thus asserting his position/identity and draws on a discourse of jobs, tasks and resources to defend both the hall's reputation and his own as manager. Rose then intercedes via a brief break in Malcolm's talk. But rather than take up Malcolm's explicitly hierarchical discourse of job titles and managed tasks, she flatters and humanises it by giving the job a name – Margaret. She then goes on to describe positively and in some detail the difficult relational work she and Margaret do to keep the dining room and kitchen operating. One of the key points for me in this is the way the statements make different kinds of appeals to the student. Rose is saying, despite the difficulties, we are managing. Malcolm is saying we were short staffed due to unanticipated events. There is pronoun difference that underpins these different appeals. Rose calls on the student to recall people's dedication (herself included) to maintain the service, '*you* know cajoling, and persuading to get people to come back', while Malcolm's third person pronoun directs attention to what would *normally* have been the case: 'so *we* were down to two staff out of a normal four'. In terms of explaining these differences we might suggest that for Rose managing is a complex set of relational activities, while for Malcolm managing is a complex set of decisions in relation to tasks and jobs.

But how far does this really get us in our explanation? We can describe the features of the text, and interpret some of the effects that these differences have, for example, highlight the discursive competencies of each manager. But herein lies the limits of such an approach. Dialogic constructivism's reverence for the utterance and for the moment-by-moment responsiveness of lived reality means that it is inevitably caught in the grip of the 'local' and is conceptually unable to draw out the broader significance of what largely is unsaid in such exchanges.

Dorothy: I've not had this experience as either a manager or an academic author of having someone else (You!) reinterpret a living text like this. I like it! In all the times that I have analysed this research conversation, I have not teased out how the warden, Malcolm, and the hall manager, Rose, use a different (moral) appeal in addressing the student, Jerome, and his lament that there should be more stodgy puddings. Or perhaps I could mention that I am struck by how it is your management author function that draws out the broader significance of the largely unsaid. But back to your point about the limits of dialogical constructivism and the limits of the moment-by-moment conversations for drawing out the broader significance of the largely unsaid. This does have implications for the pedagogical and political practice of the management author. What to do? I am attracted to Ayim's (1997) feminist analysis of the moral parameters of good talk – she would represent the good manager by virtue of talk that is caring, cooperative, democratic and honest. Compare this to Shotter's practical-ethical author who 'argues persuasively' and 'must give a sharable linguistic formulation to already shared feelings, arising out of shared circumstances' (1993a: 150). I don't think that as a manager I gave a shared linguistic formulation to shared feelings in conversations but I did as a secretary. But back to our playlet, Rose by Ayim's categories is a good manager when she *caringly* addresses Jerome directly and 'displays a readiness to listen to the other speakers' (1997: 98); when she *democratically* strives 'to see that everyone has a turn, and that no one [not even the women peeling spuds and washing sinks] is excluded from the conversation' (1997: 99); and when she *honestly* and straightforwardly does not try to deceive the listeners about the circumstances around the lack of stodgy puddings in order to protect identities or reputations. Malcolm's interruption of Rose's talk would be undemocratic but cooperative in that he builds on what others say. He falters on the honesty criterion when he is deceptive about who is in charge of managing the kitchen. So what about our good talk? Are we good management authors? I feel as if I have been interrupting you left and right and grabbing up altogether too much of the text.

Craig: Not at all. But I will slip in here and complement your response. The question of what to do is obviously important. An ethics of care, honesty and democratic cooperation clearly speaks to this question. Who indeed would work with a manager who was dictatorial, authoritarian, deceitful and cruel (many do of course but that is another dialogue). But surely Rose could make 50 staff redundant in a caring, honest, cooperative and democratic way, could she not? Of course a good ethical dialogical manager might 'jump' herself if confronted with such a task. What would the ethical dialogic manager do if, to save money, the hall's catering was contracted to a Marriott or a McDonalds? The ethical dialogic manager might stay on to manage the contract, might she not?

Dorothy: [*aside*] Are you saying (or am I inferring) that making staff redundant and contracting out to save money is outside of ethical practice?

Craig: [*responding*] Well yes, surely an ethical principle upon which we would agree beyond those of the importance of good dialogue would be that we should avoid or reduce harm to people. Redundancy does harm, not in all cases, but in many.

Dorothy: [*continuing*] Of course, I am thinking of my own practice as a manager. How about this ethical dilemma? I was often torn between the good of making higher education affordable and accessible to more students and the bad of reducing labour costs, which inevitably involved taking away a person's livelihood in a community where jobs are scarce. The ethics of this was way more complicated than just saying the good end justifies the bad means.

Craig: [*continuing*] I think this confirms the point though that while the particular issues might be different the manager is already in these contradictory positions. My concern is that while something called an 'ethical dialogical manager' might make us feel better about managing these issues, it doesn't take them away. My question is at what point does the ethical position get *really* ethical and become a major thorn in the side of a university or a business or a government? When I read Rose's statement, it is impossible not to admire her discourse. But I can admire it also in the sense that it proves itself extremely helpful in coalescing the contradictions of capitalist relations: of extracting labour power from labour for so many dollars/pounds an hour.

Dorothy: I think our experiment with writing dialogically has evolved a different reading and a different critique of the manager as practical author than we had when we entered into the artifice of composing an academic conversation. Our good manager is a pesky critter – could it be that manager as contradictory author or manager as author of contradictions is evolving as the good? My autobiographical and feminine text of re-pairing knowledge worker and service worker (Lander, 2000a) is explicitly a performance of contradictory knowing and working the hyphens. Neither you nor I want to deny Shotter's practical-ethical dialogical manager – your repeated use of 'I don't deny . . .' (a kind of double negative) [*Craig inserts*: only twice!], strikes me as an example of a management author negotiating the contradictions of the manager performing live in moment-by-moment dialogue and the manager preconstituted in the iceberg of economic relations and their mediating signifying systems. I have the sense I have gone madly off in all directions – contradictory directions – in the course of this chapter, largely in response to your arguing persuasively for a manager who is pushed and tugged between human being, labour commodity and sexed worker. I viscerally take up all of those manager identities and I suspect Rose does too. I have moved to a different take on the good manager at the end of this dialogical chapter. Perhaps *really* good managing and *really* good management writing has never been normal, has always been working the contradictions. This is arguably a valued aspect of women's locales. Bauer and McKinstry's feminine dialogic draws from the voices Bakhtin hears in the novel's carnival and theorises on the contralogic of feminine language: 'A feminine language lives on the boundary. A feminine text overthrows the hierarchies. It is absence-silence-madness present-speaking-sane. It proves the hierarchies mistaken . . . The female voice laughs in the face of authority' (1991: 11). I propose to bring my uttering and non-uttering to a close by provoking our rhetorical-responsive manager author identity(ies). To use rhetoric to persuade is to argue the 'essentially contestable' (Garver, 1978). But what if our good managers and good management authors suspended our rhetoric and pursuit of proving opposites? What if our new rhetoric were to become deliberately working the hyphens of the dialogical manager (he argues persuasively) and the transgressive carnival manager (she silently chews, doodles, gossips, takes up her sexed secretarial position, and laughs out of both sides of her mouth)?

Craig: And our rhetorical style as theory? Perhaps a playlet with the title: *Transgressive Carnival Manager Does F. W. Taylor's Hair while Karl Marx Pours the Tea*!

[*The editor enters the conversation*]

Dorothy: In our first draft of this chapter, we ended here or maybe we should say that we just stopped. David Holman's response was that 'although there is no conclusion, could this be emphasised to suggest that the conversation remains unfinished and ongoing (or something along those lines)?' I propose that we again press into service style as theory and enter into a three-way conversation with David in response to his substantive comments.

David: [*to Dorothy*] You identify one aspect of what is suggested to be good management (arguing persuasively etc.) and state that you did not do it. You conclude that you were therefore a universally bad manager. I think this conclusion is a bit harsh, although I am not trying to deny that you felt excluded from Shotter's categorisation of a good manager. Also, in the next sentence, 'As a manager, I was . . .', it is suggested that you never argued persuasively for a landscape of next possible *operational* actions. Such a statement might be read as implying that as a manager you never, for example, attempted to persuade a work colleague as to what you and/or they were meant to be doing. This sentence also suggests that instead of arguing/persuading you acted transgressively (i.e., breaking or going beyond a limit or law) with regard to operational type actions. These two forms of action are not mutually exclusive. Is it possible that transgressive activities can involve arguing for a set of next possible actions? . . . Perhaps the point that needs to be emphasised/focused on here is that Shotter's work does not point to the deeper structural milieu that managers find themselves in nor how they can address it in conversations with others (although, in his defence, he does not set himself up as a critical theorist).

Dorothy: You ask great, hard questions! I shall try to respond. Yes, yes, as a manager, many's the times I attempted to persuade a work colleague as to what I and/or they were meant to be doing – I just wanted to make the point that there are many other acts that qualify as good managing. And yes indeed, it is possible that transgressive activities can involve arguing for a set of next possible actions – though I sense that for me arguing takes a different form than Shotter's arguing persuasively. Those are the easy responses. I was struck as I read your comments and queries that I did not do nearly enough of what I set out to do, which was to look at our own conversational texts, including my autobiographical text *as text*. This is doing poststructural work in Lather's terms, which means '"doing it" and "troubling it" simultaneously' (1996: 3). I need to trouble this very text that you mention, where I seemed to be drawing the conclusion – you believe too harshly – that I was a universally bad manager. I happily troubled Malcolm's text and the way he constructed himself as the manager by othering Rose. When you (Craig) troubled Rose's text, I was not quite so happy even as you admired her discourse. The danger of doing this reflexive troubling of my autobiographical text and making my rhetoric explicit is that my authenticity and hence the performativity of the text are diminished.

Craig: [*interrupts*] Or is it destroyed? Are you going to admit you have been playing with the reader?

Dorothy: [*replying*] What is rhetoric but playing with the reader and pretending that we are not – pretending that we have a transparent, referential truth, rather than a constructed truth? Reflexivity requires breaking out of the pretence and pulling the reader out of the pretence too – or so it seems to me. By performing a reflexive analysis of my own reflexivity, I point up Shotter's '*destructive* inequality in our ethics of communication' (1993c: 105). I point up the hierarchy of my first-person rights over your (David's and Craig's) second-person rights and over third-person rights, e.g., Rose and Malcolm. The unidentified reader that I have been playing with also comes under the second-person category. To perform a reflexive analysis is to declare that I too have interests – as my management author, as my author manager, and as my other identities. At the same time, I declare my writer's 'right or a privilege to "move" [the reader] with [my] words, and [the readers] have a duty or commitment to "make sense" of the "movements" [my] utterances produce in [them]' (Shotter, 1993c: 105). I sense that there is a fine line between the management author who indulges in 'confessional monologues, whose claim to moral grace is to be "more reflexive than thou"' (Hardy and Clegg, 1997: S12) and 'reflexive theoretical positions [as] those best able to account for their own theorizing, as well as whatever it is they theorize about' (1997: S13). So here goes – I shall trouble my texts and try to account for my own theorizing of the good manager. My reflexive analysis of my reflexivity requires me to confess that I cast myself as the hero of my good manager's autobiography – or more precisely my service worker anti-heroine 'with whom the audience is basically in sympathy [or so I hope]. We identify with these outsiders because we have all felt like outsiders at one time or another' (Vogler, 1998: 41). You will now recognise that my manager's autobiography plays out the wounded quality and the 'rebel with a cause' that characterise the anti-hero. And I guess it worked because you seem to be moved by my secretary-as-manager who was not recognised as a manager. So now you have my sense of the practical author who performs the trans-gressive act of moving the reader to lose himself/herself in my story and forget that I constructed my autobiography for an audience – this is a transgressive act with rhetorical purpose where I get to argue otherwise.

Craig: Rhetorical analysis is one way into such reflexivity. I guess I prefer my reflexivity written as identities/subjects found in discourses to that of the rhetorician's finesse. But I worry about the reader. Do we have some duty of care toward the reader? Will they 'make the trip' into this reflexivity over the structures of our stories? I can imagine a patient reader getting to this point, closing the book firmly and shouting: 'Charlatans! Con-artists!'.

Dorothy: Well, yes and no. Our narrator did alert the reader at the outset that we would be talking reflexively about how Shotter's dialogical manager didn't go far enough. I was arguing – not very persuasively, I guess – that performing contradictions and feminine contra-logic identified both the good management author and the good manager. Am I hearing you say that I might be taking reflexivity a tad too far? I really wanted to show that we management authors have interests that we pretend we have not and that we co-opt our readers into this pretence.

Kenneth Burke is a rhetorical theorist who argues that 'identification' rather than persuasion is the key term in rhetoric: 'You persuade a man [*sic*] only insofar as you can talk his language by speech, gesture, tonality, order, image, attitude, idea, *identifying* your ways with his' (1969: 55–6). I know intuitively that just about any of my readers – second person and third person – can identify with my anti-hero rhetoric of being an outsider. By introducing this reflexivity into my autobiography, I suggest that my conclu-sion that I was a universally bad manager was not harsh at all, but rather ironic. In other words, I was using the rhetorical strategies of both irony and hyperbole to argue that I stand in for another kind of good manager. For me, taking rhetoric seriously requires both my author manager and my management author to take up rhetorical theory. I admire Shotter and Cunliffe's (chapter 1) examples of poetic forms of talk such as manager Rob's use of alliteration and repetitive words in tempo. I think my utterance and the hyperbole of my italics – 'obviously I was a bad manager' – was a performance of Northrop Frye's sense of irony: 'saying one thing and meaning another, as a device which a writer uses to detach our imaginations from a world of absurdity or frustration by letting us see around it' (1963: 59).

David: Could you say why you only got to be a good manager when a secretary? It seems an interesting point . . . A question being, why did you stop being a good manager when you became a manager (in title at least)?

Dorothy: Did I really say 'only when'? I wanted to point up that I did *not* stop being a good manager when I assumed the title of manager in large part because I kept on putting my secretary skills to use. I was the secretary to the manager of residences and food service for a year (1975), and when he resigned, I applied for and got the job. Of course, I did not continue all my secretarial duties but I have a strong sense that using my diverse secretarial skills comes close to Chia and Morgan's understanding of managing 'as the ongoing accomplishment of modern life in the broad sense we use when we say "I managed to. . ."' (1996: 41). My rhetorical purpose is to have my readers identify with the manager who is doing and listening and *not* talking or arguing, who is good when he or she provides the occasions for other players/employees to argue persuasively for a landscape of possible operational and/or structural actions. The 'provision of an *intelligible formulation* of what has become, for the others in the organisation, a chaotic welter of impressions' (Shotter and Cunliffe) is involved but my 'help to create in conversations . . . a mutually shared "landscape" of possibilities for action' was outside the conversation proper and was outside the manager proper. But then I would say that, wouldn't I? I sense that management authors find writing about the structural environment of managing more glamorous than operations – myself included. In Shotter's (1993a) work and in Shotter and Cunliffe, they are more attracted to examples of managers arguing for structural actions. Or is it the case that managers as participants in a research situation just talk less about operational actions? I accept Shotter's statement that 'in everyday life, much of what we talk about has a *contested* nature' (1993a: 153) but as a service operations manager working the floor, I challenge that the contested nature of our talk is often such topics as ' "democracy", "society", "the person", "the individual", "the citizen", and many other essentially political concepts'. Not abstract talk 'about' democracy or the person anyway!

David: Ayim's moral parameters of good talk seem very similar to Habermas's. Is this intentional by Ayim? In the introductory chapter by Shotter and Cunliffe (this volume), they discuss the moral parameters of good talk . . . . Also, I'm not sure how caring, cooperative, democrative and honest talk would be any more likely to 'draw out the broader significance of the largely unsaid' i.e., the icebergs, than those skills and abilities mentioned by Shotter.

Dorothy: Ayim draws on Habermas's moral analysis of communicative competence in ordinary conversations, particularly his two sets of criteria that govern 'the conditions of *truth* of the communication and the conditions governing the *process* of communication among the participants' (1997: 85). The moral analysis that is missing in Habermas's work is the gendered differences in conversational styles and Ayim is quick to point out empirical work that connects her moral criteria of language and some of Habermas's ideas of communicative competence to females' conversational style and to the private realm of the home. 'Women have historically assumed personal responsibility for maintaining a context in which conversations could flourish, in which other speakers felt "cared for" linguistically' (1997: 90). Ayim's analysis is different in that the caring dimension of good talk underpins her other criteria of democratic, cooperative and honest but she hypothesises that the 'caring was so much a part of the fabric of the conversation that its presence was seldom noticed and its need seldom felt' (1997: 90). Providing for speakers to be cared for linguistically is not the hallmark of either Habermas's ideas of argumentative consensus or Shotter and Cunliffe's 'social accountability and ethical discourse' in this volume. It is the hallmark of the manager-as-secretary who provides the occasions for dialogue and cares for the speakers linguistically, in arranging for their participation and recording their words. Following Ayim and drawing on my own experience, the caring underpinnings of good talk create the safe environment that is more likely to draw out the broader significance of the largely unsaid, that is the icebergs, and maybe especially draw out the gendered dimensions of the icebergs. Ayim's moral criteria of conversation are anti-dominant and anti-confrontational (1997: 103) and conversation takes up plural ways of getting at the truth – feelings and gossip and ordinary discussion as much as arguing persuasively. Ayim's (1997: 115) criteria are also anti-hierarchical and anti-self-centred individualism. In the new management trend which extols cooperation and communication rather than confrontation and control, women are ahead of the trends. They do not have to learn those leadership and management skills. They have been practising them most of their lives' (Beasley, 1983: 15).

Narrator (Curt, 1994): I get the sense that we're moving to a discussion of women in the workplace. I'm sure Craig would like to come back on this point about women being 'ahead of the trends', but I'm going to have to cut you off! I know also that I'm going to be accused of always having the last word and enforcing the silence on these two interlocutors. But let me remind you, dear reader, that this chapter invited you into a continuing conversation. I am merely adding, then, a rhetorical 'bracket' around the dialogue above. The conversation continues. Should you wish to join the authors, please send messages to: c.prichard@massey.ac.nz and dlander@stfx.ca.

References

Alvesson, M. and Willmott, H. (1996) *Making Sense of Management: A Critical Introduction.* London and Thousand Oaks, CA: Sage.

Ayim, M.N. (1997) *The Moral Parameters of Good Talk: A Feminist Analysis.* Waterloo, ON: Wilfred Laurier University Press.

Bakhtin, M. (1981) *The Dialogic Imagination.* Austin, TX: University of Texas Press.

Bauer, D.M. and McKinstry, S.J. (1991) *Feminism, Bakhtin, and the Dialogic.* Albany, NY: State University of New York.

Beasley, M. (1983) 'Women in educational leadership', in S. Randall (ed.), *Changing Focus: The Participation of Women in Educational Management in Australia.* Carelton, Victoria: The Australian College of Education. pp. 13–16.

Boot, R. and Tanton, M. (1997) 'The gender agenda; passion, perspective and project', in J. Burgoyne and M. Reynolds (eds), *Management Learning: Integrating Perspectives in Theory and Practice.* London: Sage. pp. 127–43.

Braverman, H. (1974) *Labour and Monopoly Capital: The Degradation of Work in the Twentieth Century.* New York: Monthly Review Press.

Brookfield, S.D. (1995) *Becoming a Critically Reflective Teacher.* San Francisco, CA: Jossey-Bass.

Burke, K. (1969) *A Rhetoric of Motives.* Berkeley: University of California Press.

Butler, J. (1990) *Gender Trouble: Feminism and the Subversion of Identity.* New York: Routledge.

Butler, J. (1997) *Excitable Speech: A Politics of the Performative.* London: Routledge.

Calas, M.B. and Smircich, L. (1993) 'Dangerous liaisons: the feminine-in-management meets globalization', *Business Horizons*, 71–81.

Chandler, A.D. (1977) *The Visible Hand: The Managerial Revolution in American Business.* Cambridge, MA: Belknap Press.

Chia, R. and Morgan, S. (1996) 'Educating the philosopher manager: de-signing the times', *Management Learning*, 27 (1): 37–64.

Cunliffe, A.L. (1999) 'Everyday conversations: a social poetics of managing', paper presented at the Critical Management Studies Conference, July 1999.

Curt, B. (1994) *Texuality and Techtonics; Troubling Social and Psychological Science.* Buckingham: Open University Press.

Czarniawska-Joerges, B. (1994) 'Gender, power, organizations: an interruptive interpretation', in J. Hassard and M. Parker (eds), *Towards a New Theory of Organizations.* London: Routledge. pp. 227–47.

Ellinor, L. and Gerard, G. (1998) *Dialogue: Rediscover the Transforming Power of Conversation.* New York: Wiley.

Fine, M. (1998) 'Working the hyphens: reinventing self and other in qualitative research', in N.K. Denzin and Y.S. Lincoln (eds), *The Landscape of Qualitative Research: Theories and Issues.* Thousand Oaks, CA: Sage.

Frost, P. and Stablein, R.E. (eds) (1992) *Doing Exemplary Research.* London: Sage.

Frye, N. (1963) *The Educated Imagination.* Bloomington: Indiana University Press.

Game, A. (1994) '"Matter out of place": the management of academic work', *Organization*, 1 (1): 47–50.

Garver, E. (1978) 'Rhetoric and essentially contested argument', *Philosophy and Rhetoric*, 11: 156–72.

Hardy, C. and Clegg, S. (1997) 'Relativity without relativism: reflexivity in post-paradigm organization studies', *British Journal of Management*, 8: S3–S17.

Harré, R. (1983) *Personal Being. A Theory for Individual Psychology.* Oxford: Blackwell.

Hollway, W. (1991) *Work Psychology and Organizational Behaviour: Managing the Individual at Work.* London and Newbury Park, CA: Sage.

Holmer-Nadesan, M. (1996) 'Organizational identity and space of action', *Organization Studies,* 17 (1): 49–81.

Isaacs, W. (1999) *Dialogue and the Art of Thinking Together: A Pioneering Approach to Communicating in Business and in Life.* New York: Currency.

Jacques, R. (1996) *Manufacturing the Employee, Management Knowledge from the 19th to the 21st Centuries.* London: Sage.

Lander, D. (2000a) 'Re-pairing knowledge worker and service worker: a critical autobiography of stepping into the shoes of my other', in C. Prichard, R. Hull, M. Chumer and H. Willmott (eds), *Managing Knowledge: Critical Investigations of Work and Learning.* London: MacMillan. pp. 141–57.

Lander, D. (2000b) 'A provocation: quality is service', *Journal of Quality in Higher Education,* 6 (2): 135–41.

Lander, D. and Prichard, C. (forthcoming) 'Life on the verandah: colonial cartographies of academic identity', in S. Whitehead and M. Dent (eds), *Managing Professional Identities: Knowledge, Performativity and the 'New' Professional.* London: Routledge.

Lather, P. (1996) 'Methodology as subversive repetition: practices toward a feminist double science', paper presented at the annual meeting of the American Educational Research Association, New York City.

McKinlay, A. (2000) 'The bearable lightness of control: organisational reflexivity and the politics of knowledge management', in C. Prichard et al. (eds), *Managing Knowledge: Critical Investigations of Work and Learning.* London: Macmillan. pp. 107–21.

Nonaka, I. and Takeuchi, H. (1995) *The Knowledge-creating Company: How Japanese Companies Create the Dynamics of Innovation.* New York: Oxford University Press.

Poynton, C. (1993) 'Naming women's workplace skills: linguistics and power', in B. Probert and B.W. Wilson (eds), *Pink Collar Blues: Work, Gender and Technology.* Melbourne: Melbourne University Press. pp. 85–100.

Prichard, C. (1999) 'Identity work – moving the "theory of the subject" from "division" to "depth" in critical organizational analysis', paper presented at the First Critical Management Studies Conference, University of Manchester Institute of Science and Technology, July.

Prichard, C. (2000) 'Know, learn and share! The knowledge phenomena and the construction of a consumptive-communicative body', in C. Prichard et al. (eds), *Managing Knowledge, Critical Investigations of Work and Learning.* London: Macmillan.

Prichard, C., Chumer, M., Hull, R. and Willmott, H. (2000) *Managing Knowledge, Critical Investigations of Work and Learning.* London: Macmillan.

Shotter, J. (1993a) *Conversational Realities: Constructing Life through Language.* London: Sage.

Shotter, J. (1993b) 'Harré, Vygotsky, Bakhtin, Vico, Wittgenstein: academic discourses and conversational realities', *Journal for the Theory of Social Behaviour,* 23 (4): 459–82.

Shotter, J. (1993c) *Cultural Politics of Everyday Life.* Buckingham: Open University Press.

Shotter, J. (1997) 'Dialogical realities: the ordinary, the everyday, and the other strange new worlds', *Journal of the Theory of Social Behavior,* 27 (2/3): 345–57.

Van Maanen, J. (1995) 'Style as theory', *Organization Science,* 6 (1): 133–43.

Vogler, C. (1998) *The Writer's Journey: Mythic Structure for Writers* (2nd edition). Studio City, CA: Michael Wiese Productions.

Willmott, H. (1994) 'Social constructionism and communication studies: hearing the conversation but losing the dialogue', *Communication Yearbook*, 17: 42–54.

Wittgenstein, L. (1953) *Philosophical Investigations*. Oxford: Blackwell.

Zuboff, S. (1988) *In the Age of the Smart Machine: The Future of Work and Power*. New York: Basic Books.

Author Index

Subject Index